LET'S SEE WHAT HAPPENS

Marvin Rees was born in Bristol and brought up by his mother. He began his career with a leading international development agency, then moved to the US to work with a social justice organization. On returning to the UK he worked with BBC Bristol, the Black Development Agency supporting the BME-led voluntary sector and NHS Bristol's Public Health team. He is a Yale World Fellow and co-founded the City Leadership Programme. He became mayor of Bristol in May 2016. Deeply committed to building a fairer, more inclusive world, Rees lives in Bristol with his wife and three children.

MARVIN REES

LET'S SEE WHAT HAPPENS

THE LAST MAYOR OF BRISTOL

PICADOR

First published 2024 by Picador

This paperback edition first published 2025 by Picador
an imprint of Pan Macmillan
The Smithson, 6 Briset Street, London EC1M 5NR
EU representative: Macmillan Publishers Ireland Ltd, 1st Floor,
The Liffey Trust Centre, 117–126 Sheriff Street Upper,
Dublin 1, D01 YC43
Associated companies throughout the world
www.panmacmillan.com

ISBN 978-1-0350-0919-0

1 3 5 7 9 8 6 4 2

A CIP catalogue record for this book is available from the British Library.

Typeset in Perpetua by Jouve (UK), Milton Keynes
Printed and bound by CPI Group (UK) Ltd, Croydon, CR0 4YY

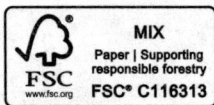

MIX
Paper | Supporting
responsible forestry
FSC
www.fsc.org   FSC® C116313

Visit **www.picador.com** to read more about all our books
and to buy them. You will also find features, author interviews and
news of any author events, and you can sign up for e-newsletters
so that you're always first to hear about our new releases.

To my grandad

CONTENTS

PROLOGUE

'Britain stands on the brink of exciting democratic change. Just over a week from now, the polling stations will go up, the voters will come out, and our biggest cities will vote yes or no to having their own mayor. Let's be clear what this moment means. It's not some trivial re-structure or fiddling about . . . It's a once-in-a-generation chance to change the way our country is run. I passionately want those cities — from Bristol to Birmingham, Nottingham to Newcastle, Sheffield to Wakefield — to give a resounding, emphatic "yes" next week.'

In April 2012, I was sitting in the audience at the Marriott Hotel, across the green from Bristol City Hall, listening to the then Conservative prime minister, David Cameron, outline his vision for the future of local government. At the time, the idea of a city having a directly elected mayor was a relatively new concept in the UK. Tony Blair's New Labour manifesto of 1997 had promised an elected mayor for London. This led to Ken Livingstone becoming mayor in 2000, running initially as an independent. That same year, the Local Government Act paved the way for cities across the country to hold referendums to discover if the local electorate wanted directly elected mayors. In 2011, following the election of the Conservative–Liberal Democrat coalition, the Localism Act took this one stage further, allowing central government to trigger such local referendums themselves. In Spring 2012, ten such votes were taking place: in Birmingham, Bradford, Coventry, Leeds, Manchester, Newcastle, Nottingham, Sheffield, Wakefield . . . and my home city of Bristol.

The argument for and against directly elected mayors swings back and forth across the political spectrum, and also between politicians on a local and national level according to how it impacts their status as councillors and MPs. In 2012, Cameron seemed to have plenty of backing for the idea: 'Next month's referendums offer Britain's cities the chance to try a new approach,' *The Telegraph* wrote. 'We urge them to seize it.' 'Opponents fear that mayors are intended to push radical reform,' *The Economist* argued. 'They are right: that is why mayors are a good idea.' By contrast, when a second Bristol referendum over directly elected mayors took place in 2022, the local Conservatives campaigned against it.

But locally, across the political spectrum, views were mixed: Labour and the Lib Dems were officially neutral, though they had campaigners on both sides. Stephen Williams, the Liberal Democrat MP for Bristol West, was considering running. Barbara Janke, the Lib Dem council leader, observed that 'quite a few' American mayors had been corrupt. 'The municipal establishment broadly opposes elected mayors,' *The Economist* noted. As for my own party, Labour, opinions were also split. Alderman Bill Martin led the 'no' campaign, claiming they were part of a plot to privatize services: a Conservative mayor would be able to pass decisions even though they were a minority on the council.

I was at the Marriott as a potential Labour candidate if the 'yes' vote won. Lawrence Hill councillor Marg Hickman had recently encouraged me to run if Bristol decided it wanted a mayor. I hadn't really thought much about UK mayors before, but I'd studied American politics as part of my degree back in the 1990s and had seen how big cities like Chicago and New York had benefitted from having someone championing their cause and that they could provide an opportunity for people and voices from outside the political establishment to have influence. When I was studying in America, I'd spent time with David Berg, a professor of psychology, who became something of a mentor to me and we'd stayed in touch. He was good friends with Howard Dean, who'd run for the Democrat nomination for US president in 2004. Dean hadn't won, but his use of internet fundraising and grassroots organization was hugely influential. Aware of my political interests, David mentioned to me that Howard had once told him that it was much better to be a governor in American politics than a senator: put simply, you got to make things happen and make your mark. David continued, 'I think it would be a better fit for you. You'd find executive politics more fulfilling than legislative politics. I think you'd enjoy it more.'

His intervention stuck in my mind, even after I returned to the UK. When Labour declared that the selection for Bristol West would be an all-women shortlist, it seemed to rule out any opportunity for me to represent the place where I grew up. But when the possibility of Bristol having a directly elected mayor came up, and with Marg's encouragement, it felt as though the stars had realigned. I took part in the 'yes' campaign during the referendum, not as a player but by helping and handing out leaflets. On one particularly embarrassing afternoon, I agreed to be driven around the streets of Clifton with a megaphone to urge people to vote yes. I crouched as low as I could with just the speaker poking out of the open window to try to maintain my anonymity.

Cameron's plans were ambitious but never fully came to fruition. He talked of creating a 'cabinet' of mayors across the UK who would meet twice a year under his chairmanship. Tapping into the ability of cities to deliver and boost the economy was the right idea. The problem with his scheme was that out of the ten cities holding a referendum, there would only be one city who voted for a directly elected mayor: my own. On a turnout of 24 per cent, the 'yes' campaign would win by 53 per cent to 47 per cent.

That day at the Marriott, the potential candidates were jockeying for position. George Ferguson, a local architect and businessman notable for his trademark red trousers, was there. He was a former Liberal councillor and parliamentary candidate but was planning to stand as an independent. Also present were Liberal Democrats, Conservatives and the other potential Labour nominees. They were all far more experienced politicians than me: both current and former councillors, already busy with their own campaigns, resources and teams.

I was all too aware of the views people in that room would likely have of me. To be honest, I carried those same perceptions within my own insecurities. But I also carried a belief that I had something to offer the city and the role. I had David Berg's words ringing in my ears, and similar encouragement from Deborah Evans, my CEO, and Christina Gray, my manager at the NHS, where I was working in public health. My CV, I had to admit, did not make me sound like the standout candidate. I was a health service manager, band eight. Before that, I'd spent five frustrating years as a BBC broadcast journalist: despite my best efforts, I just couldn't get on in the organization and I ended up resigning. I was later told that when it was announced I was standing to be mayor, my candidacy was met with laughter and incredulity among my former colleagues in the BBC Bristol newsroom.

As I entered the hotel, my overwhelming feelings were acute self-consciousness and defiance. I felt like an imposter. I knew I didn't belong there. But I was always going to run. From a young age, I have had a peculiar mix of insecurity and self-belief. In a glamorous hotel, among the prime minister and his entourage, rival candidates and the bright lights of the media, I felt like something of an inconvenient and awkward gatecrasher. Although I was certain I would be seen as a nobody when it came to their idea of politics, I knew I could hold my own when it came to understanding Bristol and how the city should be run. But glad-handing and working a room wasn't something I felt comfortable with – and never have. I took my seat to listen to Cameron's speech.

Once the presentations had finished, the jockeying to get an interview with the media began. It was the smart thing for prospective candidates to do, to get yourself an early bit of publicity to push your profile and cause. But all the other candidates had the same idea. When it comes to photographs, I've never mastered – and I haven't sought to master – the skill of pushing my way to the front and centre: I'm often the one at the side. Here, this meant that I was well down the line. With a swish of his red trousers, George Ferguson was quick to offer his opinions to the waiting journalists, who lapped him up in equal measure; my rivals for the Labour nomination were also ahead of me. I joined the queue and waited my turn.

At least Paul Barltrop, the BBC Bristol political correspondent covering the story, knew who I was, having recognized me from my time there. I continued to wait while the others were interviewed, but just as I was about to get my turn, he was called away.

'Sorry Marv,' he said. 'I've got to go off and interview David Cameron. I'll be back to do you in a moment.'

'Of course,' I said. 'I'll be here.'

Around me, the room was emptying. The rival candidates, who'd all given their interviews, were grabbing their stuff and heading off. Around me, hotel workers started to stack up the chairs. Up on the stage, I heard a 'pfft' as the sound system was switched off: the microphones were packed away, the leads unplugged, and the speakers lifted down from their stands. The clean-up of the room continued, workers saying 'excuse me' as they scurried past with their hands full of equipment. I continued to wait for the BBC journalist to return.

Finally, with the room almost empty, Paul came back. But as soon as he saw me, he shook his head.

'Sorry Marv,' he said. 'Everything's run over. I've got to get back to the newsroom. Maybe next time, yeah?'

And with that, he was off and out the door. I stood there for a moment, the clank of a sound system being dismantled behind me. I felt small. I felt belittled and humiliated. In my attempt to take the first step to getting elected, I came face to face with the fact I knew to be true, that I wasn't considered by the mainstream to be a serious candidate, not even worth an interview.

But I still knew I had something to offer. While I had never been indifferent to these sorts of slights, I had also learned the habit of not letting them stop me. *Let's see what happens*, I whispered to myself. It was a mantra that I'd been drawing on ever since I was a young boy. Life had thrown its fair share of trials at me over the years. And when it did, and others put me down, that's what I'd say to myself.

Let's see what happens.

That moment in the emptying hall was difficult to take. But I'd faced worse before, and although it wasn't welcome at the time, I had learned to always come back stronger. This was just the latest in a long line of challenges, a line that went all the way back to my early childhood.

1.

Early Years

I was born in Bristol in 1972, the mixed-race child of a white mother and a Black father.

My mum was born in Bristol in 1948, my nan and grandad's third and youngest child. My nan was the first of ten children and came from a large Bristol family called the Bryers, while my grandad was from Merthyr Tydfil in South Wales. His dad, known as Tally bach – Little Tally – was a Welsh miner, a little over five foot, but his mum came over to South Wales from Ireland. They were poor, genuinely poor – a tiny house with an outside toilet and all the rest of it. My great-grandfather swore his children would never go down the mines, so my grandad moved to England to look for work. He found himself in Bristol, where he met my nan at a dance in Old Market. My nan always remembered that it was his teeth, nice and white, that caught her eye.

Growing up, Mum, her sister Glenys and brother Terry moved between Bristol and Merthyr as my grandad followed work and sought family support. Mum always says that she moved to Merthyr with an English accent and came back to Bristol with a Welsh one, which caused her trouble at both ends. Money was extremely tight. Once, they got a lift to Merthyr with the children under a cover in the back of a flatbed truck. When they got there, they didn't have anywhere to stay and ended up living in a semi-derelict cottage in Cefn Coed. They weren't supposed to be there, so they'd make themselves scarce during the day, and sneak back under cover of darkness every evening. Eventually, my nan and grandad saved enough to be able to afford a house in Bristol's Armoury Square, which they borrowed £500 to buy. Funnily enough, my nan always told me the house had belonged to someone called Alderman Ross, a former Lord Mayor of Bristol.

My grandad was a clever man. His exam results were, apparently, up on the wall of his old school, Cyfarthfa Castle, because he got top marks. My nan told me all this because Grandad didn't talk about himself much unless it was about his days playing in Merthyr Rugby Club's front row. Nan told me he'd won a prize for his exam results but was too ashamed to go up and claim it because his second-hand uniform was so raggedy that his fellow pupils made fun of him.

He should have gone to university but he couldn't afford it. Years later, he discovered that he could have applied for a scholarship, but no one had ever mentioned it, so he had never applied. By the time he found out what might have been the moment had gone. He became a bus conductor but never rose through the ranks. I don't know if it was a lack of confidence or if his background had ground his potential out of him, but he never had the career he deserved. When I went to university – and a Welsh university at that: Swansea – he couldn't have been prouder. I was the first in my family to pursue higher education, and when I graduated, it felt like the best present I could give him. My nan told me he lived his dreams through me.

I was very close to my grandad, and it was through him I inherited my love of rugby. We lived one street apart so I would go round and watch the Five Nations Championship, as it was then, on the TV with him. He would have all the curtains drawn and the 14-inch TV almost at full volume. And rugby or no rugby, I'd go and stay with Nan and Grandad every weekend, either on a Friday or Saturday night. Nan would watch *Starsky & Hutch* with me while Grandad went for his pint at the Bus Club near the bus depot on Lawrence Hill Roundabout or the Waggon and Horses on Stapleton Road – which was one of the pubs used to film the TV sitcom *Only Fools and Horses*. When he got back at around 10.30 p.m., we'd take his dog, Ziggy, for a walk. I used to love those late-night walks and conversations.

My nan worked at a department store called Brights, though she'd also worked in a greengrocer's, baker's and at Bristol's Concorde Cinema. She was a source of great strength and stability for me. She was also a fighter and wouldn't shy away from a row when it mattered. In the 1960s, she fostered the son of a Nigerian doctor. Nan had an open-house arrangement, and Lawrence was one of a number of people she took in over the years. A white woman with a Black child at the time led to derogatory comments and Nan being spat at. But she gave back as good as she got in return.

It frustrated me, however, that Nan always showed such deference to professional people, such as doctors, as though they were better than her. I guess it was down to something within her, but it was rooted in her working-class background. She always wanted to give them gifts to thank them for whatever they were doing for her, which used to make me really cross. I felt it was because she felt herself to be lower than them. She was giving money away to people who were doing their jobs, even though they were paid far more money than her. I'd say, 'Nan, they're not better than you.' That early belief became a key driver when I went into politics: whether it was individuals or institutions, I'd decided to leave any sense of inferiority at the door.

My dad is from St Thomas in Jamaica. He also had a tough upbringing, albeit in a different way. His mum, my grandmother Lilian, was very hard. My grandfather, William, had lots of children with different women – as my father would also go on to do. The result is that I've got a lot of aunts and uncles: some of whom I'm close to, but many others I've never met.

William went to the US and that side of the family, the Walkers, are very close-knit. And successful too – one uncle was in banking; a cousin works for the US Department of Agriculture while others are entrepreneurs. There are a lot of high-flyers in my paternal family. I first met them when I went to the US as a nineteen-year-old to participate in Camp America. That was the first time I'd seen my grandfather. It was a big moment for me. I'd say my soul stirred. He stared at me, wide-eyed, in silence. And then, finally, in his strong

Jamaican patois, he said, 'If me did see you pon de street, me'd never even know you was mine.' Those words are all I have of him.

At the same time as William went to the States, my grandmother and my father came to the UK. They went to London first, then moved to Bristol. My father met my mother at one of the dances that Jamaicans and other West Indians used to hold in St Pauls at places like the legendary Bamboo Club run by Tony Bullimore. Bullimore was a larger-than-life businessman who helped to break down racial barriers in the city. The club welcomed both the Black and white communities at a time when many pubs and clubs were closed to Black people. It also brought in an amazing range of acts: Bob Marley and Tina Turner played there. The Bamboo was a place people went to for the atmosphere, the music and the dancing.

When my mum became pregnant with me, she was advised not to go through with the pregnancy. The health workers took one look at this unmarried twenty-two-year-old white woman with a Black boyfriend and Brown baby on the way and told her that if she were a good woman, she should consider having an abortion. After I was born, the pressure to give me up continued. This was real-life *Cathy Come Home* culture and attitudes.

When asked about the things that shaped me and made my politics, I used to go to my own experiences of growing up poor and mixed race in a city where race and class inequality and hostility were entrenched. But increasingly, I have realized that my mum's experiences have motivated me. I was thinking about it recently and reflected that it wasn't just about me being mixed race, but also about my mother's social standing. That people believed they had the moral authority to say she shouldn't be a mother and what she needed to do to be a 'good' woman – my mum had to carry that. Fortunately, that prejudice wasn't the only voice in the room – another health worker who was there stuck up for her. 'You leave her alone,' she said. 'The Bryers take care of their children.'

I got the name Marvin after Lee Marvin – when my mum was in labour, she could hear in the background 'Wand'rin' Star', the song from the film *Paint Your Wagon*. Lee Marvin's character was a red-faced drunk. When I was born, I had a red face too, so the name stuck. Despite that one supportive health worker, with whom my mum recently reconnected, she found herself having to do things the hard way. More helpful 'advice' came her way. Now she was told that she should give me up for adoption.

I love my dad. He is my father and I know he had it tough as a child, especially as a newly arrived teen migrant surviving and navigating 1960s England. But he wasn't there at my birth and nor was he around much in a practical way. He wasn't the father I longed for when I was growing up. That absence has left me with a sense of vulnerability I have always carried, and the belligerent resilience I developed to overcome it.

My mum first lived in City Road, in a house with multiple occupants. It was one of the few places that would take her as a white woman with a Brown baby in 1972. Like so many, she fell foul of the 'No Irish, No Blacks, No Dogs' rental practices of the time. Moving there wasn't easy – a number of Black women who lived in the area didn't like who she was. They saw her as a white woman taking a Black man and harassed her as a result. Sometimes, that got physical. One of my early memories is of her in a fight after a woman attacked her. I was about three. My mum smashed a bottle and cut her hand. In our family album, there is a photo of my mum with bandaged fingers. It's a picture that always speaks to the vulnerability I felt in her.

Mum's situation wasn't helped by my father. He was well known in Bristol, which meant that everyone also knew who she was. And he had children with other women as well. After me, there was Natasha, who had a different mother, my sister Dionne with mum, then Martin and Leon with Pauline, then Haley with yet another woman. Then there's Shamira, whose mother is Angela, and Carleon whose mother is Sue. Beyond my full sister Dionne, none of my siblings were introduced to me by my dad.

Early on, my mum went round to see Pauline and said to her, 'It's not the children's fault.' Their relationship was made possible by the fact that both Mum and Pauline had become Christians. The two of them became close and Pauline was soon like a second mum to me. Martin and Leon would spend a lot of time around my house while I was growing up, too: when Pauline went into hospital to have

Leon, Martin stayed with us. The four of us – me, Dionne, Martin and Leon – were close.

I came across my other brothers and sisters later. When Leon became manager of Foot Locker in town, he once spotted a mixed-race girl standing outside, looking in and staring at him. Leon was getting ribbed by his friends – 'She's checking you out, man' – when she walked in and asked, 'Are you Leon Walker?' When he said yes, she replied, 'I'm your sister.' On another occasion, when I was about twenty-four, Martin came round to my mum's house, bringing a three-year-old mixed-race child with him. 'This is our brother, Carleon,' he said. I shrugged and said, 'Come in.' It wasn't a surprise to discover I had another sibling. We loved him straight away.

I had a complicated relationship with my dad growing up. My mum told me about his background and how hard it had been, adding that he could be a good man and that he did love me. But he wasn't around when he should have been, and when he was, not in the way we needed. When he did turn up to play football or cricket in Rawnsley Park near my house with my friends, it was always quite the show. He was a great athlete, and I would be torn between being proud of him and conflicted when it made me see what I was missing the rest of the time. I felt safe when he was around but there was always tension when he turned up at home. I resented him for assuming he could walk in and take the status of the man of the house when he hadn't, as I saw it, put the time in.

At the same time, his reputation in our community could be useful. I used to have a pair of ice skates – Bauer Turbos – and one time on the bus back from town, this other kid decided he liked the look of them. Now, I wasn't a weak kid. I was reasonably athletic. But I wasn't tough or bad and so this particular kid, who was a bit of both, decided I was fair game. He asked me if he could have a look at my ice skates, and not thinking anything of it, like a fool I handed them over. At which point, he took the skates and said, 'I'm keeping these.'

The way boys worked, it was down to me to initiate the fight with the kid to get the skates back. I fancied my chances. He was older but all mouth and I was boxing at the time; I thought he was a noisy fool. But I could see a few other kids on the bus who knew me, and I saw the opportunity to make another kind of statement. So I didn't take the bait but said 'OK' and smiled and rang the bell to get off at the next stop with the aim of going to my dad's. One of the older boys, whose family, like my dad's, was part of Bristol's tight-knit Jamaican network, went over and whispered in his ear. I saw his expression change. 'Have your skates, man,' he said, handing them back.

A lot of people liked my father, but others less so. There were always stories floating around about what he had or hadn't done. On the occasions he'd pick me up and take me out, we'd go to any number of older Jamaican family houses where they'd welcome us in and give us food. I came to see these women as the local matriarchs. People like Mrs Wynters and Mrs Davis were our pioneers: I continue to have huge respect for what these women of the Windrush generation had to overcome as they sought to make homes for their families and establish our communities.

My father's life was a hustle. For him and so many others, it had to be. His experiences even ended up in a book by Ken Pryce, published in 1979. *Endless Pressure* was a ground-breaking investigation into the effects of racism and discrimination on West Indians living in the St Pauls area of Bristol. The book describes the 'endless pressure' of racism on daily life and the lengths people had to go to to keep it together. I faced my challenges, but to be Black in 1960s and 1970s Bristol was another level.

My father was primarily a businessman, owning a shop and a night-club called Crystal Dove that was particularly well known. It was on the corner of Grosvenor Road and St Nicholas Road. While other nightclubs would close at 2 a.m., Dad's club would carry on into the small hours. He had a pool table there which was available during the day, and I used to work there every Saturday from the age of four-teen. I'd do everything from sorting the change for the pool tables to flipping burgers. But while my dad owned all these businesses, I never remember him having a house of his own for me to go to. He could have done – he was often cash rich and houses in the St Pauls district of Bristol were cheap. But he seemed to prefer having a room here, a place to stay there, always ready to move on.

He treated being a parent the same way. He was around and then he wasn't. Although he lived nearby, there were periods when I didn't see him for what seemed like months. Then he'd suddenly reappear as a big presence and show off his football and cricket skills in front of my friends. That's my dad, I'd think, swelling with pride.

Once, when I was about eight, he turned up at the house having been in a fight. He was covered in cuts and bruises. I was in bed when he arrived, and I remember hearing the shock in my mum's voice when she saw him: 'What happened?' He shrugged it off – 'It's nothing' – and came up to see me. I pretended to be asleep, but he sat down on the bed and put his hand on my head. That wasn't the only time I heard about him being involved in fights. Another time someone said to me, 'Your dad is a serious man.' And we both knew what he meant. Growing up, I was proud of him for that. The Bristol of the time could be a tough, violent place and that Windrush generation had to be able to take care of things.

One evening I was at home watching the local news when my dad's name flashed up on screen. The police were looking for him because, apparently, he had beaten someone up. It was a local rivalry between him and this other guy. Years later, a police officer told me that he was glad my father had done it because the rival was a real troublemaker. When I got to school the next day, everyone had seen it. *Marvin, man, your dad was on TV last night!* To be honest, I felt good about the attention, not to mention the fact he'd won!

While he didn't seem to have a home, what my dad did have was a car that he was really proud of – a beige Jaguar, Arthur Daley-style. He had two doves that he kept in the car that would sit looking out of the back window. Despite the crime rate in the area at the time, my dad made a show of never locking it. It was a point of principle: everyone knew who he was, so he knew they would leave it alone.

That said, there was the time he left a video camera on the back seat and it got stolen.

I was fifteen then and one of my mates told me they thought they knew who'd done it. It was another boy from school. He was in a posse – and a serious one at that. Most of the kids in it were two to three years older than me. I wasn't in anything, but still got it in my head I had to do something about it. It seems crazy thinking about it now, but I went to this kid's house to confront him. But when I knocked on his door, his mum answered instead. He wasn't in, so I told her why I was there: 'I think he's taken my dad's camera.' His mum gave me a look, and said, 'I don't know anything about that.' I'm sure she didn't, but I still told her, 'He needs to bring it back.' I then went looking for him in one of the pool halls.

While I was risking my neck for him, it transpired my dad had found out who had actually taken the camera. He'd tracked it down to a basement club in St Pauls – the sort of place where most people would be afraid to go. Another school friend of mine happened to be in the area and told me what happened. My father had sauntered down into the club with one of his doves atop his finger. He'd then emerged five minutes later, the dove still perched on one hand and the video camera in his other.

None of which helped me. It quickly got back to the kid I'd accused that I'd been looking for him. Now he and his people were looking for me. I was told they were going to beat me up. With sticks, one friend warned me. For the rest of the week, I stayed on my side of Easton. There was a dual carriageway between where he and I lived. As long as I stayed on my side of it, I reasoned, I should be OK.

Come Saturday, however, it was the norm for everyone to head up into town. I decided I couldn't hide for ever and had to go in. Sure enough, it wasn't long before I ran into this kid and his people. My heart sank. It was a bright, sunny day, and I remember my mind racing as he came up to me. I stood my ground in an effort to suggest I wasn't afraid. There was a pause while I braced myself for the verbal threats and first punch. Instead, he said, 'All right, Marv?'

'All right?' I replied, feeling anything but. The moment, though, was defused. Inside, I breathed a huge sigh of relief. It was high-stakes stuff for a fifteen-year-old.

I never told my dad that I'd gone looking for his camera. But three years later, when I was eighteen, I did speak to him properly. My life was moving on: I had been invited to Lympstone to take the Royal Marines Potential Officers Course, had completed my A Levels and had offers from universities. I decided the time was right to confront him. Over the years, I'd built up a lot of sadness and anguish towards him, from all the times he'd let me, my sister and mum down – there is a level of resentment and antagonism that can only be found in relationships with those you deeply love. Finally, I felt old enough, strong enough, confident enough to take him on.

'I've done it – I don't need you any more,' I told him. 'You've never done much for me. I'm the one who is going to look after Mum now. You don't need to worry about us no more.'

I could feel the anger coursing through me as I spoke, and I wondered how he was going to respond. Growing up, he'd been a disciplinarian – by which I mean, step out of line and you could get a 'beatin'. 'That's how you discipline kids in Jamaica,' he'd tell me. I always resented it – as far as I was concerned, he couldn't just turn up and start disciplining me like that. It didn't happen often but because I didn't want the threat to become real, I'd do what I was told. All the time, the resentment was building up.

Hitting eighteen, I had years of frustration inside me, and that evening, it all came out. My father stared at me. I could see he wasn't happy and didn't seem to know what to do or say. He didn't respond. How could he? He knew what I said was true and there is great power in that kind of truth. He couldn't come back. And neither would our relationship, for many decades.

Perhaps unsurprisingly, with all the challenges she faced, Mum struggled with depression. Which was part of the reason why, when I was three, we moved to a refuge – Bystock, in Exmouth. We moved there in secret with only Nan and Grandad knowing where we would be. The day the social worker put us on the train at Temple Meads, even Mum didn't know where she was going. The social worker got on with us to explain what to do when we got off at Exeter. She took so long explaining, that the train started moving while she was still on board. Although life was tough, it was all Mum could do not to laugh.

Bystock was an old stately home and an incredible place for a child. I call it a refuge but those running it saw it as a community in which residents supported one another. We had a bedsit main room and a separate kitchen, which smelt of gas. The children who lived there would knock on one another's doors in the morning and we'd wander the spacious halls or head off into the grounds. There was a very special older man there called Dougy, who wove baskets in a workshop on the estate. I still remember the smell of that place and him taking me for walks. He was like a real-life Father Christmas.

Whenever we left the estate to head into town, I'd look at the suburban houses and see everything I longed for but didn't have: safety, stability, security. To that list of things I wanted, I would add whiteness. I was aware of my brown skin very early on and understood, even before I had the words to describe it, that whiteness gave access to a world not accessible to Black and Brown people. All the successful people I saw in life and on TV were white.

On my birthday, the other residents gave me a book: *Hilda Boswell's Omnibus: A Treasury of Favourites*. It's a collection of short stories, poems and abridged tales. The book is one of my oldest possessions and I can't open it without experiencing a mixture of hope and vulnerability, a wish that I could reach back from where I am today and tell my mum it was going to be all right.

One poem in particular captured a mood that shadowed my childhood: 'Foreign Lands' by Robert Louis Stevenson. The accompanying illustration is of a boy who has climbed a tree and is looking over some cottages and a stream to the green hills in the distance.

> If I could find a higher tree,
> Farther and farther I should see,
> To where the grown-up river slips
> Into the sea among the ships,
>
> To where the roads on either hand
> Lead onward into fairy land . . .

As a child, I wanted to be that boy. Firstly, he was white, which meant he had access to the security I wanted in my life. Secondly, there was an open expanse of land and sky in front of him. Later, when I moved into the physical confines of the Long Cross estate in Lawrence Weston and the emotional limbo of my teenage years, the openness of that poem came to represent the escape I wanted in my life. I still feel connected to it even today.

In 2017, there was a reunion at Bystock. I took my children and tried to explain to them the safety and hope the place encapsulated for me. The house and grounds were significantly smaller than I remembered them and the land that had sat on either side of the country road leading up to the main house had been developed for houses. Nevertheless, returning there touched me deeply.

One image that stands out from my childhood is standing at a bus stop in the dark with my mum, my sister Dionne in the pushchair, waiting for the bus to take us home. I didn't feel scared, stood there. But I did feel vulnerable – both for myself and for my mum and sister – and very aware of us waiting there in the cold while others drove past on their way home in warm cars.

In 1976 we returned from Bystock and moved into a flat on the Long Cross estate in Lawrence Weston, on the edge of Bristol: later, we'd move to Easton. The flat was a long way from my nan's, so we used to stay with her every weekend. The return journey was usually around a forty-five-minute bus journey along Stapleton Road, through the city-centre, over the Downs, through Sea Mills, down Kings Weston Lane and along Long Cross to 1 Humberstan Walk. Now and again, one of my nan's neighbours, Joe, who was also a close family friend, would drive us back in his light blue Ford Cortina. I remember him taking us on one occasion and I pretended to be asleep. Joe carried me into the flat through the cold, dark evening air. I'm sure he wasn't fooled by my acting and must have known I was awake. I was only about five but I can still remember how safe I felt in the warm car. I knew the safety was temporary and hoped that if I stayed asleep, they might turn around and take us back to Nan's house.

I couldn't escape that sense of financial and physical vulnerability as a child, of money being tight – that sense of a lack of support or safety net. I remember Mum being worried a lot. It rippled through our lives in all sorts of small ways. Sometimes, we didn't have much food in the house. And there were times we had little in the way of drinks. There was water if we were thirsty. But a squash or Ribena felt like a luxury of the good times.

The vulnerability was exacerbated by the early taste of racism I had to face. I had friends, but some of the older kids would call me 'Blackie Sambo'. My mum would get annoyed, but I never wanted her to confront any of the children for fear that she would end up in an altercation with the other parents. It felt like we had no back-up. My mum told me to say 'I might be Black but my name's not Sambo', which sort of worked.

When I cast my mind back to those bus trips to my nan and grandad's for the weekend, I picture travelling into the sunshine. Leaving the estate and going there was like travelling to safety. My mum was – and is – amazing but she was a single mother living on a housing estate on the north-west edge of Bristol, miles from the city centre and her family. She had little money and two Brown babies in 1970s England. That inevitably took its toll on her. Going to stay with my nan and grandad, with our family all around, in a part of the city where there were kids who looked like me, meant everything.

I used to feel really down about travelling back on a Sunday evening. We'd sit at the bus stop at the top of Armoury Square on Stapleton Road, waiting for the number 23 bus to take us home. Nan would come and wait with us. I'd sit there, hoping that the bus wouldn't come and then I could stay on for a bit longer. There was a slight dip on the other side of the Easton Way junction, which meant the top of the bus would appear first. I hated the sight of that. I hated the journey home, too. The bus weaved its way through the suburbia of Westbury, past streets of houses with driveways and gardens, bushes and hedges. I'd watch them glide past with my face pressed against the window. I wish we could live in one of those, I'd think. Then the bus would drive on and the landscape would change. We'd be back to the estate, the walk back from the bus stop in the dark, past the communal bin area, the all-too-familiar echoes of the entrance hall, the scratch of the key in the doorway, and home. My nan's house was warm in more ways than one. Open our door in the winter, and the crackle of cold would rush out.

Yet I'm nostalgic for those childhood years, and the magical moments we shared. I remember Christmases fondly. I remember watching *The Six Million Dollar Man* with my mum, sleeping in her bed and watching our tiny black-and-white TV when I wasn't well. Once at nursery, we read *Mr Tickle*, one of the Mr Men books, and the nursery had large cardboard cut-outs of the characters. In the book, there's a train guard whom Mr Tickle tickles, and because he's laughing so much, he can't wave his flag to let the train go. It doesn't sound like much, but they let me take the cut-out of the train guard home with me: I was so excited, bringing that back and having him standing there in my room.

I also had an early belief or faith. I had a sense of a God who knew me and cared for us, my family, from an early age. I think it's one of the reasons I had such a sense of purpose despite our circumstances. At Bystock, we had met a French Catholic woman called Christina, whose daughter was also there, and we formed a connection. She became very important in our lives. Christina prayed for me every day and sent me hand-drawn pictures and letters telling me how special I was and that I was loved by Jesus. She also told me that guardian angels were looking out for me.

But even with this child's faith, I still carried with me the challenges that my mum faced in bringing me up. We didn't talk about it. My mum isn't expressive in that way. And nor am I. But that has never stopped us being extremely close. We're very tight. There's a shared silence between us, filled by the memories of what we went through.

Even people you thought were on your side could try to take advantage of you. It wasn't just the doctors telling my mum to abort the pregnancy or have me adopted. Once, members of the Labour Party were canvassing for a local election. A man stood in her doorway, looked at this white woman with two Brown children, judged her and propositioned her: 'It looks like you could do with some help. Maybe I could help you, and you could help me in return?' A vulnerable woman being put in that position by someone who was standing for public office.

Recently, while we had work done on our house, we stayed with Mum back in Easton, which was the house we ended up in after the Lawrence Weston flat. It stirred up all sorts of emotions. It's funny being back in your old family home as an adult – everything seemed smaller and we seemed to bump into each other a lot more. But it felt good being there. And I felt lucky she was still living in the same place, that this connection to my past was still there.

I caught myself looking out of her bedroom window, remembering how far we'd come from Bystock to Lawrence Weston to Easton to mayor. I remembered staring out of the same window, just before my A Levels, watching my friends play outside. They were on the grass having a kickabout with a football while I was trying to revise. They've got a better life than me, I thought. They're relaxing, playing football. It was the same feeling I'd get as a kid having to go to bed early and hearing the other kids still playing outside. I had these revision cards I'd made and had spread them out across the bed in front of me. It would have been so easy to pile them up and head outside to play.

I often tell my kids this story. I tell them how horrible that feeling is, that it feels terrible at the time, but later on, I was glad I had invested in myself. My friends outside might have been having fun, but their lives went in a different direction to mine. It wasn't because I was smarter than them: far from it. They had a lot more ability than the course of their lives suggested. But many never reached their full potential.

When I got my first car, I drove it to my mum's house in Easton. It was January 1996 and it was cold outside. I took her shopping – door to door – then I drove to Lawrence Weston, retracing the bus route we used to take, but this time safe in our warm car. We parked outside the flat where we used to live.

'You won,' I said to Mum while I was staying there. 'You won.' All her life, she's had people looking down on her, disrespecting her, making judgements on who she is and what she has been through. It happened on a human level and on a class level, too. A lesser person might have crumbled. But her inner strength saw her through. Mum seems unable to comprehend this or take any credit, though. She told me she'd always prayed God would be a father to the fatherless and directs the credit accordingly. That is certainly part of the story, but she doesn't recognize her strength. I've pointed out how many others might not have made it, never seen their children coming out OK. I have made the point several times since. 'All those people who've disrespected you and people like us,' I've told her, 'and now you've got a daughter, my sister Dionne, living in Switzerland with two great kids who go skiing at the weekend, and a son with his own family who became mayor of your home city. How many people wouldn't have wished that for their children? Look where we came from, and where we are now. That's what *you* did.'

2.

Fighting Chance

I was eight when the first of the Bristol uprisings took place in April 1980. And on both that occasion and its successor in 1986 I was closer to the action than I should have been.

The 1980 uprising happened after a police raid on the Black and White Café on Grosvenor Road in St Pauls. The history of the Black and White Café is one of competing and overlapping narratives. In the story told by police, press and council it was associated with drugs and other criminal behaviour (and to be fair, some people in the Black community felt the same). But to others, it was a symbol of Black safety, power and defiance in the face of a politically and physically threatening city. For both these reasons, by the time it was shut down permanently in 2004, it had been raided by police more times than any other property in the country.* In 1980, the local community was reacting to Bristol's hostility toward Black people and police abuse of the new 'Sus' laws, which gave them the powers to stop and search anyone they deemed suspicious – a power that led to Black youths being disproportionately targeted, abused and criminalized. On this occasion, a raid on the Black and White Café led to a confrontation with police.

* https://www.theguardian.com/uk/2003/feb/09/drugsandalcohol.tony thompson

The police were driven back by bottles and bricks. Over the next few hours, buildings and vehicles were set alight: over a hundred people were arrested, and scores injured on both sides (though to give some sense of the opinions at the time, *The Daily Telegraph* headline describing the Bristol events was '19 Police Hurt in Black Riot'). St Pauls was the first of three major riots that took place in the early 1980s, fuelled by ongoing racial discrimination and harassment faced by Black people. It was soon followed in 1981 by both Brixton in London and Toxteth in Liverpool.

By this time, we'd moved to Easton, having been offered a two-bedroom house one street away from Nan and Grandad's. In 1980 I was in my first year at St Nicholas of Tolentino Junior School and I'd been thinking about my eighth birthday party. Rather than ringing people up, because so few of us had phones in those days, my mum was taking me around friends' houses to invite them. We were walking back along Brook Road, heading for Grosvenor Green, which is at one end of Grosvenor Road, where the Black and White Café was.

It was the shouting we heard first – a roar of human voices. We knew immediately that something was going on. Then we saw the police cars and vans parked up. As we came out the bottom of Brook Road, a police car came tearing past. There was a glass bottle lying on the road and the police car went straight over it. I felt a sharp thump against my head, like a bee sting. A piece of the shattered bottle had flown up and hit me on the eyebrow. Looking back, I was incredibly lucky that the shard of glass didn't land a few centimetres lower, and hit my eye. Mum grabbed me immediately, and we hurried home, in the opposite direction down Lower Ashley Road – away from the noise and the shouts and the smashes and the fighting.

That night, after I'd gone to bed, my dad came round. I remember listening to him and Mum talking about what had happened. I couldn't hear everything, just snatches of the conversation, but from their tones, I knew it was serious. My dad came upstairs into my bedroom and switched the light on. Taking his thumbs, he started brushing them against my eyebrows, asking me where the glass had hit me. He went all over my head, checking for any scraps or shards that might still be there.

Six years later, there was a second riot in St Pauls. The underlying issues that had triggered the first uprising were still unresolved – unemployment, unfairness, racial abuse and hostility – and, once again, it was a police raid that was the starting point. This time, the disturbances went on for several nights. I was now fourteen and far more aware of what was going on. As I walked back from school with some friends that day, one of whom was my next-door neighbour, Dean, we could all sense the tension in the air. I felt more excited than frightened as I saw the rows of police vans lined up and a helicopter circling overhead. Together with another couple of friends, we decided to walk over to St Pauls to watch what was going on and ended up sitting on a wall at the junction of Grosvenor Road and St Nicholas' Road, as the police numbers and the crowd built up. All the time, the buzz of voices was getting noisier, angrier. By this age, we had experienced enough racism to share the collective anger that was felt towards society and the police. We stayed there and waited while the atmosphere thickened, and then suddenly things began to kick off. As the first bottles began to fly, it felt like it was time to leave. When we got home, we turned on the news to see what was happening from the safety of our living rooms. The following morning at school it was the only thing anyone was talking about – and we could say, 'Yeah, we were there.'

Like many Black kids, I had a complex relationship with the police growing up, with the balance being towards the negative. There were exceptions: lots of kids who grew up in my area would remember George Row and Ian Moore, white police officers who used to run a football club on a Saturday morning. Those two were decent guys. Sometimes we'd head along to Trinity Road Police Station, go to the front desk and ask if they were there. The officer would look at us with a mix of suspicion and hostility. Then George or Ian would come out, greet us and take us into the office for a drink. It felt like we were crossing a line, going to a place we either weren't supposed to go or were simply not welcome. Overcoming that front-desk hostility was a small victory, my Virgil Tibbs moment. (I sometimes felt like that as mayor of Bristol, too. And it can be a good feeling.) Ian Moore didn't just help run our local football club: he also went on to challenge the local professional teams about not recruiting Black players. The common belief was that one in particular had an unofficial no-Black-player policy. Ian persuaded the club to let him run his own scouting sessions in St Pauls – he made a real difference.

But Ian and George were the exceptions. I may still remember their kindness and support, but I will never forget the time when I was eight years old, and their fellow officers came to our house looking for my dad. He wasn't there, but they barged their way in and turned the place over, supposedly trying to find him. They were rude and disrespectful to my mum and having not found my dad, they left the place in an absolute state for us to clear up. We went down to Trinity Road Police Station to complain. As we got there, we saw the two plain-clothes officers parked in a car in Trinity Walk, the lane next to the station – the two who'd just been to our house. They laughed at us as we walked past them into the station. Inside, things weren't much better. They stared at me, then at Mum, an unmarried white woman, with her Brown children – she was carrying my little sister Dionne. Mum's complaints were, of course, dismissed out of hand.

It sometimes felt as though the police were hostile towards us for the sake of it. There was a kids' nightclub in town that I used to go to, Studios. It was on a Wednesday night and was for under-fifteens. It finished around ten, and then we'd get the number 48 or 49 bus from the city centre back to Stapleton Road and home. These were the Black kids' buses because that's where we lived. One night, as the bus reached Old Market, it was pulled over and a group of police officers got on, again plain-clothes officers, not uniformed. One of them started speaking in a mock-Jamaican patois accent, trying to wind everybody up. I don't think he was looking for anyone in particular. He just wanted to get a rise out of us. He started kissing his teeth in a really exaggerated fashion. We stared back at him in silence. That's all we had. We couldn't do anything, and he knew it. Anyone who reacted would have been arrested. It was pure provocation.

On another night, I was heading home from Studios with Dean and another school friend. It was about 10 p.m. and we were walking through Broadmead Shopping Centre when we saw a commotion up ahead. Heaps of clothes were spread out across the precinct and kids were running in and out of a shop. It turned out that someone had been messing about and leaned on the door of a shop called Citizens' Leisure, only to discover that a member of staff had forgotten to close it. After that, it was a free-for-all – everyone was taking stuff. This was at a time when ski jackets were all the rage: there was a pile of yellow-and-white Pierre Cardin ski coats scattered across the floor. One of my mates grabbed one, but almost as soon as he did, a bigger kid snatched it off him. 'I'll take that,' he said. We walked on.

We didn't take anything else. I was too nervous to grab anything, though in my head I was cursing myself. *Man, I should've got some stuff. I could have picked this, grabbed that.* That was only natural – it was free gear, right? As we headed off, we had to cross a footbridge over the road. Just before we got there, this kid ran past us, carrying a handful of clothes that he'd taken. He was being chased by the police. As he climbed up the steps and was halfway over the bridge, a second group of officers came up the other side. He was trapped in the middle and had no choice but to hand himself in.

We watched this scene play out. That was lucky, I thought. If we had taken something, that could have been us. But before we could get any further, an unmarked police car rolled up behind us and flicked its headlights on full beam. We stood blinking in the glare as a guy climbed out, a plain-clothes officer again.

'All right boys?' he said. 'What are you up to?'

'Going home,' I replied, and started to explain where we'd been. But the police officer cut me off.

'Do you mind getting in the car?' he asked. It sounded more like an order than a question. 'It's OK,' he reassured us. 'You're not being arrested. We just want to ask you some questions.' You do what you're told when you're a thirteen-year-old interacting with the police, right? So we got in the car and were driven to Bridewell Station. There we were taken up to the front desk. The sergeant who was stood behind it looked at us and asked, 'Do you know why you've been arrested?'

'We haven't been arrested,' I said.

I looked at the officer who'd brought us in. He just stared back at us and shrugged.

'Yes, you have,' the sergeant said, laughing. Before we knew what was happening, we were taken down and put into the cells. It turned out we weren't the only ones who had been picked up. The police had obviously gone round, sweeping up everyone they could find. Or, more specifically, everyone they could find who was Black.

It was a strange feeling, being down in the cells. Part of me felt emboldened: we knew we were in the right; we had done nothing wrong. If nothing else, at least we'd get off school tomorrow, I thought. To be honest, we were also a little excited. It would make a great story. At a time when the lines of separation between the Black community and the police were clear – if occasionally blurry in places – a night in the cells wouldn't do our image any harm. Through the cell door, we were able to hear the other kids coming and going, and could hear people shouting. We knew several of those coming in, including some who had well-earned reputations, and others who didn't. We were taken off to be interviewed in turn: in our thirteen-year-old minds, there wasn't anything to worry about because we hadn't done anything. Much to the officers' frustration, there was simply no evidence and we spent much of the interview laughing because it was so ridiculous. Looking back, we were lucky. We'd already been arrested when we'd been told we hadn't been. It wouldn't have taken much for the police to pull out some of the clothes and claim we'd stolen them. As it was, we were sent back down to the cells again.

Back home, my mum was frantic with worry. It had gone one in the morning, and I still wasn't back. She later told me she'd gone out and found a police officer on the street, explaining I hadn't come home. She gave them my name. The officer checked in with the station, but they denied I was there: 'No, we don't know where he is.'

My mum rang the pastor of our church – a lovely guy called Andy Paget. It was the middle of the night but that's the pastor's life – they're always on call. Andy was an educated white man and the police took him more seriously: he found out that I'd been taken to Bridewell Police Station and came to collect me in his car. I felt safe when Andy arrived: I had a respectable white man coming to pick me and my friends up. Even by the age of thirteen, I knew my association with Andy would assure the police I was OK, would elevate me in their eyes. I had someone who could talk and stand up to these guys (and they were all men) and be heard in a way a Black advocate couldn't. It was a real-life version of Chris Rock's famous sketch in which he advises Black people to travel with a white friend as the best defence against getting beaten up by the police.

The next day at school, everyone knew what had happened. *Man, you got arrested.* They all wanted to know what it had been like in the police station. One kid said to me, 'You think you're bad now, don't you?' He had his finger on a bit of truth there. I didn't want to be in trouble, but at that time, in a city that sometimes seemed to despise us, coming into conflict with the city's institutions, in whatever way it had happened, and coming out on top, felt like doing my bit.

We were lucky it never went any further. Others in that situation were not so fortunate and – despite being innocent of any crime – their earliest interactions with the police set their lives on downward spirals they struggled to escape.

I'd always wanted to box as a child. I liked fighting. I had two older cousins – Denys and Anthony – and they made me play fight. Like so many, I idolized Muhammad Ali. Most Black families and Black heritage families would watch boxing in the 1970s and we were no different. It was a place where people who looked like us could not only rise to be kings of the world, but punish the oppressor, the bully, on the way there. One fight I remember was the world title fight between Alan Minter and Marvin Hagler at Wembley in 1980. It was an ugly occasion. My dad had taken me to London at the time of the fight. We drove through Brixton as the radio talked through the build-up. We were all 100 per cent Hagler, a loyalty that was cemented when it was alleged that Minter had said that he 'did not intend to lose his title to a Black man' (although Minter himself claimed the statement was misrepresented and taken out of context). Hagler took him apart in three rounds. As a result, the British fans erupted. Bottles and cans rained down on the ring and Hagler had to be escorted to safety by police. Minter might have been British, but migration, racism, class and poverty make belonging a complicated affair. Hagler's victory was our victory.

Even today, I like nothing better than going on YouTube to watch old highlights or a documentary. Boxing is about so much more than what happens in the ring and I am gripped by the stories behind it – there are so many I draw on for inspiration. People like Jack Johnson, who at the height of the Jim Crow era became the first Black heavy-weight champion of the world. At a time when Black people were being lynched, he married a white woman, had an expensive car and all the trappings of success. There's a story of him being pulled over by police while driving: the policeman fined him $10 for speeding but Johnson handed him $20, saying, 'I'm coming back this way.'

In 1908, he won the world title by beating Canadian Tommy Burns in Australia. For years, Burns had refused to fight him. When they finally got in the ring together, it was clear to the crowd why. Johnson took Burns apart in front of an all-white crowd. There's a moment when Burns wants to drop but Johnson holds him up, so he can continue to punish him. Throughout the fight, Johnson is talking to Burns and his corner. There was a myth that Black boxers couldn't take body punches. So Johnson goads Burns to hit him there. When he does, Johnson tells him 'You hit like a woman.' After he beat Burns, Johnson took on Jim Jeffries, the former world champion who came out of retirement to stop him – the original 'Great White Hope'. 'I am going into this fight with the sole purpose of proving that a white man is better than a Negro,' Jeffries boasted. Johnson took him apart as well.

Although I was interested in boxing, I didn't know how to get involved. That was true of sport more generally. Instead, I used to play football and cricket with other kids on the Rawnsley Park patch of grass outside my house. There was a whole load of us who used to play. It was all self-organized but good fun – and it helped keep us active.

I liked football, but I wasn't a particularly skilful player and didn't support either of the Bristol teams. I have been asked so many times on the campaign trail over the years whether I support City or Rovers. My answer is always that it's complicated. The sad truth is that when I was growing up, in the mid-1980s, Black kids weren't that welcome on the terraces. When I was ten, my junior school took us to a Rovers game. They were playing against Tottenham Hotspur at their Eastville Stadium. I was nervous, convinced the men in the stands were going to call us names or beat us up. I ended up watching them rather than the game on the pitch. It doesn't matter how old – or rather, how young we were – we didn't feel safe in an environment like that. It would start with verbal abuse and lead on from there. Even at ten, my sense of self-protection kicked in. Following a local football team simply wasn't an option.

Instead, football was something we watched on the television:

Match of the Day on BBC and *The Big Match* on ITV. When I moved to Easton, our next-door neighbours were Liverpool fans, and that's who I ended up supporting. I always liked the grit of Graeme Souness and the finesse of Kenny Dalglish. The clincher for me was when John Barnes was signed. After that, I was all in. There's an iconic photograph of Barnes backheeling a banana off the pitch that had been thrown at him from the stands. That one image summarized both his skill and poise, and the abuse Black people had to put up with. As mayor, I have shared how common it was for us as kids to have adults drive past and shout out racial slurs or tell us to go back to our own country. I see the shock on people's faces when they realize I'm talking about the city they thought they knew, rather than somewhere from a TV documentary or history book. That abuse is amplified if you're a Black figure in the public eye: this is something I've had to learn to deal with. Sometimes I could have done with some of John Barnes's elegant response.

It was when a boys' club opened near me that I got into boxing. Broad Plain Boys Club moved from Bedminster to a new building ten minutes' walk from my house. There was a kid down our road called Michael who found out about it and told us they had a twelve-foot snooker table. Pretty soon, a whole group of us were spending our evenings at the club. They had great facilities. There were table-tennis tables with proper bats, ones that still had rubber on both sides, rather than being worn down to the wood. There was also that full-size snooker table, a pool table and a sports hall. And they had a boxing club.

I used to watch the guys going in and out of the small room with the ring in it. They were genuinely tough. I went back to my friends to tell them what I'd found, but they didn't share my enthusiasm.

'I ain't boxing.'

'You get punched in the face.'

'Do you want to end up with a flat nose?'

I couldn't persuade the others to join me, but I was determined to give it a go. I've always been a bit like that. If I've wanted to do something, I've done it, even – and sometimes especially – if those around me won't. The next time I visited the club, I went over to the boxing room and asked if I could start boxing. The club was run by Jimmy Hill and Jimmy Robottom. 'Come on Wednesday,' they said. That night I ran home humming 'Eye of the Tiger'. From that evening on, while my friends were playing snooker and table tennis, I was skipping and sparring instead.

I fought at light welter, which was around ten stone. At five-foot-ten, I was tall and thin, but my body strength was building. Once at school, I grabbed one of the ropes in the gym hall and pulled myself up to the ceiling using only my arms, surprising even myself. But it taught me that I was stronger – both physically and mentally – than I realized. I could punch hard, too. I didn't have a single knockout punch but I had a good hard jab that I walked forward and through as I pushed it out. I could hit someone straight and strong. I also learned pretty quickly that I could take a punch. One of the guys we used to spar with was Mickey Ray, a local doorman. He was in his mid-twenties, a decade older than me. Mickey was a nice guy and a gifted boxer. He had a big punch on him. When he hit you, you knew about it. If we had to spar with him, me and the other kids developed a strategy of going through the motions for two minutes and fifty seconds and only then actually trying to hit him hard, calculating we would be able to evade the inevitable punishment for the final ten seconds of the round!

Boxing began to change me. I wasn't just feeling better physically from all the working out, but mentally, too. The training and atmosphere in the gym filled in some of the gaps in my life. A relationship with a good coach can take on a father–son dynamic and that's what I tasted with Jimmy Hill and Jimmy Robottom. Whether they knew it or not, I was taking a lot from these new relationships. For the first time, I had structure. I had people making demands of me. I was being tested and discovering an ability to overturn adversity. I learned the value of self-discipline and control. The first time I sparred, I glared across the ring at the lad in the opposite corner, Martin Williams. He took no notice. I went out to swing and he just picked me off. The madder and wilder I got, the more I got hit. I ended up through the ropes with him just standing behind me. I came out of that experience realizing that giving in to anger didn't work for me. If I was going to fight, I needed to think.

I began feeling more confident in myself. I was being tested three nights a week and I felt like I belonged somewhere. I calmed down, not feeling the need for bravado to cover my insecurities. I remember saying to myself, 'I don't need to fight any of these kids to prove myself. I was in the ring with Mickey last night.' It wasn't about being a tough guy. I was never a tough guy. But I was – finally – proving myself to myself.

One of the reasons I loved boxing was because the fight wasn't personal. One night, I was put up to spar against another kid I knew. He was a couple of years older than me and a bit of a 'bad man' on the street and hung out with a crew that was notorious among my age group. In the world in which I knew this kid, there was a pecking order, and he was above me in that. But he was new to boxing. What would happen if he and his crew came after me on the street because I hit him? The first time we fought was on a Monday night. I was tentative – dancing around, going through the motions. I even took a few punches, as they weren't that hard. A few of my friends were watching. Jimmy put us back in together on the Wednesday. After about a minute, I thought, *Ah, stuff it!* and I just let some go and hit him hard. Nothing wild, just straight, controlled punches. The next time I saw him out on the street, I was really nervous, but he just said, 'Yes Marv!' and couldn't have been friendlier. He hadn't ever really talked to me before.

The more I trained, the better I got. I often sparred with one of the older guys, who was a good fighter. Once, he threw a jab at me and I managed to duck underneath it and jab him in the face. At the end of the round, he turned to my coach and said, 'He's fucking good, Jim.' After that, it was only a matter of time before I was put in for my first fight. I was seventeen.

Jim Hill, my main coach, was exactly the sort of person you wanted in your corner. He was ex-navy, had had a few bare-knuckle fights and wasn't afraid of a tear-up. He was blunt, swore like the sailor he was, but he loved his boys and wrapped his arms around us. Decades later, when, sadly, he was diagnosed with cancer, I went to visit him in his bungalow shortly before he passed away. It was hard for me seeing this monster of a man now frail and vulnerable. But we sat together and watched an old Benn–Eubank fight on my iPad. At the end, he said, 'I love you, Marv.' I felt the same.

For that first fight, Jim picked me up in his car, a silver Audi 80, and drove me down to Brean Leisure Park, near Weston-super-Mare, where the bout was taking place. I was taken to the dressing room – which wasn't a real dressing room, just a room off the main dance hall. One of the other boxers from our club, Mark, a lad with an explosive right hand who was yet to have his first fight, gave me a nudge, pointing to someone getting changed opposite.

'That's the guy you're fighting,' he told me. 'Shane.'

I looked over at my opponent. While I was tall and skinny, Shane was proper stacked, muscular and fully developed. I swear he was covered in hair.

'That's a man,' I said. 'I can't be fighting him.'

But when it was time for the fight, I was taken into the ring, and as I climbed in, ducking under the ropes, I saw Shane looking at me. He *was* my opponent. The pair of us walked up to the middle, the crowds around the ring cheering us on. I think some may have been making bets: if they were, they probably weren't putting much money on me! I was nervous but too overwhelmed to be affected by my nerves. I looked my opponent in the eye. The referee was talking away but whatever he was saying, I wasn't taking it in. I went back to my corner, got my final words of instruction from Jim, and then the bell went. Round One.

Shane was a southpaw and came straight at me, hitting me with two big left hooks. I heard the crowd let out a deep 'ooooh'. I just remember two big thuds. I staggered from the force of them but was relieved that he'd only knocked me off my centre of balance rather than actually hurting me.

I stood up tall and hit him back. Straight punches. Double jabs and left-rights. I stepped forward every time I threw. Each time, his head was snapping back. I didn't hook or upper-cut – I didn't have those sorts of punches in my locker – but I could jab as well as anyone. By the time the bell went for the end of the round, I was well on top. I walked back to my corner, where Jim gave me the corner instructions.

'That's great, Marv. Just keep doing what you're doing. Don't stop. We'll have him again.'

The bell went for the second round. I continued to hit him. My straight punches continued to power home. A couple of times, he came back and got me on the ropes. But on each occasion, I'd come off and hit him back. By the end of the fight, I'd completely dominated him. I was given a trophy. A trophy! I was seventeen and I'd never had a trophy in my life. Back in the dressing room, everyone was all over me. There was a guy who wanted to sponsor me: he was a butcher. 'If you ever need some meat to hit, you come down and see me.' By the time I got home, my mum was in bed. I showed her what I'd won, the trophy glinting from her bedside light. I remember walking around, thinking, I just beat a guy.

My second fight was back at my own club. Funnily enough, Shane was also on the bill. He came out and knocked his opponent out within about thirty seconds. One punch, on the canvas, out. Wow, I thought. And I beat that guy. By then, I'd had in my head something we used to say in the gym – to do to them what you don't want done to you. So when it was my turn to fight, I came out fast and went straight on the attack. At one point, I dropped down and hit my opponent in the gut. I must have hurt him, because he turned his back to me and started walking back to his corner. His coach was screaming at him – 'Get back in there! Get back in!' I spoke to him, too: 'Hey, we're still fighting.' He turned round to face me, but I could tell he didn't want to fight. He took to the ropes: I hit him three more times before the referee stepped in and stopped it.

That season, I had six fights: I won four and lost two. The first win was my victory over Shane. In all three of the other wins, the referee stepped in to stop the fight. Both fights I lost were against the same opponent – Glenn Catley. Glenn was more than a decent fighter: in fact, he would go on to turn pro and eventually become World Middleweight champion. The first time I fought him, I got all my preparation wrong. I was so nervous, I didn't eat during the day. I even swam in the afternoon. So I was tired and lacking energy even before I got into the ring. He beat me up.

I then had a fight against another lad and stopped him. As a result, Jim couldn't get another boy to take me on, and asked, 'Are you OK to fight Glenn again?' Inside I thought, *What?!* Outside I said, 'Sure!' The second time I was properly prepared, but Glenn was still too good. Looking back, I can see that I was fairly raw as a fighter. With more emotional coaching, and more understanding of how to handle a fight, I might have done better. But Glenn was special, at another level. (He's a decent man too. Our sons now go to the same boxing club and recently, we sat together to watch them on the same bill. I think we were more nervous for them than we were for our own fights!)

Sadly, my boxing career was over almost as quickly as it began. I started getting headaches, so I went to see the doctor. Having checked me out, he sent me to be looked at, at the Bristol Eye Hospital, where they diagnosed keratoconus. It's a condition that means your cornea is too thin. It can lead to blurred vision or astigmatism. Lots of people have it, I was told: it was just that for most people it doesn't develop. But continuing to box would be a real risk. If anyone hit me near my eyes, it could cause irreparable damage. I had to give up fighting immediately.

I was gutted. Boxing had given me a purpose and a goal. It gave me discipline and did wonders for my confidence and self-belief. I once got into trouble at a Labour Party constituency meeting for sharing that boxing was a more important intervention on my journey than libraries. I was trying to offer a little perspective to a campaign for libraries that suggested they were the single most important intervention to educational inequalities. There was outrage on social media at the time and it has followed me ever since. But I stand by the importance of boxing for me. It wasn't itself an academic pursuit, but it vested in me the skills and sense of self I needed in a way that little else did. That's the way it was.

And though I had to stop going into the ring, my love for the sport didn't change. My boy is now a boxer and it's all a bit different. When I was fighting, there was no headgear or any other protection – you went in the ring with nothing more than a gum shield. And while I was sparring in the ring right from the start, today they take it much more slowly – you body spar for months with no hits to the head. My son goes to a club with a good set-up, and I hope he gets as much out of it as I did.

Broadening Horizons

Giving up boxing didn't stop me from pushing myself to see what I could achieve. Thanks to my older cousins, Denys and Anthony, I had long been instilled with a real sense of adventure. Denys and Anthony are my mum's sister Glenys's boys, six and four years older than me. Growing up, I idolized them. They were well known locally: Mum says everyone in St Pauls knew them when they were little because they were among the first generation of post-Windrush mixed-race kids, and it was a tight community.

They were heroes to me. They took me under their wing, taking me on escapades and making up little scenarios: *imagine you're a stuntman – an assassin.* In the 1970s, there were so many building sites around Bristol. There were so many places that had fallen into dereliction during the war and which, decades later, still hadn't been sorted out. You weren't meant to play in them, of course, but that was part of the fun of it. Looking back, they were really dangerous places to hang out: we'd clamber over pools of water on creaking planks of wood, or climb up several floors of a half-built building, standing there on the scaffolding.

Sometimes we'd walk the five or so miles from their house in Montpelier to Blaise Castle on the edge of Lawrence Weston, climbing trees and scrumping the odd apple from a garden on the way. We had no money: if Denys had a packet of crisps, he'd call them our rations and make the packet last the whole day. In the summer, we'd swim in the rivers in Eastville Park and Snuff Mills and walk home wet. Sometimes my Aunty Glenys would take us all camping on holiday, to Brean or South Wales, where we'd explore further. They didn't know it, but they instilled in me a craving for walking up and down hills carrying a backpack. That and the fact that we were all crazy about Action Men led me to an interest in the military and expeditions and, when I was in the sixth form, a life-changing trip to the Arctic Circle.

My school took part in the Duke of Edinburgh scheme, and I was encouraged to do it. I had to fulfil several criteria, including community volunteering and developing new skills. I really wasn't into all the organizing and record-keeping that went with this. But there was one section that really excited me: planning, training for and completing the expedition. In fact, it was the only part I completed in the end. When I got into sixth form, though I had decided not to go for the full award, the school still let me take part in the expedition.

One day, my head of year, Mr Jennings, asked me and my friend Tyrone to come and see him. He showed us a leaflet: it was from the British Schools Exploring Society (BSES).

'I thought you might be interested in this,' he said. The leaflet was about a six-week expedition to Iceland. It sounded amazing, but it came at a cost: £1,600, which was money I didn't have.

'But we can work with you to raise it if you want to go,' Mr Jennings said. 'You should be able to get sponsorship.'

Tyrone was my best friend. Our lives have been mirror images. He was a mixed-race kid growing up with his white mother, while his dad was a contemporary of my father. I still wasn't sure how I'd raise the money, but with Mr Jennings's encouragement we applied. The Society came back and turned our application down: they said we didn't have enough winter expedition experience to take part. I was disappointed, but by this point Mr Jennings was on a bit of a mission. He went above and beyond his role as a teacher, arranging for us to take part in a winter skills course up at Loch Eil in Scotland the following February and working with the school to cover the costs of the course and the train tickets to get us there.

It was an adventure in itself just getting there. We had to take a train to Birmingham, then Glasgow and cross the city to a different station to pick up the Fort William train. I was genuinely scared. This was the 1980s and it wasn't unusual for people to drive past us and shout racist abuse. I really don't know what I was expecting, but I'd been chased more than a few times by people wanting to beat me up because I was a Black kid in the wrong place at the wrong time. And this was Glasgow! Tyrone and I weren't confident we'd get across Glasgow alive, a belief not helped by school friends sharing their 'insights' into Glasgow. But we made it safely, caught the train and were soon up in the most incredible Scottish countryside.

On the first full day, we climbed a mountain. It was much bigger and awe-inspiring than anything I'd done on the Duke of Edinburgh trips. I remember looking up at it from the base before we started, watching snow being blown off the top. We climbed up through drifts of snow that were knee-high in places. At the top, the wind was so strong that I could lean into it as much as 30 degrees and not fall. On the summit, we crouched down in the shelter of some rocks to have a cup of tea and a slice of Kendal Mint Cake. I loved it. Being in direct contact with the enormity of nature was thrilling. I was like the boy in the tree from the Robert Louis Stevenson poem. I looked out across the hundreds of snow-covered peaks, hardly able to believe we were still in the UK. As we made our descent, I was buzzing with excitement. I looked over at Tyrone, but he had his cagoule hood up and the drawstring pulled so tight that only his eyes, nose and mouth were showing. There was a circle of ice around the edge of his hood, too.

'Ty, that was amazing,' I said.

'I'm not into it, Marv,' came his reply.

He completed the trip, but decided to focus on his football rather than applying for another BSES trip. But I did. And this time I was accepted onto the 1990 expedition to Svalbard.

Of course, I still had to raise the money. Yet again, Mr Jennings was brilliant. He helped me with the fundraising and support came from all sorts of places: Avon and Somerset Police had a sponsorship scheme, Bristol Rovers players helped through my boys' club and I did a sponsored abseil with the Gloucestershire Regiment. The army set up all the kit and helped me do it down a tower by the old Bridewell Police Station. I loved it. I felt like I belonged.

The Prince's Trust gave me money too: many years later, as mayor, I was working with Dame Martina Milburn, then the chief executive, about a possible scheme in Bristol. I mentioned how they'd supported me as a teenager and how important that help had been. As a result, I was invited to record a video for the Prince's Trust Awards, describing the impact that donation had had on my life. It wasn't a huge sum of money, but it was the right amount at the right time, and it opened up an experience I otherwise wouldn't have been able to have. I asked Martina to extend my thanks to the then Prince of Wales and she did. Later, I met King Charles and was able to thank him personally.

We flew to the north of Norway, then took a second plane to Longyearbyen, Spitsbergen. From there, we boarded a ship to Bohemanflya, the peninsula where we were going to have our base camp. We arrived at two in the morning and the sun was up. Incredible. In total, there were around a hundred of us on the expedition. We were divided into sub-groups of around a dozen, called Fires. Our group leaders were an army major called Glyn and a school teacher called Malcolm.

Each Fire was assigned a scientific project to complete. Having set a trig point, we had to map a cirque glacier (which we named Friday) and take sea-level readings. This was more dangerous than it might sound: I'd seen a crack in the surface of the snow. I stepped on in and went through the snow up to my knees. It was a fun and curious experience. But then I went straight through. My legs were in the air and my foot hit the side wall of the crevasse. I knew immediately that I was in trouble; I needed to keep entirely still otherwise I'd fall through. I cupped my hands, reached forward and dug through the snow, then eased myself up and over. Once out, I slid onto my stomach to spread my weight and as soon as I was on the solid ice of the glacier, I stood up. It genuinely was a near-death experience, and I spent the rest of that day shaking with nerves.

Measuring the sea level, meanwhile, turned out to be an exercise in sleep deprivation. A reading had to be taken every hour and we were put on an eight-hours-on, four-hours-off shift pattern over twenty-four hours. But once the work was over, we were given free rein to explore. We divided into even smaller groups. I was with three other guys: Jeremy, John and Swithen. The four of us looked at our map, identified a mountain that no one had climbed before, then took off with a commitment to be back at base in two days. Four eighteen-year-olds off up glaciers and mountains without a mobile phone or any way of contacting anyone.

The feeling of adventure, of freedom, was something I'll never forget. We walked all day and set up camp around nine at night, up near the summit of this peak. We then used water made by melting the fresh snow around our tent to heat up our meal. By this point, we thought that was the height of convenience. After we had eaten, we set off for the summit, walking up the top. It took about twenty minutes, and we got there just before midnight. The four of us sat on the four sides of the peak, in silence with our backs to one another, and we watched as the sun moved around the mountain. It was the most amazing experience: we sat in complete silence, no sound apart from our breathing and the occasional low rumble of the glacier cracking.

I remember looking down at a crevasse beneath us and thinking, if I fell down there, no one would ever see my body again. But, as I took in the view, I also thought, no one has even been up here before; no one has ever seen what we're seeing. I scoured the skyline and felt an incredible sense of how fragile and small my life was in comparison to the mountains and the glaciers that surrounded us. In that moment, I found my significance in my insignificance. Looking back, I realize I was as close to feeling awe as I ever had been. I was suddenly incredibly aware and in the moment. It's an experience I still speak about, especially when I'm talking to young people at the beginning of their lives.

Today, I'm president of the British Exploring Society (BES), as the organization is now called. I was hugely honoured to accept the role. When I went on that expedition, I was – as Michelle Obama described the experience of being one of the very few Black students at Princeton in her memoir – a poppy seed in a bowl of rice. That's all changed now, and the BES and CEO, Honor Wilson-Fletcher, work incredibly hard to ensure children from all sorts of backgrounds are involved.

The BES headquarters are at the Royal Geographical Society in

Kensington Gore, London. It's a grand old building, full of amazing artefacts: Sir Ernest Shackleton's helmet, Sir William Parry's compass and the oxygen kits used in scaling Everest, among them. As a child, I used to look through my mum's catalogues and dream my way through the camping section. I desperately wanted my own rucksack and eventually got one of those large metal-framed ones. Before I signed up for the Duke of Edinburgh trips, I used to put it on and walk around the house, imagining myself going on an expedition somewhere. Decades later, being invited to the Society's illustrious building as president of the BES meant a lot. The transition from my teenage years had been quite the journey.

Boxing and exploring were two of my most important teenage experiences. The third, equally significant in terms of the person I became, was my attempt to join the marines.

My cousins Denys and Anthony suggested that I should apply. I knew nothing about the marines, but they talked to me about them, and it got me excited. Then, when I was fifteen, Anthony joined the Gloucestershire Regiment along with a few of the other guys his age from Easton that I'd looked up to growing up. When I said I might be interested in following them, Anthony said, 'You're smart, Marv. If you join, don't join as a private, join as an officer.' His friends all said the same.

It was advice that came not only from his fondness for me but also from his own experience in the army. Anthony had suffered the kind of raw racism that wouldn't be allowed today. One corporal referred to him as 'spoon' as in 'egg and spoon – coon'. He and his friends told me stories of fights in the barracks. One night, some guys pinned him down by pulling his sheet over him and beating him in his bed. But Anthony proudly told me that as he established himself in the regiment – a phenomenal athlete, he became their youngest Lance Corporal – he had had the opportunity to pay some back. And I was proud he did. The more we talked, the more I realized that though becoming an officer would be tough, it would also present more opportunities and put me in a position where I could make everyone proud.

Soon after, there was a careers fair at school. The hall was full of stalls with people from lots of different businesses and organizations. One of them was for the Royal Navy. I sat down in front of the officer behind the desk.

'I want to be a marines officer,' I mumbled.

He looked up from whatever it was he was reading. He gave me the once-over, then said, 'You're going to need some A Levels, then.' With that, he turned back to what he had been reading. As far as he was concerned, the conversation was over.

The officer had been both matter-of-fact and dismissive. I suspect he hadn't anticipated coming to a comprehensive school and meeting a mixed-race kid who wanted to be an officer of the Royal Marines. He probably forgot about it as soon as our brief encounter ended, but what he said stayed with me. At that point, I was underperforming at school. I knew I had something in me. I'd always been in the top classes and got good grades. But when my grades started to slip, I got fearful and just stopped doing the work. I began to play up and mess around. I wasn't a bad kid, but if you weren't one of the teachers I'd connected with, I wasn't pleasant to have in class. And as time passed, my grades slipped.

The fear was of failure. 'Marvin, you could get really good grades, but you're not doing any work' became a common refrain from my teachers. But I found comfort in that space. What if I worked hard and still didn't get good grades? I was terrified of being exposed as not as good as they thought I was. That paralysed me, and as a result, I stopped doing any work. I wasn't enjoying life, I wasn't enjoying school. All I could see was an approaching cliff edge – the day I'd leave school. I might fail my GCSEs and end up with nothing – no direction, no structure, no one to believe in me or guide me. What would I do then?

But the boxing, combined with the naval officer's brusque words, helped to give me a focus. The latter gave me the goal I needed to work towards: the former some of the tools to get there. One of the lessons I learned in boxing was how to lose. The self-esteem I'd built up from learning to fight helped me to deal with that. I understood that though I could get in the ring with someone on a Monday and they could beat me, I could get into the ring with them again on

Wednesday and beat them. Nothing was set in stone: I could swap defeat and victory at any point. I wasn't good or bad, clever or stupid, I realized. I just was. I could do it. Realizing that the power to change things was in my hands was important.

Help came from other sources too. The deputy head at school was Mr Jenkins, a big Welshman. I connected with him because of my Welsh grandad. Mr Jenkins was also my physics teacher and made it his job to look out for me. At break time, he'd come and find me.

'I've been to check. You haven't been very good today,' he'd tell me, as he put me in a firm but gentle headlock and rubbed his knuckles on my head. The fact that he did that meant a lot – I liked him coming to find me. I knew he'd be annoyed with me for not working hard and not fulfilling my potential. 'Come on, Marvin,' he'd say, 'I want better.' The same was true of Mr Jennings. In my fifth year he wrote in my school report, 'Marvin, the world could be your oyster, but the way you're behaving at the moment, you're not going to go anywhere.'

That really hit home, and at just the right time. I went home that night and read and reread his comment. I decided to be different. With a few months left until my GCSEs, I started to work. By this point, the school had put me down for only six subjects. I should have done computer science as my seventh but the teacher called me out in front of the rest of the class. 'Do you want to do this subject or not?' he'd asked. And because I didn't want to lose face in front of all the other kids, I said no, and I was dropped. I was also dropped from chemistry, although my teacher seemed genuinely frustrated and pained by it.

In 2012, when I began my first campaign for mayor, I contacted Mr Jennings and invited him to the launch. I used an assembly at my former school to make the announcement. After the round of press interviews had finished, I told Mr Jennings about that school report and asked him if he remembered writing the words, which still meant so much to me. He said no, no memory at all. I was grateful that I was able to let him know how important he had been. I share that story often. I shared it with a teacher I met while out canvassing who seemed down. I told her, never doubt you are making an impact. You may say a few words that make all the difference to someone's life without even realizing it. They may thank you straight away. They may come back in twenty-five years and thank you. They may never thank you at all. But never doubt that your words matter.

To get into sixth form, I needed to get five Cs. I tried to cram, but I didn't know how to revise. Even today, I reflect on the fact that taking in, processing, developing and owning knowledge is a skill, one that can be acquired and developed. I hadn't ever done either. I remember being stuck inside, listening to all my friends chatting and messing about out front. Some seemed to be paying no attention to their exams. Looking back, I suspect it was more that they had checked out of a system and a city that had checked out on them. I was lucky to have had those seeds of hope and belief planted in me and that's what carried me through.

I vividly remember the day the results came out. I was lying in bed when the envelope came. We lived in the same two-bedroom house and Mum had moved my bedroom into the downstairs front room so my sister (who was twelve at the time) could have her own bedroom. It was late morning and my curtains were drawn. I wasn't feeling particularly hopeful about anything. As soon as I saw the envelope, I knew what it was. To begin with, full of fear, I didn't want to open it. Not opening it made me feel like I was in control, a rejection of all I felt had rejected me.

Finally, I plucked up the courage to tear the envelope open. I had five Cs and one D – just enough to get into the sixth form and do my A Levels. Part of me refused to allow myself the space to admit I needed anything from either my school or the world around me. But underneath, I was relieved. I had no plan B if I'd failed to get in. I had no college application, no training course, not even a Youth Training Scheme place. Despite all the internal turmoil and confusion, I also felt some hope. I was going to turn up and do my best.

On the first day of sixth form, some of the teachers had their eyebrows raised. I don't think they had expected me to come back. But for me, it was a fresh start and I buckled down. It wasn't easy. My learning, thinking and writing skills were not where they needed to be and I had a lot of catching up to do.

I found that the hard way early on. The first essay I can remember being given was for physical geography on plate tectonics. I agonized over it. I must have had twenty pieces of paper with different versions of the opening paragraph. The essay should've taken a weekend. I worked on it for weeks. Even thinking about it now makes me tired. Eventually, I cobbled something together. I wasn't confident, but I'd written lots and thought it would be OK.

A week later, we got the essays back. Our geography teacher praised the class for our effort, then said she'd call out the essays in order and we'd each have to walk to the front of the class to collect them. She called out the A grades. I dared to think I might just sneak in because I'd put so much into it. But I wasn't one of them. Then came the Bs. I thought I would be called forward. I was wrong. Now the Cs. More names were read out, but not mine. Not me again. I began to feel disappointed and embarrassed. I can't remember how many went forward for the Ds, but I wasn't one of them. Finally, she called the Es: 'Marvin and Tyrone'. We walked to the front of the class to get our essays back. It was humiliating, the fulfilment of the fear that had immobilized me for years — *what if I do my best and they find out I'm not actually as smart as they think I am?*

An earlier me might have resorted to self-sabotage to cover the shame. But this time, I stayed at it. I was going to turn up and keep putting one foot in front of the other. That change of attitude wasn't an overnight shift, though. It was a slow burn, a realization that my previous approach wasn't working, buoyed by the self-worth I had begun to develop through boxing. Now I was aware that giving up guaranteed failure, but trying gave me a chance. For the first time, too, I had a real goal.

Towards the end of my A Levels, the head of sixth form pulled me to one side. 'When you turned up, I didn't think you were going to make it,' he said, 'but you've worked hard.' I had. In the final year of sixth form, I went down to the recruiting office for the marines and repeated what I'd said to the officer at that careers fair several years before. This time, remarkably, I wasn't dismissed out of hand.

I mumbled my way through that first interaction. I was nervous. The naval officer who followed my journey — Tim Kenealy — later told me he thought it was a joke when I went in and presented myself at the recruiting office in Bristol City Centre. But he didn't shut me out. I was sent some promotional material in the post and after a second visit to the recruiting office, they offered me the opportunity to take part in a training course at a place called Mockerkin in the Lake District. Sixteen of us were sent up: twelve aspiring naval officers, and four of us who wanted to be officers in the Royal Marines. They sent me a rail pass to get up there, rather than having to pay for my train fare myself. I was excited and even this small gesture made me feel part of something special.

The journey to the Lakes was an adventure in itself. I began to spot the other guys getting on the train on the way up. I'd seen one lad when I boarded at Bristol Temple Meads and wondered if he was coming too. They all looked similar: about seventeen, with short hair, suits and sports bags.

When I got to the centre, I felt a dual sensation – both of belonging and detachment. I was with a group of people who wanted the same thing as me: I'd always wanted to be part of a group like this and now I was – kind of. At the same time, I stood out from the other candidates. The colour of my skin was part of that, but also my class background. There were quite a few posh kids there: one candidate was a young farmer; several of the others had been to boarding school. Even so, I didn't feel daunted. I had half expected it, as I was on a course for potential officers. And I knew I was fit, thanks to the boxing. I was skinny but had reasonable strength and stamina: I knew I could keep going.

A Royal Navy officer was waiting for us at the station. He lined us up and told us we'd be giving three-minute talks about ourselves when we arrived on-site. There was no messing around. The course had started, even before our train had pulled out.

The course was only a week long but remains one of the most pivotal weeks of my life. I learned so much in so many different ways. There were lectures and discussions about the navy and the marines – their history, organization and values – to help prepare us for the Potential Officers Course (POC) and the Admiralty Interview Board (AIB). We were also tutored in public speaking, problem-solving and leadership. I loved the practical exercises. We were set a mock rescue. We were told a guy was stuck up a mountain and we had to find him and bring him down safely. We had to work as a group, deciding what each of us should do to get the best outcome. And while we were doing that, the course leaders were watching, noting who emerged as leaders, who played positive team roles, who worked out a workable plan of action, and who slacked off. The atmosphere was full of testosterone. As we set off to find our subject, everyone ran, no one wanting to be the first to stop. Lungs were heaving and snot was dripping from our noses – not a pretty sight!

At the end of each day, we gathered for a debrief: the course leaders gave feedback on what they had liked, and what they thought was missing. The key element for me was the importance of clarity. In a real-life situation, lives would depend on it. Everyone needed to know what their role was. If they got it wrong, it was the leader's responsibility. We all got pulled up at one time or another for suggesting that the reason a team was not working well together was because we assumed the other team members would understand exactly what we wanted. That got short shrift. They gave us a routine to follow when leading: *This is the task. This is the plan to deal with it. This is my job, that is your job, this is your role. Any questions?* It was up to you to create an environment where people felt comfortable enough to ask all the questions they might have so that they could be absolutely clear about what was required.

We also did practical leadership tests, or PLTs. I had no experience of running things: but on that trip to the Lake District, I learned for the first time that I could lead. We'd typically be given something like a bucket of water and three or so planks of wood: the challenge was to get everyone in your team across from A to B with the water, and without anyone touching the ground in between. On one level, the task was all about cantilevers, but really, it was about organization – working out what needed to be done and communicating with everyone about what their role was.

As the week went on, I not only learned about myself but also about the world around me. I saw pretty quickly how comfortable the public-school boys were in assuming leadership roles. I did OK when it was my turn to be in charge, but they had been bred to be in charge and seemed to have an easy belief as they stepped into the role, while I lacked that confidence and certainty. I had stumbled my way through school, and this was a step into uncharted territory.

The first PLT I was put in charge of was a disaster. I was embarrassed. In previous form, I might have imploded and started acting up, as though I didn't care. But this was no place to do that. They'd have just sent me home. So I looked at what was coming next and decided to put my all into it. I learned – in a way that has stayed with me ever since – that even if the present moment went badly, I could put it behind me with the intent of making my next moment world-class. And that's what I did.

I enjoyed the togetherness with the others in the group. One night, we went to a pub in a nearby village. One of the guys was Asian and a bit of a star, probably the best potential officer on the course. As we went to the door, there was a suggestion that the two of us were the first to go in. The village was very rural, and everyone there was white. What followed was one of those 'time-standing-still' moments. The whole place turned to look at the Black kid and the Asian kid. The pub fell completely silent and people started to stare at us. Then the other fourteen boys barrelled in. We were together. It was an empowering moment, that feeling of being part of a team. And, with all of us together, I felt safe.

We looked out for one another that whole week. One task was a physical test that ran us ragged around the local hills. But it was more than that; it was also another test of our leadership skills and our ability to work together as a team. After a while, I noticed that the young farmer who wanted to join the navy was struggling. The others trying out for the marines pushed ahead, but my instinct was to hang back and help this guy. So I stepped back and stuck with him. On the uphill I got behind him, put my hands under his backpack and pushed it up, so it lifted off his shoulders a bit. We walked up the mountain together, with me pushing his backpack and helping him to go on. That evening, at the debrief, he told everyone what had happened in front of the instructors. Fair play to him. But it was a real high point for me.

During that debriefing, a serving Royal Marines officer said something about leadership I have never forgotten. 'You guys think that being a great Marine is about carrying 100-pound backpacks up mountains,' he told us. 'There is an element of that that's true. But the best officer will find the best map reader and give them the map. The best shot and give them the rifle. The fittest guy and give them the heaviest bergen. Then they'll get by on four hours' sleep while they plan for the next challenge and make sure their troop can have six hours' sleep.'

I've shared my interpretation of that speech with my children more than once. In fact, I share it with anyone who will listen. Great leaders don't have to be the best at everything. Those who solely try to be the best, whether through their talents or by suppressing the talents of those around them, become liabilities. Great leaders get people doing what they are good at, ask them to excel and create the conditions in which they can do so. And they have to be able to be comfortable leading a team in which there are people who are better than them. Since becoming mayor, I have come across more than my share of people who are smarter than me, so much so that I have often questioned if I am of any use at all. But the ability to be comfortable in that situation, to resist the temptation to suppress them or ask them to be less than they are to make yourself feel comfortable, that's, perhaps, the real leadership superpower.

That last line about sleep has stayed with me as well. True leadership is sacrificial. You aren't the person on top of the pyramid, with all the layers below holding you up. Leadership inverts the power pyramid: it is the leader who supports it all so that everyone in the organization can flourish.

The week ended on a sobering note. When I got my grades at the end of the course, I was marked down for fitness. The other three candidates for the marines all got an A. I got a B. I was gutted but also irritated. I was sure I'd held my own. The other potential marines shook their heads, saying, 'That's not right,' while the Asian guy added, 'They don't want the only two non-white guys on the course to come top.' I was grateful to him for that. And although my fitness was marked down, my overall grades were good. I was invited to the Royal Marine Commando Training Centre in Lympstone, Devon, to take the POC.

The course runs over two and a half days. We took the United States Marine Corps fitness test, consisting of push-ups, sit-ups, burpees, chin-ups and five 60m shuttle runs. There was also Lympstone's famous obstacle course, rope climb and fireman's carry across the bottom field, and a ropes course. And then there is the endurance run – a cross-country challenge including tunnels, water obstacles and a submerged tunnel known as the 'sheep dip' before a one-mile race and speed march back to base. You had to hit all the targets and show maximum effort.

I wanted it so much. On the night before I went down, I was so nervous that I made myself sick. I barely slept and by the time I got on the train, I was exhausted. I hadn't eaten – I didn't know anything about nutrition and was running on empty. I thought if I ate I would make myself sluggish. When we stopped at Exeter, I saw the boys with suits and sports bags getting on the Exmouth train. Lympstone has its own station, and when the train stopped, it felt like all eyes were on us. We got off the train and were met by marines in their green berets. Even though I was nervous, I was also so proud.

Maybe because I was so keyed up, the course itself was a bit of a blur. It was tough but I enjoyed it, especially the fact that the course leaders were expecting and demanding so much of us. At the end of the tunnels course was the mile race. The officers lined us up and set us off. I fell back to eighth while a few lads raced off up the incline and into the trees. Immediately, an officer ran up beside me and yelled right in my ear. 'Mr Rees! Stretch those long legs of yours and fucking MOVE!'

It was like a shot of adrenaline. He wanted more out of me and almost out of nowhere I started to really run. The recruits who had been so far ahead of me that they were out of sight began to come closer. I'm catching up with them, I thought. And at the end, that painfully long final 200-metre stretch, I almost did. I finished third.

Next, we had the speed march. We ran in two rows and though I was feeling pretty energized, the guy to my left started to struggle. Instinctively, I did the same as I'd done for the young farmer on the mountain in the Lake District. I reached out and put my hand on his back to help him along. At one point, the route swung us right, but he kept going straight. I tried to pull him over but he went on, head-first into the bushes. For a moment, I thought I'd pushed him over. But he had run himself into the ground to the point he could go no further. He was out of it. I went over to help him.

'Keep going, Mr Rees!' the instructor shouted.

'But he needs help,' I said.

'Fucking get going, Mr Rees!' the instructor ordered.

And so I did. I pushed on and caught up with the other recruits, while the guy who keeled over was bundled into the van and driven back to base.

Waiting for the results, I was very nervous. Eventually, I was ushered into a small room with the course officer. 'Well, Mr Rees, you've passed,' he told me to huge relief, so much so that I barely took in what he said next, '. . . but by the skin of your teeth. You've got in but we think you coasted. You needed pushing. You can't afford to coast.' I shouldn't have needed the officer to shout at me to get moving. I should've just moved. I knew I was fit, but I had sometimes kept within my limits. By contrast, the lad who collapsed had nearly made the grade because he had shown his willingness and ability to give every last drop of himself. An officer told me they can get anyone fit if they are prepared to do the work, and he'd shown himself to be that kind of person.

The final selection took place a few months later in Plymouth at the Admiralty Interview Board. This was two days of written tests, practical leadership tests and psychological interviews. They told me if I passed that I'd be the first British-born Black marine officer, which felt both exciting and daunting. We went through the process in batches of four. Two of my four I had met up in the Lake District. The fourth had been on my POC and we hadn't got on well. He came into my room on the first night and launched into a strange conversation. He wasn't being deliberately provocative, more unthinking and unaware.

'Do you know,' he said, 'we used to have great fun in my school because there were only two wogs, and we used to send them to the back of the dinner queue.'

'Why are you telling me this?' I asked.

'Oh, don't take it personally,' he said.

I told him to get out of my room. He didn't seem to think it was that much of a problem. There was a bit of a confrontation, but we weren't going to fight in the AIB. So he left. At breakfast, I told the two candidates I'd met in the Lake District what happened. When we did the tests the next day, and it was this guy's turn to be in charge, they queried his commands and suggested alternatives. The test fell apart; he had clearly lost control. Those two guys – one of whom went on to serve – had decided that he wasn't someone who should be allowed to join the marines and did their best to make sure he had difficulty getting in. It meant a great deal to me and it says a lot for them and the Royal Marines. We all passed. He didn't.

When I then passed the Interview Board as well, I had an incredible sense of self. All that was left was the medical, which was a formality, and I would be in. The next morning, I was taken through all the tests. The hearing test was first and was fine. Then came the eye test. I sat down in front of the chart and started reading the letters off the board in front of me. My left eye was fine, but when I switched to my right eye, I could only get through a few rows. As they got smaller, I couldn't make them out at all.

'I can't read that.'

The medical officer looked up. 'Really?' He seemed surprised.

Then, trying to be helpful, I said, 'I've got keratoconus.'

At that, the medical officer left the room. A few minutes later, he came back with what looked like a large lollipop – a disc with black and white concentric circles on it, and a hole in the middle. He looked through it at my eye and shook his head, explaining that if you've got keratoconus, the circles would be distorted.

'We don't take people with keratoconus,' he added, and asked me to wait outside.

It took a moment or two for it to sink in. I'd passed the tests and the interviews, but because of my eye condition, they wouldn't let me in? It hadn't even crossed my mind that this might be a problem, but the medical officers were adamant. I could not join the marines. I made my way to the train station with the two candidates from the Lakes who had passed. Nice guys that they were, although they were themselves elated, they felt terrible for me. Not long after, I received a hand-written letter on blue Royal Marines-headed notepaper from a Major Reynolds saying how sorry he was that they hadn't taken me on. It was a nice letter, but though it was heartening to receive, it didn't help me.

The marines were out, but I had also been talking to the Army – the Glosters and the Royal Regiment of Wales. But keratoconus held me back again. A colonel in the regiment suggested that they might be able to help me get treatment, maybe an operation to sort it out.

I was touched that a high-ranking officer would go above and beyond to try to help me. But they couldn't find a way to make it work. Even if I'd had treatment – assuming they could fund it – I was told that I'd still be considered a liability. In the end, the army, like the marines, said no.

It was desperately difficult to take. The goal I had set for myself of getting into the marines had kept me going throughout my teenage years. It had given me drive, purpose and self-esteem. It was going to give me a path through life, and – above all – a sense of belonging. Even now, I still have dreams about that fitness test in Lympstone – only now I am fifty years old and utterly unprepared. Having it all taken away was really hard. I felt lost. Where do I go now? I wondered. How would I find a structure for my life? How would I find a place where I belonged? In many ways, it took me twenty-five years to find it. It was only when I became mayor that I fully felt I had come home.

Searching for Elijah

I was working towards my master's degree when I saw an ad for a job at Tearfund.

My first degree was in Economic History and Politics. When I got offered a place to study it at Swansea, I was elated. As I mentioned, going to university, and university in Wales in particular, meant the world to my grandfather. It also mattered hugely to me: this felt like an opportunity to escape. But I turned up without a clue of how the place worked. I hadn't been to the open day so the first time I saw the university was when I arrived on campus. The first time I saw my accommodation was when I turned up at the student village. I didn't know I was in self-catering until I arrived.

I felt inferior to some of the other, wealthier students. I remember one ridiculing me when I said hello to him in the library in a way that must have emphasized the Bristol accent. 'Queen's English, my man,' he said, trying to impress a girl he was with. They looked at each other and laughed. Looking back, I should have asked him how much his parents had spent on his education: hundreds of thousands of pounds to end up in the same university as me, who'd paid nothing. Hour for hour, opportunity for opportunity, I'd done better than him, doing more with less, showing more resilience. That's the story I tell students from poor backgrounds who go to university now:

you shouldn't feel inhibited but empowered by your background. It would've been great to know then what I know now.

My master's was in Political Theory and Government with a focus on Black American politics. I had approached my tutor, Professor Paul Kelly, and asked if I could have a place on the course. 'You can if you get a 2.1,' he said. We both knew I wasn't really equipped to do a master's, but with the military no longer an option, I still hadn't worked out what else to do. But then, with an average across my final exams of 61 per cent, I scraped it. I was in. Just.

The stakes were high. It was a two-year programme and if I failed – which seemed a very real possibility – all that time would have been for nothing. I wouldn't have been able to account for it to myself, let alone a potential employer. Somehow, I managed to get through it, but then I had to complete my final dissertation. And that was when I got stuck. I had written about 8,000 words but then spent days staring at the screen, typing in a few words and almost immediately deleting them. I'd put in a shift and have nothing but a few paragraphs to show for my efforts. By this point, I'd been working on it for months. I realized that I needed to start again. It was a huge decision and I remember sitting in the common room, literally tossing a coin to help me decide what to do. It landed tails, which meant I would start the whole thing over, throwing away everything I'd written to that point. It felt strangely liberating.

It wasn't that I wasn't interested in what I was working on. American politics, and particularly its relationship with the Church, was of deep and personal interest to me. My faith had always been important. It was something that had always given me self-worth, a sense of existence and significance. But while doing the research for my dissertation, I read the Bible from cover to cover and gained a much deeper understanding. I particularly drew inspiration from stories, from Abraham and Moses to King David and Mary, where God had chosen the lowly over the great and powerful.

I focused on the civil rights movement. One particular aspect of it fascinated me: at the heart of the movement and all that came before and after was the complicated and contradictory relationship between faith and politics. The Church, particularly white Christianity, preached 'the Word' of the Lord while simultaneously serving as a cover, a source and a justifier of racism and slavery in the US. The way I came to see it, the Church had no problem with members of their congregations preaching to their slaves on a Sunday, sending them to work without pay on a Monday, beating them to the edge of death on a Tuesday, raping their wives on a Wednesday, selling their children on a Thursday, selling their husbands on a Friday, requiring them to profess love and loyalty to 'Massa' on a Saturday and then preaching to them on the Sunday for the cycle to begin again. In fact, these atrocities wouldn't have been possible without the support, complicity or indulgence of the white Church.

Yet at the same time, the Black Church in America became the centre of rebellion and resistance, with Martin Luther King Jr eventually rising as its talismanic leader. I was particularly moved by King's 'Letter from Birmingham Jail', written in 1963 from his Alabama cell in response to the white clergymen who had written an open letter criticizing his strategy of non-violent direct action. 'I have travelled the length and breadth of Alabama, Mississippi and all the other southern states,' King wrote. 'On sweltering summer days and crisp autumn mornings, I have looked at the South's beautiful churches with their lofty spires pointing heavenward. I have beheld the impressive outlines of her massive religious education buildings. Over and over, I have found myself asking: "What kind of people worship here? Who is their God?"' These words have always resonated with me, and the challenge they pose remains wholly relevant today.

That reality led me to quite a challenging place. One of my closest friends, Asim, was Muslim and I started attending talks with him. At the time, I had the belief that there was only one way to God and that all other religions were counterfeit: I was in part joining Asim to learn, but also to defend my faith as I saw it. Yet when I went to those talks, not only was I welcomed as a brother, but the Imams spoke about the things that were important to me: poverty, racism and politics. While my church talked about personal morality, theological correctness and the imminent return of Jesus, my Muslim friends were dealing with the world as it was right here, right now. Part of me wished I could be as proud of Christianity as they were of Islam.

I didn't join the Christian Union at university, but instead signed up for – what seemed to my immature self – a cooler group called

Christians in Sport. It was only for people who played sports at university level, but as I played rugby for the university I qualified. At one of their meetings, I came across a copy of *Tear Times*, a magazine put together by the Christian charity, Tearfund. I flicked through it, reading stories about poverty and social action. And I saw an organization that would enable me to put my political beliefs into practice, to live out my understanding of God and the sense of purpose I had developed. At the back of the magazine, there was a job advertisement for the position of South West Youth Co-ordinator. It felt as though the job had my name written all over it. On top of that, the timing couldn't have been better: I had about six months before I finished my master's, and I was starting to think about what I might do next. I showed the ad to Tom, my housemate. He took one look at it and said, 'That's your job, Marvin. That's exactly right for you.'

I put the application in and was rejected. But then, three months later, I got a letter from Tearfund, saying, 'We'd like to invite you in for an interview.' The people they had shortlisted hadn't worked out and they hadn't appointed anyone. I joked with Tom: 'It's too late, I've withdrawn my offer.' But I still really wanted the job.

It was my first proper job interview and as part of it, I had to give a presentation. I went up to London and, not for the first time, I really didn't know what I was doing and had limited experience of speaking publicly. I thought, I'll just go in as me, and see what happens. They asked me a question about why I wanted the job, and I said, 'I'm passionate about poverty and changing the world.' This was before talking about being passionate had become part of the standard political vocabulary. Brendan Bowles, the co-ordinator of Tearfund's Youth Team, told me later that after I left the room, the interview panel looked at one another, smiled and said, 'That's the man.' I was in. I completed my dissertation in December and began the job in January.

One of the perks of the role was a company car. I had passed my driving test but I'd never had a car before and was presented with a brand new Vauxhall Astra. It was a 1.7 turbo diesel and I can still remember everything about it, right down to its number plate: N62 SPM. It was red and shiny and smelled new. The first time I climbed in, I thought to myself, I've made it. Then I turned the engine on and reversed it straight into the car behind me, smashing its headlamp. I was mortified. It was day one – they were bound to sack me!

I drove up to see the leader of the youth team, Brendan Bowles, who lived in Cheshire. I had a two-day orientation session with him, feeling very unconfident, which I attempted to cover up by trying too hard. I didn't feel I had the credentials, that I wasn't the type of young Christian they were looking for. I didn't feel good enough in general. This lack of confidence has recurred throughout my life, and it's something I have learned to work with despite myself. It might not be obvious from the outside, but that internal struggle is still very much there.

After the two days, I drove back down the M6 and M5 to Bristol. As I mentioned earlier, I parked up outside my mum's house, went in and said to her, 'Get in the car. We're going to Tesco. You don't have to get the bus anymore.' From Tesco, I drove Mum down to Lawrence Weston and parked outside the flat we'd lived in. I wanted Mum to feel how free I felt. I followed the same route the bus and Joe had taken. Later, I went around the corner to pick up Nan and Grandad. From when I was little, Nan had always said to me, 'You'll take me for a drive when you're older.' We had this routine where I would tell her where I was going to take her. Now I could keep my promise, although in my childhood stories, I said the car I'd take her out in would be yellow. This one was red.

I don't want to put the Lawrence Weston area down. I still drive down there when I need grounding and I have many fond memories of my childhood in the area. However, I can't help but associate my time living there with my mum and my sister as one of the most vulnerable periods of my life.

The president of Tearfund was a theologian, John Stott. He described the job of the youth team as getting people to understand God's concern for the poor and then offering Tearfund as a means through which they could act on that knowledge. As a youth co-ordinator, I was part of Tearfund's communications team with a particular focus on young people.

The job involved lots of 'preaching'. I cringe today when I think back on it. Once, I was in a church in Newport and had droned on for so long that a woman at the back of the church repeatedly drew her hand across her throat to encourage me to draw it to a close. I had got caught up trying to copy some of the 'energetic' preachers who used to shout at their congregations, almost attacking them. As a result, I thought I had to challenge them to care more. Before too much time had passed, my team leader, a great man called Mark Rudall, gently told me, 'You need to love your congregation, Marvin.'

As well as going up and down the country, talking to and encouraging people to support the work we did, I participated in leading visits to Tearfund Partners' projects overseas. One scheme we ran was called Transform, which involved a group of teenagers being taken overseas to help to build a school or to run a youth programme with a local church. As well as helping on the ground, the idea was that the teenagers would come back with a greater knowledge of poverty and its drivers, and therefore become lifelong supporters of the charity.

I visited some extraordinary places across Asia and Africa and worked with some remarkable individuals. I will always remember Pastor Greg Sobrabas, whom I met when visiting Mindanao in the Philippines. He would pick destitute people up off the streets and take them to live in his church. When I visited, he had just over ninety people living there, including an old blind man in his sixties or seventies. The man had been a charcoal burner and his job had almost certainly cost him his sight. Pastor Greg was keen to introduce me to his latest community member, a nine-month-old baby boy with no family, whom Greg had named George Muller. Muller was a German clergyman who lived in Bristol in the 1800s. He took over ten thousand orphans off the streets during his lifetime, and provided educational opportunities for them to the point where he was accused by some of raising the poor above their natural station. Greg's own mission had started when he'd read a book about Muller. He'd been so inspired by Muller's life that he'd committed to lock himself away to pray until God granted him the blessing of being like George Muller.

I also spent time with a remarkable couple, Jonathan and Thelma Nambu. They founded a charity in Quezon City called Samaritana, which helps Filipino women who work in the sex industry. As a man,

I felt uncomfortable, even compromised around the women, but Thelma explained how important it was for the women to see and interact with men who were not abusing them. Jonathan revealed that he had felt similarly until – with his wife's help – he realized that being a respectful husband showed the women that they could have new relationships with men that were neither sexual, exploitative nor transactional.

They took me to the home of Laurie, one of the women they were working with. What I saw broke my heart. When I say 'home', I should say it was a shack in a shanty town.

There's something about visiting a shanty town that you can't really explain unless you've been to one. It's one thing to see images of such places on the news, but the shock of being there is difficult to capture. The people who live there have their dignity still, but it felt so hopeless. The woman invited us in. As a relatively rich Westerner, stepping in to see her in her poverty made me feel so awkward, but she was just being hospitable. Her shack was tiny: it was made of wood, with a tin roof and slats on the side. She'd saved to buy material to decorate it. The fabric was silky and beautiful, purple with tiny flowers all over it. She had been learning to sew and had stitched it into a valance, which she asked us to help her install. Luckily, one of the people in our party was good at DIY. There was such beauty in what she'd created. I stood back and cupped my hands to block out the rough wooden structure and the shanty town around it, so all I could see was what she had made. It could have been pictured in any interiors magazine. Despite all she had been through, despite the almost total absence of opportunity that lay before her, she had this vision of life that remained pure.

When we finished, she took us to a neighbour's shack. It was a bit larger but it was still a shack. She went away and then came back with three bottles of Coke for the three in our party. She presented the bottles to us. I looked at Jonathan and said, 'I can't take the Coke. That's too much. I should be buying *her* a drink.'

'You've got to,' Jonathan said. 'It's giving her back her dignity.'

It's a point that C. S. Lewis once made: sometimes to receive is to give. It was a lesson learned for me. I took the drink and showed her proper respect. She had given me something, and through receiving it, I was able to give in return.

We also visited Angeles City, which was a deeply upsetting experience. The area was close to the volcano Mount Pinatubo, which had just erupted. Lots of people had been displaced because of the eruption and we were sent to meet those working on the relief effort. One night we were wandering around when we were stopped by some people who were selling all kinds of stuff out on the street. They were all Aetas, members of an Indigenous group of Filipino people. One of them had a crossbow. Being polite and wanting them to know they were visible, I gestured to ask the man if I could look at it.

Everywhere I went in the Philippines, I felt I had to solve any hardship I saw. Seeing someone like this who was out on the street, really struggling, it was impossible simply to walk by. So, I asked if I could see the crossbow. He passed it over to me, at which point I realized that though I had been trying to be respectful by showing interest, he thought I wanted to buy it.

I forget the exact amount the man suggested. I tried to explain I wasn't looking to buy it and that I didn't have any money on me. He then – of course – thought I was haggling and dropped the price. Every time I said no, the price continued to drop. I felt terrible watching this man, who must have been in his forties, exposing his lack of power to me, a Westerner, barely in his twenties. I didn't want that kind of power. I didn't want this man to be almost begging me to buy this from him. My misguided attempt to 'see' him and treat him with dignity had gone horribly wrong. What was even more complicated was the fact that our economic and political identities – he an impoverished, Black, Indigenous, South East Asian man, and me a Westerner – separated the solidarity I wanted to have with him as a Black man. In the end, I felt so awful, I borrowed some money and bought it. It was a working crossbow. I brought it back to the UK with me. It was only when I got home that I realized it probably wasn't the brightest idea I've ever had. It was a good job no one checked my suitcase!

Another interaction that seemed to capture the state of the world came one night when we went to McDonald's, craving Western food. There was a young boy outside, begging. He was barefoot, in khaki-coloured shorts and a torn purple T-shirt covered in dirt. He looked about eight. He was making money by helping people park their cars – guiding them into spaces and asking them for cash. His little body looked so vulnerable in the dark evening, lit up by the reversing lights of the SUVs he was darting between. We walked past him and into McDonald's, where we ordered our food. I took a seat facing the window and I could see him working. I'd been looking forward to this meal, but watching that child, I couldn't eat. He was right there, on the other side of the glass, but our lives were worlds, universes apart.

I went out and asked him if he wanted anything to eat. I don't speak Tagalog and he didn't seem to speak English so I gestured as best as I could. I bought him a meal for a few dollars and took it out to him. He looked at me, smiled, took the burger, fries and drink and sat down on a raised pavement next to the SUVs. I went back and sat inside the well-lit, air-conditioned restaurant and watched him eat. It was all wrong.

When we left, the boy was standing there looking at me. He had the soda in one hand, the burger in the other and one fry hanging from his mouth. I tried to say something in Tagalog to acknowledge him. One of my team mates looked at me and asked, 'Marv, what's the matter?' That set me off. I had to go around the corner to cry. I wiped my eyes, and when I came back the boy was looking at me. I couldn't save this child, and he needed saving. I felt pathetic. We travelled around on motorbikes. It was a warm, muggy night, and I remember clinging on to the back of the bike, with tears in my eyes, angry at myself, at the world, and questioning God. I found it hard to equate what I was seeing with my faith. Where are you, Jesus? I asked. This isn't right.

One of the Old Testament stories that has always stuck with me is that of Elijah. Elijah was a prophet during some of Israel's darkest days. God not only told him to anoint two kings but also to find and anoint Elisha as a protégé. Towards the end of Elijah's life, Elisha asked to be blessed with a double portion of Elijah's spirit. Elijah would eventually anoint Elisha as a prophet who went on to perform twice the number of miracles.

As a younger man, I was continually on the lookout for my own Elijah figure. It's the same thing I'd sought in boxing and also in the military. I felt I had something to offer and needed someone to help me understand what it was: a guiding figure who could teach me and help me fulfil my potential. My faith was important to giving me a broader sense of self and purpose, for sure, but it needed grounding. It was also bound up with a desire for the father figure I had missed. Whatever the impetus, that constant, restless search for an Elijah to *my* Elisha, hung over me.

Around this time, I read a book called *The Soul of Politics* by Jim Wallis. Wallis was a white American evangelical who had been involved in the aftermath of the civil rights movement, a fusing of faith and politics. He challenged the evangelicals who'd either opposed or failed to stand up against racism and poverty in America, and were now actively or passively part of the white backlash of the 1970s. I found the book really inspiring. It echoed many of the arguments and discussions that I'd had when I'd done my master's. At the same time, I was beginning to have doubts about my work with Tearfund. It had been an amazing first job, but I couldn't see where it was going. There was no obvious career path or progression: if there was a route upwards in the organization, it wasn't being offered to me.

At Tearfund, a lot of the talk was about Christian development and a debate about what that meant. The more I thought about it, the more I was interested in a slightly different discussion regarding Christian politics. Did such a thing exist? The concept didn't resonate so much in the UK, but in the US it played an important role. I applied to Sojourners, an American faith-based campaigning organization, and became an outreach assistant intern in their Washington offices.

It was quite a shift. I went from a full-time job on around £18k with a company car to being on $20 a week. I joined towards the end of Bill Clinton's second term, and the first thing I worked on was welfare reform. There were concerns that, because of the policy changes being enacted, some Americans were disappearing from the system. Organizations like Sojourners had argued that churches should not just be telling people that Jesus loved them but proving it by engaging in social action. There is the famous story of Jim and others cutting out of a Bible all the verses that referenced poverty, then holding the book up in front of a white church congregation, saying, 'Here is your bible, it's full of holes.' There was also a question over whether the government was taking advantage of the fact that they could cut billions of dollars from the federal budget in the expectation that faith-based groups would step into the gap.

The internship should have been a great opportunity, but in reality it was a bit of a let-down. Looking back, the scheme was more suited for white suburban Americans to step into another world and come into contact with the inner cities, the racism and poverty their white suburban lives had shielded them from. I didn't need to learn that – I knew what racism and poverty felt like.

I was also surprised by the attitudes of the others on the scheme. I was the only intern who wasn't a white American. We were all housed together but there was only one other intern, Kris, who I bonded with: we came from similar backgrounds and she had grown up in care in California. Kris was super smart, was doing her master's at Berkeley, and we got on really well. I was frustrated that our group sessions were shaped by the interns who were telling stories about how bad their lives were – it seemed we were all there to counsel each other. One of them complained that her father had been a visiting professor at Oxford, so they had never properly settled down.

I kept quiet for a few months, but on another occasion, during one of our evening discussions, it started up again. I had to speak. I explained, 'You are rich, white Americans, life just isn't that bad for you. We're living in Columbia Heights . . .' – this was pre-gentrification – 'The best thing for this middle-class angst would be to go outside, and see the Vietnam Vets, Black people, Hispanic people out on the streets. They're living on the grilles, so they can stay warm from the steam coming up.' The room was silent. Then there were some tears. I started to feel a bit bad. But I said what I had to say and it was true. I realize now that I was sharing the historical frustration that Black people have often felt with middle-class white radicals when they make the anti-racist or social justice movements more about themselves than the racism or injustice they claim to be fighting against – a frustration I have also experienced as mayor of Bristol.

In the end, I resigned from my internship six weeks early. A whole group of us did. I'd gone to be inspired by Jim and the community, but that hadn't happened in the way I'd hoped. When I handed my notice in, I told the organizers why. I told them the scheme felt like cheap labour. 'You've got us doing jobs for $20 a week that you could be employing local people to do.' The responses from the organization split along racial lines. The white workers felt affronted. 'But I am radical,' one of them said to me. Sojourners had a well-deserved reputation for consistently being on the right side of history. But that doesn't give anyone or any organization a pass to ignore privilege. The Black staff, who had seen the dynamics at play, reacted differently. 'We hear you,' one of them said.

Despite my disappointment, my time at Sojourners did produce opportunity. While there I had worked on the Call to Renewal programme. Its aim was to build a faith-based movement, in the model of the civil rights movement, to tackle the consequences of welfare reform. One of the big names there was the Rev Dr Tony Campolo, Bill Clinton's spiritual adviser, and a hugely inspiring individual. I saw in Tony someone having the kind of impact I wanted to have in the world.

Tony was a prominent speaker, known for inspiring, challenging and calling out in equal measure. He was larger than life. Like Jim, he was one of several evangelicals who were fighting to ensure God and the Church's agenda weren't captured by the religious right and the coalition that made up the moral majority. He was something of a serial social entrepreneur: he was always starting up programmes to tackle poverty, all while being a professor at Eastern University, just outside Philadelphia, and one of the leaders of a well-known master's programme in Global Economic Development. I met him at one of the Call to Renewal events and told him that I wanted to join the programme. 'Write to me,' he said. So I did. I explained that I wanted to participate and learn but didn't have any funding. He wasn't fazed. 'Just turn up,' he wrote back. 'I'll pay for you.' That was Tony all over and I took him at his word. I went home to Bristol for a few months after I resigned from Sojourners in July, then flew back out to Philadelphia in January 2000 to start the programme.

The course built on what I'd learned at Tearfund and also, I hoped, might help me embark on a career in the media, which was something I was beginning to think about. This was around the turn of the millennium, and Jubilee 2000, the campaign to cancel developing world debt, was big news. They'd taken an issue that felt distant to most people and turned it into an issue ordinary people could relate to and campaign on. I witnessed the importance and power that the media and storytelling could have. I began to see the course as an opportunity to grow my understanding of international development with the aim of becoming a foreign correspondent for the BBC.

Working under Tony Campolo was a bit like working for Jim Wallis — he was hugely in demand, both as a speaker, mentor and advising the president. I remember him coming back from the White House with an overview of the latest conversation he'd had with the president and the actions we needed to take as a result. When he was around, it was exciting and inspiring, but he wasn't there anything like as much as I'd hoped.

One person who *was* around was a young undergraduate from the Boston area, Kirsten, who had grown up in Beverly, Massachusetts. She used to come along to events I had organized for fellow students. To begin with, it was a question of smiling and saying hello. But then we became friends. I was attracted to her from the start, but was very conscious of the fact that I was older, and also that she was a white American. This was America, where there can be a lot of sensitivity about interracial relationships. When we started hanging out, I was careful to always meet off campus, to minimize gossip.

My course finished before hers and I went back to England. We continued to email each other, and I always felt a buzz of excitement when I saw her name in my inbox. She had a strength and a vulnerability about her, like an angel, I thought. I believed that I would be able to achieve anything with her in my corner, but I didn't want to scare her off by trying too hard, so I always gave her space to do her own thing. After she graduated, I wrote to her, saying, 'Why don't you come over?' I also told her that I'd always had feelings for her, to which she replied, 'Well, why don't you phone me, then?' I called her that evening. We chatted, and I invited her to come and visit and she said, 'Yeah, I'll come.' And that was that. I may not have found my Elijah, but finding the person I wanted to spend the rest of my life with more than made up for that.

5.

Media Pressure

In 2001, not long after I returned from the US, I joined the BBC as a broadcast assistant at BBC Radio Bristol. I wanted a meaningful job that would allow me to do something about the global problems I'd witnessed working for Tearfund. I increasingly thought that journalism was the answer. My travels and master's degrees had given me a good grounding in international affairs, and I hoped that, ultimately, I might become a foreign correspondent. But instead, my five years at the BBC sucked the life out of me, affecting both my self-confidence and my mental well-being. And I can't deny that the memories of my time there frame my interactions with journalists to this day. Both the profession and the organization spat me out.

My editors repeatedly told me, 'You can't speak properly.' I was endlessly corrected for not pronouncing 'ing' rather than 'in' at the end of words. I didn't know what to do – I was speaking exactly as I'd always spoken and, although I was still learning about broadcasting, I knew I could string a sentence together. Yet I had this constant barrage of criticism, which was complicated by the fact that I wanted to be part of the BBC so much. When I got my staff pass, I was incredibly proud. So much so that I submitted to their criticisms in order to fit in. But it was embarrassing and humiliating and the more conscious I became of the way I spoke, and my not fitting into their culture, the more tongue-tied I got and the more distant I became.

But it wasn't just about the way I spoke. I didn't fit in and one editor in particular went out of their way to draw that out. I had built up great networks and I knew how to find a story. But when I brought in ideas about investigating poverty in the Bristol area, the growing fair-trade movement or the anti-war protests that were building, they said, 'That's a bit worthy.' The *Bristol Post* had run a column during the Iraq War by Barry Beelzebub, a pseudonymous right-wingish provocateur, suggesting British soldiers used 'pork bullets' to shoot at the 'towelheads'. I took it to my editor and suggested we speak to members of Bristol's Muslim community because it was outrageous. I took it to the station manager, who told me, 'There's a rule, Marvin. Journalists don't criticize journalists.' I looked around the all-white, almost entirely middle-class newsroom and realized that it was a serious problem – and dangerous, too. The media was then – and remains – one of the most racially and class-elitist professions in the country. (Jon Snow spelled this out in his 2017 James MacTaggart Memorial Lecture in the aftermath of coverage of the Grenfell Fire: a powerful, rare and welcome moment of self-reflection from a member of this elite.)

My lack of progress was painful. As well as my diction and worthiness, comments were also made about me being too 'Radio 4'. Then I kept being given Sunday producer shifts – the ones no one else wanted. On one occasion, the Monday Radio Car reporter called in to ask if I could do his shift the following morning so he could stay with friends. Of course I would: I was excited to be doing it. Less than an hour later he called back telling me not to worry. I knew exactly what had happened – the editor had found out that I was going to be speaking on the radio, and found a way to take me off. It was this sort of episode that sent me down a rabbit hole of anxiety.

Despite these experiences, I still showed up every day. And when a dream job came up at *Newsnight*, BBC2's flagship TV news programme, I went for it, despite being told that I wouldn't get it and not to apply. But I was never not going to give it a go, and thankfully, I was offered an interview. I decided before going there I'd write to ask if I could go for a day's work experience with the team, to give me some insights, and also to give them a chance to get a look at me. They agreed, and to help me keep it off my manager's radar, I took a day's leave, booked my coach ticket (travelling by train was too expensive) and travelled up to White City.

It was 2003 and England had just won the Rugby World Cup in Australia. At the editorial meeting, the discussion was about how the country might build on this success to make rugby a mass participation sport – rugby union was still, in England at least, a public-school game, but was trying to break out beyond its traditional fan base. From my time in the US, I knew that basketball had been taken from the viewing doldrums to a mass audience game. I proposed we should reach out to some of those involved. Instead of being dismissed out of hand, as had happened when I tried to make a suggestion at BBC Bristol, they listened. I carried on, knowing the BBC had been talking about using more voices from outside London, and suggested they speak to Mike Dick, a friend of mine who taught and coached rugby at Fairfield High School in Bristol, which had a very diverse, working-class student body.

I gave Mike a call, and *Newsnight* booked a local camera team to film a training session. It was broadcast that evening. I was really pleased: it showed that I could make a contribution. After two years at the BBC, I needed to know that. Unfortunately, the interview didn't go as well. Although I'd shown what I could do, it wasn't enough to get the job.

But I genuinely believed I had journalistic mileage in me and it didn't stop me trying to find a way in. When another opportunity came up, an attachment with BBC World Affairs Newsgathering, which provides stories for the World Service, I picked up the phone. I've never been afraid of cold-calling people so before I sent off the application I called the head of the department to arrange a visit: I wanted to introduce myself to as many people as possible. As before, I took the day off work and booked my coach ticket. It was an early meeting so it meant a very early start. When I got to Broadcasting House, the front desk rang through to his office, then gave me a look. 'He's not in today,' they said.

'But I have come up to meet him,' I replied, feeling deflated and embarrassed. I took a breath and carried on with the application. This time I got the job, covering stories in Africa and Spain.

On a couple of them, I worked with Mark Doyle, the BBC's Africa Correspondent at the time. Doyle was a really fascinating guy and we got on well. After I'd put together a story about the import and export of sugar between Ethiopia and the EU, Mark seemed to be impressed, telling me: 'That's a really nice tape.' I got positive comments from Radio 4's 5 o'clock news team too. 'We really want to support you getting on,' I was told. But once again, nothing happened. There was no plan and no structure, much like the missed meeting. I couldn't work it out: was it me? Was it the system? No matter the quality of work I produced, I just seemed to get the same non-response.

While I was working at the World Service, an email came round asking for ideas for stories. I sat at my desk and knocked out five suggestions for features: one about people of mixed heritage whose parents come from either side of a conflict, one about albinism, and the other three focused on the debt economy and fair trade. I'd read somewhere that 50 per cent of the roses sold in the UK came from Kenya. So, I suggested following the journey of a flower from producer to consumer, telling the story of the different people who were involved in that process along the way, from the farmer and field labourers to the consumer at the other end.

I got an email back from someone at *Panorama*. He told me he really liked the idea and asked me to flesh it out for him with more details. Fair trade was still a relatively new idea at the time and I was really excited. I worked away on the outline, sent it over and . . . nothing. I had about three weeks to go on my three-month attachment before I had to go back to BBC Bristol. As the weeks ticked down, I grew increasingly desperate for a response. But once again, it was the same cycle of good work being rewarded by silence.

My break didn't happen. I was back at BBC Bristol, my tail between my legs. I wasn't happy to be back – and no one there was particularly pleased to see me, either. To make matters worse, a documentary then aired on *Panorama* about the journey of a piece of fair-trade clothing. I'm not saying they stole my idea, but it seemed extremely similar to the one I'd pitched. Instead of a rose, the programme followed the journey of a dress, where the material was sourced, who made it, all the way to the catwalk where an actress who presented the show modelled it at a London Fashion Show. I emailed the *Panorama* editor but didn't hear back.

It was time to admit defeat and I resigned from the BBC. I wasn't getting anywhere, it was sapping my confidence, and my mental health was deteriorating. I had no job to go to, so tried to make ends meet by going freelance. I got a gig working night shifts for Radio 5 Live. They used to have a show called *Up All Night*, which started at ten or eleven in the evening and ran right through to three or four the following morning. I was part of the production team: booking guests, writing cues for the presenter, that sort of thing.

It was a challenging existence. I'd get a coach up from Bristol — which took three hours — then do the shift which started at about 7 p.m. and finished once the programme came off air at about 3 a.m. The first coach back to Bristol wasn't until six and with nowhere else to go at that time of night, I had to sit in the studio, watching the hours click by. I got £120 a shift. Once I'd taken off the cost of travel and totted up the hours spent getting there and back, it was barely worth it. I wasn't in a great place and felt increasingly embarrassed and ashamed that my life had come to this.

But I didn't stop trying. I pitched a programme idea to *It's My Story* on Radio 4 about Jamaican women who had been used as drug mules. I had got to know a charity called Hibiscus that supported the women involved. At the time, there were lots of stories in the media about Jamaican women swallowing drugs and bringing them back into the UK. They were portrayed as criminals but I saw them as victims. I wanted to counter that narrative at the time and Hibiscus were interested, but the idea wasn't picked up.

I tried again with a slightly different pitch — what happened to these women when they were deported back to Jamaica at the end of their sentence? The depressing answer is that not only were they socially ostracized, but the women were then at the mercy of the gangs who had given them the drugs, accused of failing to deliver the goods, and as a result owing the gangs money. On top of this, they were dealing with the social stigma of having been in prison and often trying to reconcile with their families and children whom they hadn't seen for many years.

Radio 4 came back and said they really liked the idea but couldn't afford to employ me to make it. Instead, they said that I should come up to London and they'd pay me to research it for two days.

I was desperate and thought it was such a good story that it might lead to more commissions. So I contacted Hibiscus and we got the trust and agreement of two women who were about to be deported and the producers brought in Lucy Ash to front the programme. She met the women and flew back to Jamaica with them. As disappointed as I was not to be working on it more closely, I was satisfied because it was meaningful journalism. This was the voice of the voiceless, women who were victims of their poverty, the gangsters and the callousness of our criminal justice system.

This, though, was a rare success story. Part of my failure to break into journalism may well have been personal, but there were other issues at play too, ones I have come up against on the other side of the fence, dealing with the media as a politician.

In 2006, on the eve of the 200th anniversary of William Wilberforce's 1807 bill to abolish the slave trade, I pitched a documentary to *Inside Out* about the history of racism in Bristol – the BBC commissioning editor turned it down, telling me that he didn't think there was a story in it. This was symptomatic of the Bristol media view on race issues at that time. Years later, when I was mayor and the statue of Edward Colston ended up in the city harbour, the BBC interviewed me on *Points West* and asked me why I hadn't taken the statue down. Yet the media's culpability in all of this was never questioned. Because they couldn't 'see' a story in terms of Bristol's past and present relationship with slavery and race, they had never helped create the conditions in which the city could have a sensible conversation about memorialization and who gets remembered and what that meant for modern Bristol. They ignored it and then, when events blew up, wanted to know why I hadn't done anything about it. Sometimes a question needs unpacking and questioning. I was asked the question by the flagship presenter. 'Hold on, you wait hundreds of years for a Black political leader, then I'm elected the first in Europe and the fact there is a statue of a slaver up in the middle of the city becomes my fault?'

I thought it was a question that could have only been generated by a newsroom that lacked insight and connectivity into the society around it. This incident involves the local BBC, but they are not alone. And it's not all their fault. Like the rest of society, they are, in part, the outworking of our country's social immobility. When most people in the media are from similar backgrounds, maybe it's not a surprise that some important stories are either missed or not properly understood.

I believe that quality journalism improves our politics and the world. The opposite is also true. I saw that first-hand in my Jubilee 2000 days. And that is why I am so often frustrated with the way our news is reported, with the pressure on the workforce to generate drama and sensation in the name of generating clicks over the need for space for insight and nuance. There are fault lines running right through the way our news is reported, but let me give you just one further example of how the media work. One of the political issues I had to deal with as mayor was the introduction of a clean-air zone into the city. Environmental groups had rightly campaigned for action to be taken to clean up air quality and a number of cities were mandated by government to introduce clean-air zones.

But putting a clean-air zone in place is not always straightforward. At first, I was criticized by environmental campaigners and opposition parties, who complained that I wasn't delivering the zone quickly enough. But as with the majority of political decisions, there is complexity, and positive outcomes overall can still have negative consequences for some people. When we announced the scheme design, the first letter of complaint I received came from University Hospital Bristol. The proposed area of the zone went right in front of the main hospital. That affected their suppliers, and would make deliveries more expensive for them. They warned me it would have the effect of imposing financial cuts on the NHS. They also raised questions of patient access: if you needed to get to the hospital but only had an old, non-compliant car, what would you do?

The then environment secretary was Therese Coffey. The press was briefed by government that Bristol was dragging its feet over the scheme, which was untrue. In fact, I'd had several conversations with the secretary of state about the unintended consequences of the scheme, particularly the hospital's concerns over increased costs. I suggested she needed to talk to the health secretary about who would swallow those costs. I raised concerns, too, that the financial penalties a clean-air zone would bring in could negatively impact the lowest-income households and businesses. But Coffey was unsympathetic and said we just needed to get on with it.

The media picked up on the story. About four months before the final design was announced, I was interviewed on Radio 5 Live about the situation. Their questioning was over the delay: why are you dragging your feet? Don't you care about the environment? Three hundred people are dying every year from dirty air and you're missing a deadline to put one in place? It was frustrating, as the line of questioning wasn't a reflection of the situation, or a considered probing of the issues. I repeatedly made the point that while we had an environmental, moral and legal duty to deliver clean air in the shortest possible time, we also had to be aware of the dangers of the costs falling disproportionately on those least able to cope.

A few months later, we announced the clean-air zone, having managed to negotiate a £42 million package of mitigations to help businesses and households through the transition.

Two things happened at the point of announcement. First, all the environmental groups that had been campaigning and pushing me to move faster and harder to put a clean-air zone in place disappeared. Not a single one came out in public to defend or support the scheme. The second thing that happened was that I was invited back onto Radio 5 Live to talk about the scheme. Now they were grilling me about the impact the scheme was going to have on businesses and households. Why haven't you considered them? What are you going to do to help?

I replied, 'You probably want to listen back to the interview you did with me three or four months ago, pressing me to deliver the CAZ, when I listed all the things that you are mentioning now, that there were difficulties for businesses, households and public services, which was why we had been taking time to get it right.' They had me in a seesaw of conflict, only able to position me in one camp or the other, rather than facilitating a discussion about how every solution came with a price tag.

I think the media should be a bit more upfront about the pressures on the news business. There is ferocious competition for our attention and the news business is competing along with everyone else. That introduces a pressure which drives it toward the sensationalist. That's not to say there isn't quality journalism. The loss of nuance and accuracy is sometimes the price that is paid for an industry that must produce volume (quantity and noise) to keep our attention.

Locally, we have platforms that must sell advertising, which compounds the pressure further. A journalist working in one of our city's main outlets complained to me that they were under pressure to produce clicks. That was what the editor would assess them on at the morning team meeting. And what gets clicks? Conflict. The result is that news reporting becomes more heat than light. Informed debate becomes binary, simplistic anger, because this is what is going to get eyeballs. I understand that in many organizations that are struggling for revenue, journalists are fighting for space to keep their jobs. But the metric that decides who stays is how many clicks their articles are getting. And conflict is ramped up even further.

We're left with a situation in which we lack the framework to assess politics properly. As a politician, I'm frustrated by that. And it's frustrating for the public, too. They don't benefit from an informed debate, which makes it more difficult for them to make informed choices. Of course, the public should better inform themselves, but the media bears a huge responsibility. Things could be better.

I was listening to the *News Agents* podcast, which presenters Jon Sopel and Emily Maitlis left the BBC to launch. Jon Sopel was describing the benefits of not working for the BBC news machine and said that the podcast format allowed them to get 'off the hamster wheel' and to have the room to dig deeper into a story rather than always trying to get that 'gotcha' moment.

It's an important point. If, as a journalist, you're constantly looking for a gotcha moment, it's about getting one over on your interviewee. Gotcha moments and getting one over on the interviewee aren't the same as getting to the truth. It can overlap, but the two are not necessarily the same. If gotcha has become the aim, then we have a subtle but significant shift in the purpose of news. That's not really any individual journalist's fault: it's the machine they're feeding to make ends meet. But if more journalists could get off the hamster wheel, it would be better for all of us.

6.

Late to the Party

My early approach to politics wasn't couched in terms of party politics. In the 1983 election, I instinctively chose Labour and even had
an argument with one of my friends: 'You shouldn't be with the Blues;
you should be with the Reds.' But that was about as aware of party
politics as I got. My formative understanding of politics wasn't about
ideology but about the everyday struggles and how we attempted to
make sense of and overcome the challenges of racism and class and
poverty, for me, my mum and others like us.

That said, Labour has always been my natural political home. In
the Labour Party, I found the closest thing to a group of people in
the political system who cared about and worked for the issues that
matter most to me: poverty, inequality, fairness, social mobility, environmental justice. I eventually came to the view that here was a group
of people in a party closer than any other to the things I cared about,
and I wanted to be part of it and learn from it.

I never joined a political party at school or university. That kind of
politics wasn't available in any form during my school years, and by
the time I got to university I had effectively edited myself out of it.
I'd developed a mantra: I will never do anything mainstream. It was
born of a youthful self-righteousness. I thought party politics was
corrupt, corrupting and something that could not be saved. Why
would I want to align myself with that? I thought I would shout in

from the outside – and sometimes, as at the World Bank Protests in Washington DC, for example – I was quite literally shouting in.

I was far more motivated by American politics than British. That was partly because of how the American story dominated the world's story, and because the Black victories and leadership I desperately needed to see – from Jackie Robinson to Joe Louis, Martin Luther King Jr to Malcolm X, Public Enemy to Jesse Jackson – were more obviously accessible there. US politics seemed more overtly concerned with issues I cared about – race and poverty – and it was in the growth of the civil rights movement in the US that I found my inspiration. I'd studied the movement and it had shaped much of my political theology. I didn't know what the British equivalent was, which isn't to say it didn't exist. It was partly my ignorance, but it was also a reflection of our education system: the Black element of British history was simply not taught or explored in the schools I went to.

I see the same political characteristics I had back then in some of the activism directed my way as mayor – it's a curious mix of cynicism and idealism, self-righteousness and hopelessness. I felt to take part in politics was to engage in a broken system that would compromise me and take my soul. By extension, I had a judgement that those involved had sold theirs. But I have come to see that not engaging is a middle-class luxury. It's great if you have assets that mean you can weather any storm, but it's the most vulnerable members of society who most need politics to work for them. Ironically, those least served by politics are those least able to give up on it.

I am frustrated when I look back at my younger self, and frustrated, too, when I hear arguments from those whom I call lifestyle activists: *it doesn't matter who is in charge, they're all just the same.* Among my team we talk about those for whom changes in party and policy don't make a difference. If you're fortunate to have that sort of life, good for you. That means you have assets that make you immune to the wider socio-economic system. It probably means the economy works for you without government intervention forcing it to. But for most people, a subtle change in policy can make all the difference to whether or not they can get by. Policies like Sure Start centres, the living wage, the minimum wage, changes to housing allowance or the willingness or not to extend free school meal provision: these have the capacity to change people's lives.

As I grew older, so my politics matured. I made peace with myself, with our imperfect system, and joined an imperfect political party, to work in a broken political system in a perverse and unjust world. I do what I can within the system and sometimes things line up and we get a win. Sometimes we don't. That's politics. It's far from perfect, but then neither am I and nor is life.

Some lifestyle activists live their lives as though the world is as privileged as they are. They seem to prefer getting nothing to compromising to get something. They'll push for everything at the potential cost of everything and call that radical. But it's not really radical because the changes sacrificed in the name of perfection can cost the most vulnerable the most, while making no difference to those whose family wealth or race and class privilege shield them. Since becoming mayor, I have been on the end of campaigns by activists I have come to view as people who are not used to the world not bending to their will. And what they are sometimes angry about is not the failure of their cause, but their first experiences of the world, of someone, saying they can't get everything they want.

All of which is not to say we should not strive for greatness nor that we should settle for less. But we need to approach things with a bit of humility. I've grown to realize that while we can't solve everything, politics has the power to make some things better, and that is worth fighting for.

Politics can be a bit like rock climbing: only reach up for the next handhold if you've got a rope attached, otherwise you're going to fall off the side of the cliff. The lifestyle activists have a safety net: their parents' money. But many people aren't so fortunate, and I have to make decisions that minimize the risk I put into their lives. If I don't reach that next handhold, I could take down a lot of people depending on me.

My political wake-up call was Operation Black Vote. This is an organization that originally came into being in the 1990s to encourage Black and Asian people to mobilize their untapped political power by registering to vote. But as the organization expanded, so they also started to encourage more Black and Asian people to move beyond lobbying others to running for office ourselves. I first heard about them in early 2001 while a student at Eastern University. By the time I'd returned to the UK later in the year, I'd missed the deadline to participate in their Magistrates Shadow Scheme. But I called and asked if I could turn up to their training events anyway, even if I was not formally in the scheme. They kindly let me participate and that, in many ways, was the beginning.

The organization was then run by Simon Woolley, now Lord Woolley, who was to play a pivotal role in my journey. With his support, I went on to participate in two Operation Black Vote schemes: the Commissioner Shadow Scheme where I shadowed Trevor Phillips, who at that time was the chair of the Commission for Race Equality; and the MP Shadow Scheme through which I shadowed Bridget Prentice.

While the schemes were invaluable, the key moment for me came during one of the training days. Simon and I were discussing politics when he turned to me and said, 'You've got a great analysis on why the world is rubbish, but what are you going to do about it?'

When I started to bluster about overhauling neo-liberalism, he quickly cut me off, telling me, 'You can't do everything. But you can do something.' He then asked if I was in a political party. I shook my head.

'You can't get elected if you're not in a party,' he replied. 'My advice to you is join a party, become a candidate and get elected. *Then* you can do something.'

Simon's words hit me like a slap in the face. All these years later, I still recall how hard they hit home. *You can't do everything. But you can do something.* It was like being given the missing piece in the jigsaw between my passions and a way I could carry them out, philosophy and pragmatism. There was never any real debate for me about which political party I should join. I signed up to be a member of the Labour Party and finally started to do something real.

I was picked up by Bristol Labour as someone with potential. There was some talk about Bristol seats. Then, when the national Labour Party needed someone to present some events, they asked me. In

2006, when Tony Blair undertook his 'Let's Talk' tour, I was asked to host the Bristol event, which was held at a sports centre in St Pauls. Hazel Blears, then Minister of State for Policing, was in Bristol for the event and I was asked to interview her for a podcast. I was sent a set of questions by Labour's head office. I immediately thought, *Oh, these are all under-arm deliveries. No one's going to believe this is a real interview.* So I switched the questions for some of my own. When the interview started and I asked Hazel my questions, she looked down at her notes and then at her team. I thought that was a good sign. But it wasn't. I thought they were suggested questions but they had been carefully crafted for a podcast and I wasn't on script. It was a really good interview in the end, even if I gave the press officer who got me the interview, my friend Matt, a few tense moments.

It must have been OK because I was then asked to host the Let's Talk events with Tony Blair in Bristol and Nottingham. And from there, I was asked to go to Downing Street to interview Tony Blair again, this time for a podcast.

This all took place when I was coming up to London to do the night shifts for Radio 5 Live. I was struggling to get noticed at the BBC, but now here I was, being invited to Downing Street to interview the prime minister. It all seemed quite incongruous. I was ushered in, and tried to take in my surroundings as I waited. It's quite easy to get carried away by the history. The PM was running behind schedule and so I took the opportunity to ask to go to the bathroom. While I was in there, I found myself thinking of all the people that might have been there before: Winston Churchill, Bill Clinton, Mikhail Gorbachev or Ronald Reagan.

I'd interviewed Tony a couple of times by this point so knew him a little bit. When he came in and said, 'Hello, Marvin,' it made me feel like I existed. The interview went really well; he was happy, and his people were happy. Before he left, he shook my hand and said, 'If you're ever going for selection anywhere, let me know. I'm really keen to support you.' I was thrilled. I'd arranged to meet Matt at Labour Party HQ straight after and when I got there, I was taken to his desk where he was working. After a couple of minutes, Matt asked me if I wanted a cup of tea.

'Sure,' I said, thinking that I'd lived with Matt for a while and he'd never made me tea. He took me to the kitchen. Once there, he turned to me. 'Mate,' he said, 'your flies are undone.' I realized, in horror, that they must have been undone since I'd gone to the bathroom in Downing Street and that I'd done the whole interview like that. I had no idea if the PM had noticed, but I really hoped not.

Back in Bristol, people were beginning to talk about me running to be the candidate for the Bristol West seat in the 2010 election. Linked to that, an opening came up to stand for a council seat in the ward of Ashley, which was in the same constituency. I felt well placed: it included St Pauls and Montpelier, where my family was from and where I'd spent much of my childhood. To win that would give me a good platform which would help any future parliamentary campaign. The sitting councillor, Shirley Marshall, was a Liberal Democrat. I knew Shirley and, although she was in a different party, I felt loyal to her as the only Black woman on the council. We spoke, and she told me she had decided she was going to stand down at the next election.

As a result, I put myself forward and won the Labour nomination. Standing as a local councillor might not sound like a huge deal, but it meant a lot to me. I had my first foothold in the political process. But then Shirley made an about-turn: her party leader had convinced her to run again.

I was now faced with a difficult choice. If I stood as the Labour candidate against her, then I would be launching my career by attempting to defeat the only Black woman on the council. The whole point of Operation Black Vote was to increase Black and Asian representation – not pitch us against each other. If I ran against her, I would have to argue that she wasn't good at her job. But being a Black woman in a posh white man's space gave greater weight to Shirley's position. She might have represented a different party, but she was ours and I couldn't tear her down.

At the same time, if I didn't stand against her, I knew there'd be repercussions within the local Labour Party, which would affect my chances of being selected for the Bristol West seat. I was warned against stepping back. 'Don't do it,' I was told. 'It's going to cost you.'

I didn't know what to do. I rang Simon Woolley for advice. He heard me out and understood my dilemma. 'It's a big deal,' he said. 'But you've got to make a decision.'

I wrestled with what to do. I knew it would damage my chances, but in the end I couldn't do it. I went back to the local party leadership and explained. 'I can't run against her,' I told them and withdrew my candidacy. They were furious.

A number of senior members of the party met me in an effort to change my mind. But I just couldn't head up a campaign to knock the only Black woman off the council. The meeting got more heated with one highly respected member almost yelling at me: 'You were supposed to run in Bristol West and you blew it. You let us down. You let the party down. You're finished now. You're finished in Bristol politics.'

It was hard to hear. My party brand had disintegrated and with it my hopes of doing anything in politics. Then the selection meeting for Bristol West came up. While I took the warnings seriously, I felt I needed to put myself forward. I was hopelessly naive. I thought – against all the evidence – that if I turned up, debated and presented well, I might win the nomination. The other candidates, who were more politically savvy than me, had spent their time contacting the members beforehand to secure support. The fact that I'd stood and withdrawn for the council seat killed any chance I might have had of being nominated. I attended the hustings and received almost no votes. I felt like a pariah and was treated as one.

I remember saying to my wife, 'What do I do now?' There was no one in the party I felt I could talk to. I didn't feel they fully understood the tension that existed between party and race. They wanted people who'd say, 'cut me open and you'll find Labour running through me' – that wasn't, and still isn't me. I rang Simon Woolley, who was sympathetic and said I had done the right thing. That was easy to say, I thought. I had nothing. But I didn't say that to Simon. I just thanked him and hung up, demoralized and really low. I'd failed at journalism. Now it felt as though I'd failed at politics, too. If I couldn't get the nomination in the seat where I grew up, where on earth could I?

I continued to freelance for a while, picking up shifts at Radio 5 Live and the odd local project before coming across a job at the Black Development Agency, supporting local Black- and Asian-led community organizations. It was a timely job with good purpose, but it wasn't changing the world. And to rub salt into the wounds, our offices were opposite my old school. Kirsten and I had bought my nan's former house, one street over from my mum's. So every day I had to walk to work retracing my walk to school through the streets of Easton. When I was at university, I remember how I used to come back on the train, walk along by the railway line, looking out over the red roofs and the housing and thinking to myself, I've made it. I'm out of here. I'm never coming back.

Except there I was. Right back where I started. I was ashamed that, for all my efforts, I was no further forward in reaching my goals. Walking to work along the same route I had walked to school was evidence of my failure to make a success of my life.

After working for the Black Development Agency, I moved to the NHS, working in Public Health. It was there that I met three people to whom I owe so much: Christina Gray, who was associate director of Public Health and my line manager; Hugh Brady, the director of Public Health; and Deborah Evans, chief executive of Bristol Primary Care Trust. It was Hugh who told me about the Yale World Fellows Program and suggested I should apply. I didn't have much personal interaction with him, but I must have done something to get noticed.

I looked up the programme and my immediate thought was, I'll never get on to that. It was set up to give 'people of character, integrity, energy and talent' from all over the world the chance to develop their leadership skills. There were fifteen places and they went to serious high-flyers. I skimmed through the profiles of people who'd taken the course: lawyers, journalists, activists, financiers, diplomats. I wasn't running to be president of anything: I was a band eight manager in the NHS. I didn't want to appear weak or needy, but I needed to be sure Hugh had really meant it when he'd said, 'I think they'd really like you.' I told him I'd looked at the programme and that the alumni were so impressive. Hugh was very aware of this, but assured me that he thought I should apply: he'd nominated someone a few years previously and she'd been accepted. It was like my GCSEs all over again. If I applied, I might fail, but if I didn't apply, I would fail.

I wasn't living under a powerful, oppressive regime. I hadn't set up an environmental organization or led a political party. Instead, in my application I did the only thing I could do and talked about what I knew. I wrote about the politics of mental health, poverty and race. I talked about the difficulties of making change when the lines between good and bad aren't always that easy to discern – about when 'bad' isn't represented by an overtly evil individual, but the way an impersonal system works. To my great surprise, I got an interview. It was a telephone call with Kel Ginsberg, the associate director of the programme. I came off the call thinking I'd acquitted myself well. And to my amazement, I was offered a place. Yale! This could be my reset. Hope.

Part of me was shocked to be accepted. But, if I'm honest, part of me wasn't. Despite all the setbacks, I still believed that I had a purpose and that something like this – at last – might be the gateway to the opportunity I had been longing for. I am reluctant to talk about my sense of calling and purpose for fear people won't understand it or think I am claiming some kind of special status. But that sense of calling is inseparable from my faith and being, and I have always felt it.

The longing and belief that I could/should/was supposed to 'do something' has been both a source of energy and a burden throughout my life. When things were going badly at the BBC, I was thirty-three years old and very low. I visited a church and, unsolicited, some of the congregation said they wanted to pray for me. So I let them. One of them suggested that I should read Psalm 139, 'Search Me O God and Know My Heart'. It was a profound moment, as only a few days before I had read that Psalm and it had stopped me in my tracks. It told me I mattered. The same person then said – without knowing me at all – that they saw me like a bush that needs pruning. No one wants to be pruned, but that is what ensures the fruit. They also likened me to a surfer who was frustrated at missing the waves passing them. They said they believed my wave was coming.

Writing and sharing this is quite strange, and makes me feel quite vulnerable. No one has to believe in the spiritual element of this, and I know that some people will read and dismiss it. But what that group of strangers said to me when I visited their church and the fact they prayed for me was an important moment and one I shall never forget.

I knew that the power that kept me going had something to do with my faith in God. The missed opportunities with the marines, at the BBC and in politics were painful enough, but what really hurt was the feeling that I might have missed the opportunity to become the person I could have been. Perhaps the Yale World Fellows Program would be the wave I caught, a breath of life.

It was an incredible opportunity. The course was fully funded: accommodation, food, flights, a healthy stipend. Looking at some of the people who were there, it still seems extraordinary I was accepted. Among the other students at the time were Sergei Lagodinsky, now a Green MEP in Germany; Ricardo Teran, a successful entrepreneur in Nicaragua; May Akl, who had worked for the prime minister of Lebanon; Lamumba Di Aping, Southern Sudan diplomat to the UN; Aziz Royesh, later recognized as one of the world's top ten teachers for educating thousands of children at his school in Kabul; and Alexei Navalny, poisoned, imprisoned and ultimately killed for campaigning against Vladimir Putin's corruption in Russia.

The calibre of the other people left me feeling like an imposter. While I was determined to take every opportunity the university offered me, I was also burdened by a belief that they'd made a mistake in accepting me onto the course: surely there were plenty more qualified people out there? While I recognize that the way my political career has gone since then goes some way to justify my inclusion, even now I'm still at a loss as to why Michael Cappello (the course director) and Kel Ginsberg accepted me. I don't understand what potential I unknowingly displayed and what they saw and heard in that application form and phone interview. The sense that I didn't deserve to be there was a challenge – and it is a challenge that, sadly, is all too often felt by people from backgrounds like mine. It's the opposite of the entitlement that going somewhere like Eton bestows upon you. A belief that you have a right to be anywhere and do anything can carry you a long way in life. For me, though, the corresponding lack of belief is something that must be consistently overcome.

I needed to talk to someone about how I was feeling. I connected with a university chaplain. I thought it was safe to open up to her. 'I feel like a total fraud here.' Her response was, 'Welcome to Yale. Half the people walking around here feel like they shouldn't be here.'

Those words were a comfort to me. But they also challenged me to recognize that privileged people can also carry insecurities and that I should avoid falling into self-righteousness about my own. My imposter syndrome, however, did mean that I was determined to make the most of my time there. I was always leaning in. The guests they brought in to speak to us were incredible, among them Tony Blair and General Stanley McCrystal. Some of the Yale fellows would pick and choose which speakers they saw. I didn't miss a single session.

Together with my fellow student May Akl, I set up sessions for Yale students of mixed heritage. We put forward a provocation that people of mixed heritage have a unique but untapped contribution to make to the way we do politics on issues of identity, conflict, peace and reconciliation. It came about because of something I had said when I first arrived. We all had to introduce ourselves and I gave what was probably a rambling talk about a number of things, including how my experiences of being mixed race had shaped my life and sense of identity and belonging. After I finished, May came to me in the break and said, 'You've just told a Lebanese story.' She described how she had a Lebanese Jewish mother and a Lebanese Christian father: 'I've got cousins called Mohammad and Moses,' she told me. Like me, she had grown up living across boundaries.

Professor David Berg was part of the Yale Faculty working on the programme and we became close. David became a really important figure in my life. A Jewish-American psychologist, he is an amazing person, full of insight and incredibly well-connected. He shared Tal-mudic stories to help with our insights and reflections, which I found profound. One of his friends from university was Howard Dean. Dean had been governor of Vermont and then ran to be the Democrat candidate in the 2004 presidential election. Although he didn't win, his grassroots campaign changed how politics was done in the States: he developed internet-based fundraising, targeting small donors and encouraging participatory democracy. After we had got to know one another, David told me that Howard had once said, 'Being a governor was much more fulfilling than being a senator.' David continued, 'I think you'd find executive political leadership much more fulfilling than legislative politics.'

This was before the mayoral system in the UK cities outside

London had even been set up, so at the time it seemed something of a misplaced comment, but one that turned out to be remarkably prescient. And funnily enough, while I was at Yale, they did try to set up a meeting for me with Cory Booker. A huge figure in US politics, Booker was then mayor of Newark, New Jersey. He'd been to Yale Law School, and someone decided he would be a good person for me to meet. The meeting never happened, unfortunately, but in terms of what I'd go on to do, it too felt prescient: the mere fact they thought I was worthy of meeting him lifted me.

I learned so much about leadership from Yale. Perhaps the most important lesson was that even if I felt like a fraud, I still turned up. And if I felt scared, no matter how uncertain I might feel inside, I'd still be there, trying to make a contribution.

I was struck by the diversity at Yale. Obviously, it's an Ivy League university and like so much of society, it has a long way to go. I am keenly aware of the injustices and social immobility which expose the American Dream as being more myth than reality. But the fellows selected on my course were truly international. And I met more Black and Brown students and professors in that short time than I could see across the UK's Russell Group combined.

One of the first events I attended was at the Afro-American Cultural Center, known as The House. It didn't feel like the sort of place you'd find at Oxford, Cambridge or Bristol. The event was entitled 'Black Defined' and involved about forty Black and Brown students debating how we each related to the term 'Black'. The students were African American, Black Hispanics, Mixed Race, Nigerian, European. Some spoke English, some spoke Spanish, some had other first languages. From the off, I felt lifted to be in a room with so many Black high achievers. The evening started with a showing of Dave Chappelle's 'Racial Draft' sketch, which got laughs. Then the debate started: 'How do you relate to the term "Black"?' As we went around the room, each person's view was subtly but significantly different. It was a profound experience. By the time they got to me, I'd had time to think, and I had seen a pattern. 'It depends,' I said and concluded that 'Black' hadn't been enough to capture the fullness of the identity of anyone in that circle, including me, but Black was essential to everyone. Without it, we lost the common connection we all needed and without which we would feel rootless and lost. Our identities as Black people felt simultaneously inadequate and essential to understanding our relationship with one another and the world.

After speaking at another debate on race, I was approached by three men who'd disagreed with some of my points. They were angling on dropping race so everyone could just be American. They were white Americans. So I asked about their identities.

'We're Irish Americans,' came the reply.

'There you go,' I said, 'that speaks volumes. Whiteness isn't enough to define you, is it? I don't think I've ever met a white American who was content to just be white or even just American. Everyone explains their Scottish, German, Swedish, Italian or whatever roots.' Whiteness wasn't enough for them – although because the world affirms whiteness, it's easier for them to go through life without having to confront the inadequacy of the grouping. The term 'American' is synonymous with white, so how could it possibly be enough for Black Americans?

All these debates and discussions fed into the wrestle with racial categories I'd had since my childhood. Growing up, my primary family, the people who cared for me every day, were white. To some I was 'half-caste' – at school, some Black children referred to me and the other mixed-race kids as 'half-breeds'. I remember being in the playground at St George Rose Green when one of the kids asked me, 'Black people would go to Jamaica, white people would stay in England, but where would you go?' Another morning, on the way to school, another kid put it directly: 'Marv, in a war between Black and white, whose side would you be on?'

I'm not white; that's obvious. I have faced the hostility of racism for being Black. But Black doesn't capture the fullness of my heritage as a person of Jamaican, English, Welsh and Irish heritage. Being described as half-caste or half-breed suggests a brokenness and an incompleteness. I have come to a view that while they are indispensable to understanding the world, if the identities of Black and white aren't enough to define those who more easily fit into them, how can they be enough to divide me?

My journey from finding my mixedness a challenge to revelling in it has been accompanied by an understanding that difference is good and isn't of itself divisive. In 2019, I became the first mayor to speak at the negotiations over the United Nations' Global Compact on Migration. I explained how recognizing my Welshness didn't take away from my Englishness and my Englishness did not take away from my Jamaicanness. I shared that when I discovered my great-grandmother had come from Ireland, it didn't take away from any part of me, but made me more whole. Difference isn't the problem. The problem is our desire for simplicity and inability to live with difference and complexity and dynamism within groups. And when that difference attaches itself to socio-economic inequalities and is exploited by predatory politicians, that's where the real challenges begin.

It was both liberating and empowering to be in the room with such ferociously smart African Americans. I've always believed I was reasonably clever: back in infant school I could do the maths questions and wondered why others couldn't. For a while, I was put in all the top sets. But when I became a teenager, the wheels started to come off. I wasn't a bad kid but neither was I an angel in school. The work got harder and my grades went down. I was embarrassed and I didn't know what to do. So I pretended not to care. That helped me fit in at the time, but at the risk of my future prospects.

I remembered walking to school with my friends years before, when I was discussing whether to go to sixth form and study for A Levels. 'No, Marvin man,' I was told, 'that's what white kids do.' There was this suggestion that further study was somehow abandoning my Blackness – an idea that had an additional edge for me, as a mixed-race kid – the same Blackness we all had to hold on to in that room in Yale. I didn't think that was right then – more than two decades later, listening to what those extraordinary minds at Yale had to say was more than proof enough.

I was inspired by so many of the sessions during the course but two in particular stand out for me. One was with the Croatian theologian, Miroslav Volf. He ran a workshop on what a good life is. In it, he talked about how, throughout history, different people had come up with different answers, whether it was happiness, or relationships, or industry and hard work. He talked about how people often respond to the question in a flippant way – they don't properly engage with it, but when you really think about it, you can learn a lot. Volf himself was taking a sabbatical year to study what it meant to flourish. I loved that word and how it turned the question round – rather than thinking about what makes life meaningful, what do we need and what does it mean for a human being to flourish?

The other session that had an impact on me, and which couldn't have been more different from Miroslav Volf's, was with a US General, Stanley McChrystal. He had been the Commander of the US Forces in Afghanistan and we were invited to join him for breakfast. I'd read up on him and made assumptions about what he'd be like. I thought he'd be a militarian Alpha male, an unthinking, even robotic, patriot. That morning, I got to the meeting early. I was one of the first of the fellows there.

'Hey, come on in,' McChrystal said. He couldn't have been friendlier. He showed us the sort of care, concern and politeness that left me feeling humbled and uplifted. And rather than having my prejudices confirmed, I met someone phenomenally intelligent – a thoughtful, inquisitive mind. Which, if I'd thought about it, I should have expected. You don't get to be a four-star general without being smart. There I was, passing judgement on him before I'd met him: here he was, going out of his way to give me his time.

During the breakfast, McChrystal talked about leadership and politics. One of the biggest fears in politics, he told us, was that the price of getting involved in public life had become so high that good people would decide not to get involved (and this was in 2010, with social media only just taking off). The danger, McChrystal continued, was that we would end up with only two kinds of people prepared to commit to public service: those who are so self-absorbed or narcissistic that they have no ability to hear criticism; or those who are willing to pay any price to get into power.

It's a thought that continues to resonate with me. If you look at some of the people who have entered politics in the last decade, McChrystal has been proven right. And for those of us who did step up to fight the good fight, the price of getting involved weighs heavy. Most of the time I find the noises on social media more of an irritant than anything else. But there are moments when I think, do I want to carry on dealing with all this?

As the culmination of my mayoral term approached, I began to think about what I wanted to do next and I can't pretend that the culture that surrounds public leadership doesn't leave me with a bit of an 'I'm done' feeling. It's only human. Michelle Obama famously advised Obama supporters, 'When they go low, we go high.' Of course, it is great advice, but it takes a discipline that in turn consumes a lot of energy. Though I would never walk away from politics for negative reasons, the temptation to take a role where the personal cost is lower is appealing. But if we leave a political vacuum, something will fill it. What we have may not be perfect, but sometimes the job is merely to occupy the space so that other stuff doesn't. In that sense, there is no neutral act. Not standing up is a decision in itself for the other.

7.

Losing . . . and Winning

The 2012 Bristol mayoral election came at the right time for me. I'd
finished at Yale in December 2010 and had applied to go to Harvard
Kennedy School, for their Master of Public Administration. I was
offered a place to start there in the summer of 2011 but didn't have
the funding, so they'd allowed me to defer for a year. If I'd taken the
offer up, I'm not sure where my life would have gone. At that point,
I wanted to work for the United Nations and I suspect I would have
ended up working in the US and never returning to Bristol.

As it was, I was back in the UK and working out what I wanted
to do. I went up to London to attend the Labour Party's Future Candidates Programme. One of the sessions looked at the Conservative
government's plan to introduce mayors into local government and
the Labour Party's search for mayoral candidates. But I didn't go. It
didn't seem relevant and I wasn't interested in getting stuck in local
government. I went to the session on becoming a prospective candidate for Parliament instead. The idea of standing in Bristol West
at the next election really appealed to me. The seat was held by the
Liberal Democrats, who'd seen off the challenge from the Labour
candidate I'd lost out to. I thought the disagreements over not standing for councillor in Ashley were firmly in the past. I was back living
in the area, and I felt I could do a good job. I'd led significant work
across the city's voluntary sector through the Black Development

Agency; I'd led work for the NHS's Managing the Race Equality in Mental Health Programme and been director of our Local Strategic Partnership – all high-profile leadership roles. But it was decided that the seat would be an all-women shortlist. I was personally very disappointed, though I do support the principle. But it's a complex matter – especially when it means ruling out Black, Asian and working-class male candidates who are also under-represented. That doesn't mean we shouldn't do it. We should, and the Labour Party has shown how it makes space for talented women that the selection process and culture, left to themselves, had traditionally failed to see. But the unintended consequence of addressing male dominance needs to be recognized.

Once again, I felt stuck. It was like the marines all over again – close, but not enough. But then Bristol voted yes to a mayor. I will be eternally grateful to Margaret Hickman, the Lawrence Hill councillor and all-round good person, who suggested that I should put myself forward. And it was Margaret who introduced me to Ben Mosley, another key figure in the local party who was working for Kerry McCarthy, the Labour MP for Bristol East. Ben was only in his mid-twenties then, but he was already a fantastic organizer. Ben took me for a drink at the Wetherspoons down by Temple Meads to sound me out. I was eager to meet him – Margaret had told me that if I was to run, he was the sort of person I needed to have on board.

Ben had a pint and I had a hot chocolate. He grilled me on all sorts of issues, including my religious beliefs: he knew I was a Christian and, although Catholic himself, there were mischievous suggestions I was homophobic. But by the end of it, he seemed convinced and went back to tell Margaret. 'This is the guy,' he said. 'This is the candidate.'

Kerry has been a constant support and immediately made space for Ben to work on my selection, and he was brilliant, immediately clicking into gear to run my selection campaign. For all my time at Yale studying leadership and all the experience I now had, I knew little to nothing about the internal culture and workings of the Labour Party, or the practical side of running a political campaign to win votes. This was where Ben came in. He turned up at my house with a membership list and phone numbers. He passed me a sheet and told me to start making calls – and I began putting in the hard yards. We spent hours in a small room at the back of my house – and at Margaret's – ringing round everyone on that list, member by member.

Soon we had formed a small team and momentum began to build. I was up against a tough field, but I was positive about my chances even though there were things I got wrong. I had a leaflet designed and thought I'd put some of my own artistic touches to it. Design is certainly not my forte – in fact, I am a liability. As it was about to go to print, I decided to add a red tint over the whole front page. Some of the other candidates had been pushing the line that I wasn't really Labour, that I was a Tory, and I thought the red tint might send a subliminal message that I was indeed Red. But the results were mortifying. The primary effect was to make me look sinister, even demonic. Thankfully, the members didn't seem to mind too much.

The other candidates I was up against included Cllrs Peter Hammond and Helen Holland, between whom the local Labour Group leadership had alternated over recent years. There was also Kelvin Blake, a former councillor – who went on to be my agent in the 2012, 2016 and 2021 elections – and Dan Norris, a former MP who had worked with David Miliband when he was foreign secretary and was then a junior minister in the Department of Agriculture. They all had successful election records. The only candidate who didn't was me. That was a problem, but it was also an opportunity. I was the one person standing who could present themselves as something different, someone new. There was a tangible desire for change in the city and an anti-politics sentiment that heightened a taste for candidates running as independents. The favourite, George Ferguson, was tapping in to that mood. He had resigned from the Liberal Democrats and was standing as an independent under the banner of his new Bristol First Party. It made sense for the Labour Party to offer someone who was also a break from the past, rather than a familiar political face.

This was the tightrope I had to walk. I needed to offer a new start, but I didn't want my opponents to keep pushing the 'no track record' and 'not really Labour' line. And I deeply resented anyone setting a bar to earn their acceptance. I had experienced that as a young man, especially when it came to racial categorization. Part of my own liberation had been – and would continue to be – overcoming that kind of thing and denying the power of those who assumed they were the arbiters of who belonged and who did not. I didn't join the Labour Party for that kind of history to repeat itself with that kind of purity test.

In the run-up to the final selection, there was a debate between the prospective candidates. It was a union-organized event in a room on Princes Street – two hundred people crammed into a small venue. The other candidates talked about their political experience and track records. I took a different tack, talking about my record in the community. 'This selection is not a general knowledge test of the ins and outs of Bristol City Council,' I told the room. 'If you make it a general knowledge test on council processes, then I won't get chosen. But that's not what this process is. Being the mayor isn't just about the council. It's about leading the city beyond the council.'

People seemed to embrace my ideas. And they seemed to warm to me, too. The more meetings I went to, the more people I talked to, the more people seemed to get on board. One of the people in the audience at the debate was Kevin Slocombe, who worked for the Communication Workers Union. He would say he wasn't particularly inspired by local Labour politics but, for some reason, he decided to attend that night. And that was the beginning of the most important political relationship in my life.

I won the nomination in July and I was thrilled. But that excitement was soon tempered with disappointment. I had expected a Labour campaign machine to shift into place, preparing for the election in mid-November. But as the weeks slipped by there was nothing. The Bristol Labour Party just wasn't geared up to run a citywide campaign of this kind. Ward by ward, yes. Constituency by constituency, yes. But a campaign for a single candidate across the city's four constituencies? No. It was a wholly new prospect. On top of this, despite winning the nomination, the party didn't seem settled on me. There were those who had opposed the introduction of the mayoral model, those who didn't believe we could win it in the face of the headwinds of anti-party politics, the appetite for independents with big personalities, and there were some who simply resented my winning the Labour selection.

I became increasingly concerned. I went to London to the Labour Party head office and met with Scott Langdon, the Labour Party director to the general secretary, to share my concerns. In the meantime, a Communication Workers Union activist Kye Dudd mentioned that he knew someone he thought I should get to run the campaign. That person was Kevin. Like me, he was a local boy and when we met at a cafe in Stokes Croft, we immediately clicked. I could tell from the off that he was one of the smartest people I'd met. He understood where I was coming from and offered to run my campaign. He was working for the CWU at the time, and a deal was struck between the union and the Labour Party to second him to me. One of the first bits of advice I'd received on getting selected came from Richard Angel, then the head of the Labour pressure group Progress. He told me to watch *The West Wing*. In one episode, President Bartlet asks a young representative if he has a best friend.

'Yes,' he replies.

'Is he smarter than you?'

'Yes.'

'Do you trust him with your life?'

'Yes.'

'That's your chief of staff,' concludes Bartlet.

A core requirement for any leader is to find people who are smarter than you, surround yourself with them and always expect them to bring their full abilities to the roles you give them. That's Kevin.

In the meantime, Party HQ had approached Simon Fletcher to help. They'd also recognized we could win the election with a proper campaign. Simon had run Ken Livingstone's campaign for Mayor of London and become his chief of staff. He would go on to run Jeremy Corbyn's selection campaign and become a senior member of Jeremy's team when he was leader of the Labour Party. At last, the core team was in place: Simon orchestrating the campaign from the regional office; Kevin running all things communications, from messaging to press relations and husting preparations; and Ben managing relationships with the Labour group and wider membership. National Party Headquarters had also become aware of some of the unhelpful Bristol Labour Party internal politics, so Emily Thornberry, then shadow attorney general, was dispatched to the campaign and spent considerable time in Bristol making it clear we wanted to win. I will always be thankful to Emily. Once she arrived, the Party culture surrounding the campaign changed dramatically. We had an office and some structure to the campaign. A Twitter feed was set up, speeches were written and it finally felt as though we were moving forward.

But there was still a lot to do. There was no clear message from the Party as to what I should focus on, no strategy on how I should be presented. And there was little information or data to work with. We did a scratch poll, which put us eighteen points behind George Ferguson. In election terms, that's a mountain to climb.

I learned a lot about politics during that campaign. I learned a lot about Bristol. And a lot about myself. George Ferguson, with his red trousers and confident manner, campaigned as the candidate of change. He was the independent, the maverick, the outsider. By contrast, because I was standing for Labour, I started to be portrayed as the establishment figure. Never mind that George was a CBE and a member of the Society of Merchant Venturers, or had been a member of the Liberal Democrats, and served as a Liberal councillor and run for Parliament before I was twelve years old, while I would have become the first directly elected mayor of Black African descent in Europe. George managed to switch the narrative from being the bookies' favourite to being the outsider: the red trousers were presented as a sign of rebellion. One of the biggest surprises of what turned out to be quite a strange election was when Massive Attack threw their weight behind him. I didn't understand that. I was the comprehensive school-educated, mixed-race kid, descended from Irish and Welsh migrants on one side and enslaved Africans on the other, running against a privately educated, wealthy white male. Massive Attack had made several strong political statements, even taking a stand against playing in the Colston Hall because of its association with the eighteenth-century slaver Edward Colston. Yet they came out for George. I had to put it down as one of those things.

I felt the same about the response of the Green Party, the first to take to Twitter to attack me. I was shocked. Being on the receiving end of an unsolicited Twitter attack from someone who doesn't know you is one thing. But when it's from people you expected to have some common ground with, it's a whole new level. It's not changed in the decade since. The Greens — in Bristol and beyond — have cultivated a brand that is friendly and caring, grown-up and beyond traditional political party bun-fights. But in my experience, they have been the most aggressive and well-organized party on social media with a well-coordinated structure of outriders ready to lead a Twitter pile-on against anyone who challenges their ownership of the moral high ground.

We tried to run the campaign differently from a traditional local Labour campaign. I wanted to try a community-organizing approach. It's a common set-up in American politics. You start with a small group of people and ask each of them to bring ten people to the next meeting. Then you get those people into a room and ask each of them to reach out to a further ten. Ed Miliband, the Labour leader at the time, had brought the political activist and organizer Arnie Graff over from the US. Arnie had worked in Chicago, Baltimore and numerous American cities, working with some of the most marginalized communities to encourage them to get out and vote. He was great. He challenged Labour to take campaigning beyond simply canvassing people on their doorsteps and trying to convince them to vote Labour without knowing if they were Labour supporters or had any prior relationship with the party. I joked with David Miliband that the traditional approach reminded me of those Evangelicals who walk up to people and just say, 'You need Jesus!' having taken no time to get to know them. Community organizing challenged us to get beyond the retail kind of politics in which we try to 'purchase' a vote by making big promises that – in truth – we may not be able to deliver. Instead, we were trying to offer a relationship which felt more authentic. We were getting people involved, people who had never been part of the political process before: Black and Asian kids, working-class people who felt they had a connection with us, that we were on their side. We were asking them to work with us.

Despite all this positivity, the internal Party squabbling rumbled on. Simon, Kevin, Ben and I were called to a meeting in the Labour offices in the recesses of Bristol's old Council House by a small group of councillors and party executives we knew were resentful that I'd beaten their leader to the nomination. They were all white men in their sixties and seventies, who told us, 'You need to convince us we should vote for you. You need to show us you're really Labour.' They then homed in on an issue that would prove highly significant during the election. All the other candidates had said they would appoint a rainbow cabinet if they won, in other words signalling the intention of having representatives from every party in their cabinet. This was partly sheer practicality. None of the parties were big enough to run a single-party cabinet: George Ferguson, in particular, was a one-man party, so would have no other choice.

Promising to have a rainbow cabinet seemed to me to be a bit of political theatre that risked ignoring the city's real challenges – inequality, housing, hunger, racism, social immobility. But it did appeal to the city and it did appeal to my desire to reconcile people across social and political divides. And I could see that the media were beginning to hold it up as a key point of difference between the candidates because it was an easy story. Yet these self-appointed Labour gatekeepers told me that I had to commit to a Labour-only cabinet to prove I was truly Labour. Looking back, I can see this is where we made the wrong call. We concluded we needed the party and would give them the cabinet, even if our plans would ultimately take city governance beyond the council. But you have to strike the balance between keeping the Party happy (or those who claim to represent the Party) and talking to the people. I warned them it would cost Labour in the polls and, sure enough, it was a criticism George Ferguson made in his campaign. I was angry that the old guard in my party had leveraged me into it against my will. In hindsight, I don't think they were that committed to me winning the mayoral election, anyway.

It's a painful thing to have to acknowledge, but although I was in the Labour Party, I still felt there was a racial dynamic at play. The opposition I came up against was full of contradictions. From some I've felt a kind of snobbery – I wasn't part of the intellectual left. Others talked as though I was some posh kid, my master's degrees and time at Yale evidence of some kind of silver spoon. I remember one hustings when a councillor challenged me, saying 'Don't come here with all your big words'. And then there is the subtle but significant idea that I still come across – that the working class is chiefly associated with white men, that my struggle was a racial struggle and not part of the class struggle. There is a tendency to identify the racial struggle

as something of a middle-class concern, closing the circle in which I
could be seen as a posh kid with big words, only there to deal with
race at the expense of class.

Fortunately, others in the Party were hugely supportive and at
national level I had a lot of encouragement. Iain McNicol, general
secretary of the Labour Party, had called me personally to congratulate me on winning the nomination and continued to check in. Then
I was invited to give the speech to introduce Ed Miliband, the party
leader, at the 2012 Labour Party conference. That was a nerve-
wracking experience. As my moment came, I stood behind the stage,
thinking, I could blow my entire career in the next seven minutes in
front of tens of thousands of people. Apart from the content and performance of the speech, I worried my trouser leg would get caught
on one of my boots, or worse still, that somehow my flies would be
undone – again. I gave the speech and sat down. It seemed to go OK.
Ed gave his speech and got a standing ovation. As he walked off the
stage, a member of his team rushed over to me and said, 'Walk off
with him.' Simon later said that if my speech had gone badly, they'd
have left me sitting there!

As election day neared, we knew we had momentum on our side.
The gap between us and George Ferguson was narrowing by the day:
by the end, we'd reduced it from 18 per cent to 3 per cent. George
and his team continued to play at being outsiders, ready to overturn
the old political order. It was as if they were mugging me of my story.
I resented a privileged man and his privileged supporters co-opting
the language of the marginalized. And I still do. It's become the thing
that politicians, journalists and self-styled activists do as a matter of
course today. Running as an independent without a party was being
held up as a sign of political authenticity, but it's really just a sign of
independent wealth. Campaigning for mayor costs tens of thousands
of pounds. Candidates like me could not hope to stand without the
Labour Party and trade unions. Their support makes it possible for
people of ordinary financial means to run for office. But my ability to
say this openly was limited. It would have been branded as class envy
and Black anger. It's one of the painful ironies of modern politics that
it's only really members of the establishment who can get away with
being openly angry at the establishment status quo. So, I let it slide

in the vain hope that the journalists analysing the candidates' political messages and conveying them to the public could disentangle the
symbolic from the substance.

Later, Kevin would remind me of my saying to him, 'My priority
is to come across as a credible candidate. I can't risk coming across
as the angry or funny Black man.' I just didn't have that luxury. What
it cost me, Kevin replied, was the chance for the public to interact
with the fullness of me as a rounded human being, and that didn't
help my campaign.

On election day there was a real buzz but it was also a sombre time.
We were out in the neighbourhoods, getting people to vote. I remember standing on a street corner and people who'd never voted before
were coming up to us saying: 'We want to vote for you; where do we
go?' But it was November, and we were out in the dark, cold evening,
looking at the cosy glow coming from house lights, and asking people
to leave that warmth to go vote for something of which many of them
had limited understanding. Winter elections always suppress the vote
and usually go badly for Labour.

The momentum we'd built wasn't quite enough. The headwinds
were too strong, and our campaign hadn't started fast enough.
George Ferguson's candidature was helped by the fact that the Conservatives' vote collapsed. Their supporters could see their candidate
wasn't going to win, so they'd voted for George instead. He cleaned
up in those neighbourhoods, while the inner city and poorer areas
went for us.

On election night, I was hopeful that we'd pull it off. I thought that
somehow the universe would step in to ensure that the old order
would be overturned and this mixed-race Black kid who grew up on
benefits would win out against someone I saw as the embodiment of
privilege. But Kevin and Simon had crunched the numbers and, just
after midnight, Kevin called me, saying: 'We can't win.' I couldn't quite
believe it: I'd spent so long working for something beyond me that I
thought it was going to happen. My response was to get into my car
and drive. I drove around the circumference of Bristol – or as close
to it as I could get: down the M32 to the M4, M5, back in along the
Portway, up to Hartcliffe through to the Brislington Trading Estate,
onto the ring road and back in on the M32. The journey cleared my

head, making peace with the city that had brought me up but had now rejected me.

The following morning I went in for the end of the count. I was ushered into a small side room with my close team and family while we waited for the final votes to be confirmed. For some reason, I still had space for the miraculous. The announcement itself was excruciating. The room was packed with our supporters and the media: cameras and microphones were everywhere. On stage was the returning officer, myself and George. He had won. His supporters cheered and broke into a rendition of 'For he's a jolly good fellow . . .' I wanted the room to swallow me up: I shook hands with George and the returning officer. As George gave his victory speech, the returning officer leaned in and whispered to me, 'You'd have made a great mayor.' I was proud of everything we'd achieved, but I felt crushed. I was embarrassed I'd failed and felt I'd let people down. The TV news asked me what was next for me. 'Back to work on Monday,' I replied with a fixed look. I didn't want anyone to see any emotion, any weakness. But it was humiliating. I was going back to Public Health – which was in the process of being transferred from the NHS Bristol to Bristol City Council. Not only had I lost, but the new mayor would be my boss. It was pain upon pain.

I had some dark times after I lost the election. Dark nights, dark moments, dark thoughts. I'm one of those people, for better or worse, who doesn't talk about things when they go wrong. I could talk to Kirsten, my family and close colleagues, but I'm far more likely to internalize everything. I know it's not healthy, but it's who I am. I might look calm on the outside, but inside, I'm turning everything over and over.

In that moment, all I felt was a sense of meaninglessness. Here I was, facing middle age and again feeling as though I'd failed. My school reports had always talked about my potential. So even when I wasn't doing well, or my grades weren't good, I knew that I had promise – that, given a chance, I could be something.

But I was no longer the bright young thing. The years of getting nowhere had chipped away at that. The shine had come off. I felt dulled – a could-have-been. Each time I'd come up short, I'd always been able to talk myself up rather than down. Now, for the first time, I was less sure. Maybe coming up short was all I was good for. Maybe the potential that others had seen in me simply wasn't there. At school, I'd done that thing of not trying hard so I'd have a fall-back: I knew I hadn't done my best. This time, though, I'd given it my all. There was no fallback from the thought that this was all I had to offer. And it wasn't enough.

I knew I had a lot to be thankful for, don't get me wrong. I had a beautiful wife, young children, my family, my faith. I was proud of them and wanted them to be proud of me. But what had I achieved? I remembered hearing the story that there had been laughter in the BBC newsroom when they learned I was running for mayor. For a brief moment, people had taken me seriously. Now I'd been put back in my box. Again.

The dark thoughts would bubble up when I was least expecting them: at night, out on a walk, at work. I am confident I would never have followed through on them, but I'd find myself thinking how I might end it all, my mind whirring through different scenarios. What if I reached fifty and had nothing to show my children and my family? What then?

Running for public office, by definition, is a public affair. Everyone knows who you are. Everyone knows what has happened. I'd pop around to Stapleton Road to buy a pint of milk from the local shop. I'd known the owners since childhood. Other customers would recognize me. I felt I could see them thinking, 'You lost'. I had a grey hoodie I'd wear with the hood up to remain anonymous.

But there were places where you couldn't wear a hoodie. At work, for example. That was tough: rather than sitting in the mayor's office, I was back at my desk, middle management at Public Health England. Not only had I been beaten by George Ferguson, but now I was work-ing for him as well. On one occasion, I came across him at an event to mark the Bristol Bus Boycott. 'This is odd,' I said, trying to make a joke about the fact he was my boss. 'I guess I am,' he said, before wandering off to talk to someone else. That was about as much input in his administration as he wanted from me.

Getting up, putting on my suit and walking to work, my feet like clay – those were some of the worst moments. Every fibre in my body was telling me I didn't want to be there. I'd get to the building, make my way to my floor and head for my desk. I couldn't tell if it was real or my imagination, but those first few days back, it felt as though people didn't know what to say. I didn't know what to say myself. I was embarrassed. I'd put myself out there in a big way and lost very publicly. I'd sit at my desk and think about what might have been and what it might have meant. And there were my dark thoughts, settling into the emptiness that was now in front of me.

Not long after I lost the 2012 election, I was invited to speak to a group of kids who were on the edge of gang activity. I felt connected to these young people, not because I had ever really come close to gang life (I'd had too many positive influences, and I knew I didn't have 'the thing' – call it strength, ruthlessness, smarts or desperation – that would have enabled me to operate successfully in that life). But I'd gone to school with people like that. A very smart school friend of mine had ended up in prison. I saw him after he got out and he told me that as tough as he was known to be, he'd often cried himself to sleep at night. That's the place I try to speak to at times like this. Beyond any bravado, there is a person who must face themselves alone at night. This is where Miroslav Volf's question hits home: what does it really mean to flourish? We all need to feel valued. And I valued these kids.

'I failed,' I told them. 'I stood for election and in front of 450,000 people I lost.' These young people were used to failure and being told they were failures, which was partly why they were there. They'd been told this so many times that they'd started to believe it, and stopped believing in themselves. They may have had a degree of confidence navigating the limited options available to them, but it really wasn't a route to flourishing. I remember speaking to a guy who grew up at the bottom of my street and became quite a serious player. He said to me that people he knew went into the life thinking they'd leave with money, a house and car, but their choices had led to jail, death or a stress-related illness.

The event took place at the Greek Hall in Easton, a three-minute walk from the street I'd grown up on. Some of them were surprised to hear me say I was local: the TV appearances and my political opponents had led them to believe I was a privileged kid. I could see they were also surprised that I was talking openly. But I wanted to be honest, not as a sign of weakness, but a sign of strength. Failure is an inevitability when we pursue our ambitions and try to step into places we shouldn't be stepping. Some of the kids in the room knew me anyway, but I wanted them to know that I grew up right here and that my background was the same as theirs.

In a strange way, talking about losing the election was cathartic. I had said in my concession speech that while it was painful, there might have been a greater good in my defeat. It's a bitter truth. I'd come so close and I was still convinced that I was meant to be mayor: I really believed that with Kevin by my side and the approach to city governance we had been developing I could do a good job for Bristol. But maybe my life wasn't going to be straightforward. I was struggling with the possibility that this was another wave that was passing me by.

We're nervous about talking about failure in this country. It's seen as a sign of weakness. But what you can learn from failure is invaluable. In American businesses, they talk about going through a company failure as being the million-dollar MBA: what you learn from an experience like that is worth more than any course you could take. In 2020, I took part in the Bloomberg Harvard City Leadership Initiative for Mayors. Fail fast, learn fast, the Harvard professors told us.

I'd had plenty of failure to talk to those kids about. For all my goals, and for all that was said about me over the years, I had failed to get into the marines. I had failed to make it at the BBC. I had failed to become mayor. Yale had been an incredible opportunity but hadn't obviously led to anything and the likelihood of taking up my place on the Harvard MPA was fading too. I had no notable outward signs of success: I was still living one street from the one I grew up on with my mum, in a ward that was in England's top 1 per cent for deprivation. Money was tight; I was driving a ten-year-old VW Golf that my sister had left for me when she'd moved to Zurich, and I had no idea which way to go. All I had to cover the sense of worthlessness that I felt was the resilience I had built over the years, a lingering sense of self and purpose that was rooted in my faith and my lived experience. I was as lost as some of these young people and I encouraged them, like me, to just keep putting one foot in front of the other.

'You should have ambition,' I told them. 'You should be ambitious for what you can do in life. But at the same time, you're going to have to buckle up. You're going to fail at some point. But that doesn't mean you're a failure.'

I told them the advice that the boxing trainer Cus D'Amato had given Mike Tyson: 'The hero and the coward both feel exactly the same fear. The difference is in the way they respond to it.' It's great advice. Swap the word fear for failure and it still holds.

What did I learn from losing in 2012? Many things, but most importantly, I learned to be more myself. I didn't want to be mayor in order to be mayor: I wanted to be mayor to be able to do things. If the conversation was about ideas, or about policy, I was happy to get stuck in and engage. But when it came to talking about myself, I felt more awkward. I was wary of telling my story and coming across like I was campaigning for a sympathy vote. George talked about Bristol having fun. I wanted to stay well away from that. I didn't want people to vote for me to have fun or because they found me entertaining. I wanted them to vote for my ideas. So, I held back, almost challenging the public to vote for me because of what I thought rather than what I was. But opening yourself up is the best way to connect. It shows people that you care – that you empathize, that you understand. Maybe it was the emotion kicking in, but I was much more open in my concession speech. My friend Rob Mitchell, who had been filming my run for mayor, told me a number of people asked why I hadn't spoken more like that during the campaign. They wanted to hear more of my personal story. The truth is that I was always selective who I opened up to emotionally. To my political opponents and local journalists I would be more careful and closed. But in rooms of young people like at Greek Hall, with people from backgrounds similar to that of my mum, my dad, Nan and Grandad, I would always open up and seek the connection. That's where I allowed myself to open up.

When the 2016 election came up, I was advised not to go for it. Ben will hate me for saying this because his political antenna is usually very strong, but I was walking along the railway path on the phone to him when he said, 'People don't like re-runs.' He was concerned another loss would finish me off politically – and perhaps personally. But I felt I couldn't not do it. I'd only lost the election by 6,000 votes while the other candidates had trailed far behind. There was unfinished business. I was older, wiser, more rounded as a person and as a candidate. I was more comfortable with myself. Kirsten and I discussed whether I should stand, and she set one key condition: 'only if Kevin comes to work with you' (Kevin and Simon had been asked to go to London to work for Jeremy Corbyn).

When the count came in, my vote had more than doubled. After second preferences were added in, I'd beaten George Ferguson by 62.5 per cent to 37.5 per cent. This time, it was George shaking my hand, offering his congratulations, standing at the side of the stage while I walked up to the lectern to the cheers of supporters and the flash of cameras – a moment I found profoundly exhilarating and humbling in equal measure.

8.

Managing Expectations

Not long after becoming mayor, I was walking along the railway path near where I lived when I bumped into a Jamaican man who had come to Bristol with my dad's generation back in the day. He'd known me since I was a baby and I had worked with him over the years too, on a few community projects. He stopped to congratulate me, but then added, 'We need to make sure you don't sell out.'

This was a sentiment I would hear time and again and it is one of the difficulties of holding office when you're Black or Asian. I asked him why he didn't understand I was stepping into a shark pit, going to places that Black people hadn't been before, places that all the traditional forces of politics say you shouldn't go to. That it was going to be hard. Why couldn't he have said, 'I am going to support you to make sure you're a success, for your sake and ours.'

I talked to Sadiq Khan, the mayor of London, about it. We were both elected on the same day. I was Europe's first mayor of African heritage and he was Europe's first Muslim mayor. We both came from communities who haven't had a political voice and we both immediately faced an incredibly high bar for success. Everyone seemed to expect instantaneous change on day one. They turned up with twenty-five years' worth of 'asks' that weren't shared with or went unheard by previous white leaders, and used whether or not we delivered on those asks as a test of our integrity.

We were both presented with a long wish list of things – things that white leaders had never been asked to deliver. They had saved it all up for Black and Asian representatives. It's often said that Black and Brown people have to work harder and be better than their white peers just to stand still. And that is true. It's also true that our own communities expect a lot more from us and judge us harder – as in the case of the elder I bumped into – and don't always come forward to help.

Historically, our communities have lower turnouts and higher needs of the political system, even if they have lower expectations. The bar is set higher for Black and Asian leaders than for white ones: it can seem as though these communities have priced in their disappointment there before they've even started. That disappointment has a different feeling depending on who is in charge. With white leaders, it's the norm for Black communities, so that sense of disappointment almost doesn't register. With Black leaders, that disappointment comes with a sense of betrayal.

This can make it even harder to be a Black politician.

While this was going on in the background, I was trying to find my feet as a leader, having to navigate people looking me in the eye – a six-foot, shaven-headed Black guy – and thinking, 'You shouldn't be here. You're not in our dining club.' It was an uphill battle and without the full support of my own community.

I was in a shop, recently, when the assistant, a Black guy, said, 'We don't see you any more.' I'm never quite sure how to answer that. There are 472,000 people in Bristol and I'm not just there to represent the Black community, but everyone across the city.

I tried to explain to the assistant, saying, 'This is how politics works. When you're campaigning to get elected, by definition your job is to go out, meet people and get votes. But the day you win, you have a full-time job that requires you to be in the office. Your job is to drive the local economy, build homes, balance the budget, sort out the education system. Your job is no longer to be on the streets walking about.'

I then asked him, 'What would you prefer at the end of my time in office? Do you want to be able to say that you've had a cup of tea with me, or that you're living in a new house that we've built for you and your family?'

There's a maturity that needs to happen in the community about what it actually means to get elected into leadership. Going back to my dad's friend on the railway path, the community needs to say, 'You know what? Even if we don't hear from you, we can see what's going on. We've taken the time to do the research and find out what you're up to. We've informed ourselves and we're ready to support you.'

I had started to develop a new framework for assessing Black politics some years earlier when I was interning at Sojourners. An African American colleague called Larry Bellinger had told me, 'We don't vote Democrat because they'll do anything for us, but because we know they won't do anything to us.' At the time, I thought that was depressingly cynical. But I have come to see it as insightful, wise and pragmatic. In 2010, I heard people assessing Obama's first term as president and measuring him against revolutionary change. It seemed he was supposed to have ended racism, poverty, police violence and more. Hold on, I thought, some people don't even accept him as an American. He is being asked to show his birth certificate to prove he is American, and you are asking him to work in the face of opposition to deliver a scale of change, at a pace no one has ever managed before. Rather than demanding radical change, it seemed to me that Obama's first job was to stop harmful people taking office, just to stop them doing things to Black and poor people. His second job was to get re-elected to keep them out and to ensure the first Black president was not a failure. If, after all that, he could get some radical stuff done, then great.

I thought it was also important that Obama understood the responsibility he had towards future Black politicians, and thus make it possible for them to get elected. Scare people too much, and Black politics becomes an aberration. Be good, and you open the door. Some would say that if you're not going to be radical (whatever they mean by that), what's the point? But not all change is revolutionary. Politics is a long game. Some change is highly visible: tackling food poverty, for example, or our scheme giving young Black people internships in professions where they are under-represented. But some changes happen because at some point someone nudges the compass bearing by one degree. It feels like nothing at the time, but ten years down the line we find that we are in a wholly different place to the one we would have been.

As I've said, this is a real problem in our communities and one that consistently deters people from stepping forward to take part in politics. We need to find a way of moving forward together, to understand that when people from our communities move into new territory, they need support when they get there. We need to inform people. In my time as mayor, we have tried to be as transparent as we can about what we're doing, making it as easy as possible for people to find out what we've been up to. Every other day there's a blog that goes out from my office – yet the number of people from our community who read it is tiny.

Once, at my sister's house, one of the other guests (who, incidentally, we had supported into a prominent position in the city) said, 'Marvin, people in the community are complaining they don't know what you are doing or what difference you are making.' This was one of my hot-button complaints. First, I would have hoped he would tell them about our work, including his own rise to prominence. But I asked him, 'Have you got your phone on you?' 'Yes,' he replied.

'Open up your browser. Type in "Marvin Rees Blog".'

I waited for him to find it.

'What comes up and what does it say?'

'Housing,' he read.

'Scroll down. What does it talk about?'

'Child hunger.'

'So, it takes eight seconds to pull up a blog we publish almost daily about all we are doing. If people can't take the initiative to search for the information, then they won't know. What am I supposed to do? Go to everyone's house and explain our record over dinner?'

When I stood for mayor in 2012, the very first hustings was held in the conference room of the law firm Burges Salmon, an excellent civic-minded Bristol company. The debate was hosted by people who were in property development and the audience reflected that. There were lots of lawyers and planners. Only three people in the room weren't white: one person in the audience, my mum's friend, and me. I was acutely aware of this while simultaneously proud that I had the audacity to be there – a boldness that had been strengthened by the selection process. There were somewhere in the region of fifteen mayoral candidates, but the organizers had decided only to invite the four they thought could win. I was positioned on the far left of the stage: the other three were John Rogers, a retired GP for the Liberal Democrats; Geoff Gollop, a retired accountant for the Conservatives; and George Ferguson, an architect. All three were white men in their sixties and seventies. I looked out at the audience and judged the room, perhaps unfairly. No one is looking at this stage thinking to themselves that the Black guy on the end looks like the mayor, I thought. The audience might have thought that, but I was also projecting my own self-consciousness onto them. Whichever it was, my presence offered a new image of what political leadership could look like. I would be the first Black or Brown political leader in Bristol's history. My sensitivity about the issue wasn't developed in abstract. It was in part a product of my experience, experience that has shown me that leadership looks and sounds like posh white men.

I'm sometimes asked what the biggest legacy of my time in office will be. There are lots of things I am proud of – housing and construction, the One City approach, opening up work experience to kids who hadn't previously had the opportunity, winning the Channel 4 Creative Hub for Bristol, our international work on climate and migration and the work we've done on child hunger and welcoming spaces. But the biggest achievement, which might not seem like much at first glance, has been to make sure that the mayor – or any other political leader – can be someone like me. This was confirmed when my friend Poku Osei told me his daughters said he looked like the mayor. We laughed because we don't actually look alike. Poku is Ghanaian-born and two shades darker. But his daughters have grown up with high-profile Black political leadership as the norm. Poku and I talked about how that opened a door in their minds.

I have said very openly to young Black and mixed-race kids, 'The mayor can look and sound like you.' One of my deputy mayors, Asher Craig, is the first Black Rasta woman cabinet member in Europe. She and I sometimes smile at the fact that a Black Rasta woman represents

Bristol not just locally, but on the national and international stage. 'Who would have thought that would ever happen?' we have asked each other. I take time to mentor young Black kids, talking to them and encouraging them, and I remind them that people will make visual judgements on what leadership looks like, what intelligence looks like. One of the most important things I can do is to be a credible leader, to string my sentences together and not embarrass anyone. Those are my initial priorities. After that, I can try to get stuff done.

Representation doesn't just stop at colour, either. Class matters too. My family is working class, and I say to working-class kids of all colours, 'the mayor comes from your background'. And when I do that, I feel like I breathe life into my nan and grandad's investment in me, and the Bryer and Rees families we are part of.

After the excitement of winning the election, starting work quickly brought me down to earth with a bump. At the time, the mayor's office was in Temple Street while City Hall was being renovated. Kevin hadn't joined me yet as he was still heading up comms for Jeremy Corbyn. Simon Fletcher had returned to London to work for Jeremy Corbyn. Ben Mosley was working in the Labour Group Office. He was the closest inside contact I had. I didn't know how I was supposed to act as mayor on the first day, so I just turned up figuring I'd work it out.

It was a challenging start. I was shown to a glass-walled enclosure set centrally on the Senior Leadership Team's floor – my office. And then I was pretty much left alone. There was no coherent orientation or handover meetings. Just, here you are, get on with it. I later learned from one member of staff that a document containing all the key phone numbers for staff was put together for me, but someone on the leadership team said I wouldn't need those numbers. They blocked me from having them: I had to find out myself, one by one. Thankfully, I was given invaluable support from Gabriel Scally over the initial weeks. He was a public health physician and a former regional director of public health (RDPH) for the southwest of England. He helped me navigate those early weeks despite the absence of any support from the senior executive team. Gabriel and I initiated our own tour of the building to meet the staff. After a few days, one of a small group who'd been sitting politely outside my office came in to see me and said, 'The team are feeling a bit neglected.'

'What team?' I asked. She pointed to the group of people sitting around a long desk next to my office. No one had told me I had my own team, nor bothered to introduce me to them, let alone explain how they were supposed to work with the mayor.

I was shocked but not surprised. It was a continuation of what I'd experienced from the moment I'd won the party selection. The result was confirmed by the Thursday afternoon. When I arrived at work on the Friday, my line manager said to me, 'I've been told you need to resign on Monday.' I was at a loss. I reached out to my union but they said there was nothing I could do, so after a few days of trying to find a way through I resigned.

During the election itself, senior council executives had been as unhelpful as they could be to the candidates challenging the incumbent. We were offered a briefing a few weeks before polling. In my view, this should have happened at the start of the process, when the candidates were announced. We could have been briefed on the ins and outs of the council budget and what sort of state the finances would be in. But whether it was deliberate or simply disorganized, it didn't happen.

Instead, we were offered a one-hour briefing at the very end of the campaign period. At that point in an election, time is everything: you're fighting for every vote and an afternoon not campaigning is an afternoon when you're losing support. I had considered not attending but, in the end, I decided I would go with Kelvin Blake, my agent. I sat in a small room with the four most powerful people in Bristol City Council. The only purpose it served was to give us an insight into what would happen if we won. As we came out, Kelvin turned to me and said, 'Well, that was fucking awful.' And it was. They spent the whole time looking at and talking to Kelvin, even in response to questions I asked them directly. In the end, I gave up, letting them talk to Kelvin as he valiantly attempted to get them to address their points to me. Recently, I heard that they were aware of the awkward dynamic, too. After the briefing, one of them apparently turned to his colleagues in exasperation and asked, 'What are you doing? He might win.'

Unfortunately, that's something I've become accustomed to over the years. I commented to Kelvin as we left that it wasn't the first time in my life that I hadn't been taken seriously. Let's see what happens, I thought to myself.

The comments about my suitability for the job had come up again and again before election day, even though we thought our campaign was going well. I remember one event at the Watershed, where I got talking to Cllr Simon Cook, a Lib Dem and a member of George Ferguson's cabinet. 'You've run a good campaign,' he told me. 'I just don't think you're experienced enough or have the credibility to step in and run the council.'

He wasn't the only one. George's cabinet had a vested interest, of course, in him being re-elected, but the same was true of others in the council. Some senior officers were saying, 'He's never had the big job. He can't do it.'

But these criticisms didn't bother me. I had thought about it a lot and I had concluded that they didn't understand the role of mayor, and this was something that had played out under George. These were council people with a council perspective. But the mayor is a city leader. It's an approach to leadership we described as moving from local government – and the disproportionate focus on the local authority – to city governance, and the understanding that cities are collective acts. They are the product not just of the local authority, but the decisions made by organizations, businesses and unions working across the public, private, voluntary and civil society sectors. The mayor doesn't just run council services but has to convene people and find common alignment around shared city goals.

Besides that, the mayoral position is directly elected. I had to impress the people of Bristol, not the council establishment. And the latter point was incredibly important. I said my candidacy wouldn't have been possible without the Labour Party and the trade unions. My election wouldn't have been possible without being able to directly appeal to the people of Bristol. By this time, I knew I had a better relationship with the public than the city's political establishment.

* * *

However, now I was mayor, it was as though the people running the council just hadn't prepared. My swearing-in had been planned to take place in an anonymous and hard-to-access room on the top floor of the M Shed Museum. When I arrived for my first day in the office, I walked into the building alone and there was no orientation, no handover, no briefing pack, nothing. They gave me the office but continued to run the show. Everything I tried to do created problems. I had a friend who worked in the housing department. We'd grown up in church together. I'd known her since I was eight. I gave her a call and invited her up to my office for a cup of tea.

'We're not allowed up there, Marv,' she replied.

'What?' I asked. 'Why not?'

'Our passes won't let us into that part of the building.'

It was evidence of the hierarchical system and culture set up in the council, whereby normal council workers' passes would not let them into the areas where the senior management team was based. When I tried to flip things around, it proved equally problematic. The result was a silent war over which passes would allow people where, with me trying to open the building up while the senior officials kept trying to lock it down.

But I was determined to open a channel of direct communication between the front-line staff and senior leadership. When I had been working in public health, I had a mentor, Madeleine Vaughan, then the director of HR. She had once told me, 'When you're at a senior level in an organization, it's really important that you have contacts on the frontline. Because otherwise, you'll never hear bad news. By the time that news is filtered through layers of management, that bad news will become good news.'

I wanted to meet the staff. I wanted to talk to them and tell them what I wanted to do, but I also wanted to hear their concerns and their ideas. I wanted to hear from them what we could do to create the conditions in which they could excel at their jobs and get good outcomes for Bristol. The idea went down like a lead balloon. The senior management team didn't want me to do it and passively refused to facilitate it. In the end, I sorted it out myself, with Gabriel, going from floor to floor and introducing myself to everyone.

I didn't feel that I could trust the leadership team already in place.

It's never easy when a team has been selected by your predecessor, but I never felt that they were pulling for me. They would turn up in my office, presenting limited options on decisions that had to be made by close of play. It seemed a number of significant issues – from the need to put money into the controversial Colston Hall to investing in heat networks – had been delayed until after the election. It felt as though I was being taught a lesson for having had the audacity to run and win.

It was a tidal wave of urgency. Shortly after taking office, I met Michael Berkowitz, who was heading up Rockerfeller 100 Resilient Cities, of which we were one, but had been part of Michael Bloomberg's team when he was mayor of New York. He told me their first year in office was like having their mouths around a fire hydrant. It was overwhelming but I knew I just had to sit tight. At some point, I knew we would begin folding the wave back on itself.

I began to re-organize my team. The constitution allowed me to make one political appointment and I chose Kevin Slocombe as my chief of staff. Immediately I felt more in control. I had someone I knew who I could develop with. He would have my back. There was an inevitable period of readjustment with the rest of the senior team, though, and one of them told Kevin, 'Marvin just needs to learn to trust the executive directors.' Kevin's response was, 'Why?' There was no response, so he continued, 'The senior directors need to earn Marvin's trust.'

That was the moment things began to change.

As time went on, some of the senior team left, while others adapted to our way of doing things. I wanted people I could trust. I meant what I said when I was standing for mayor – I was there to lead; that meant a politically led council working with us to lead the city. Leadership is about giving people the space to do their jobs. We created a framework where people could work together. And the team we built has been brilliant in delivering what we wanted to achieve.

In the July after my election, I hosted a meeting on the top floor of We the Curious, Bristol's hands-on science museum. I had invited around seventy leaders of the city's biggest organizations and sectors.

I had people from health, academia, further education, public policy, trade unions, the voluntary sector, faith groups and transport providers. I had been planning for it since before the 2012 election. In one early hustings, when I was asked the first thing I would do if elected, I said I would pull the city leaders together and try to get everyone organized around common goals for the benefit of the city.

We made space for people to talk about their priorities, for their organizations and, most importantly, for the wider city of Bristol where they lived, worked and operated. They spoke not just to the needs and opportunities of the here and now, but how we might prepare the city for the next ten, fifteen, twenty years. People raised the importance of delivering affordable housing and the need to deliver more on brownfield land in active travel distance from the city centre. They shared the need to understand that childcare was as much part of the city infrastructure as transport. They raised the climate crisis. We raised the importance of being ambitious and driving a strong economy, but the right kind of ambition and economy, one that was inclusive, provided good jobs, included a living wage and tackled the city's entrenched, intergenerational inequalities. It wasn't just the lists of priorities that came out of that time, but the evidence of our interdependence. Affordable housing was important to the big employers. An ambitious, strong economy was important to the unions. The impacts of climate change were important to the voluntary community sector. We didn't have easy solutions, but we had a shared knowledge of our common goals.

At the end, I thanked everyone for coming. 'My office has done a quick calculation,' I told the room, 'and found that together we have a £6bn to £7bn financial footprint in the city. And between us, we employ over 70,000 people. So we have phenomenal power and reach in the room today. We all face challenges, but what could we *not* achieve if we worked together, agreed to focus on one to three city priorities and then committed our organizations to helping the city achieve them?'

This was the beginning of the City Office and first of what we came to call our City Gatherings.

*   *   *

One of the important takeaways that I took from my time working in public health was how health was set by things other than people's interactions with their local NHS. Public health professionals refer to this as the wider determinants of health. The 2010 Marmot Review showed that socio-economic inequalities have a clear effect on population health outcomes and pointed us towards a social gradient in health.* In the 2014 paper 'If You Could Do One Thing – Nine Local Actions to Reduce Health Inequalities', the authors refer to an American study that found 'as little as 20 per cent of influences on health were in the gift of clinical health services – to do with access to clinical care and quality of care. The other 80 per cent of the influences on health comprise health behaviours (30 per cent), socio-economic factors (40 per cent) and the physical environment (10 per cent).'

When I was in the NHS I had run the Race Equality in Mental Health programme. I had no clinical background. But what qualified me for the role was an understanding that the racial inequalities in mental health that characterize our country are political outcomes – the results of inequalities in housing, employment and financial security, education and access to quality nutrition. A GP once said to me, 'If a single mother with three kids is living in substandard accommodation, in debt, socially isolated and tells me she is depressed, that's not a medical condition. It's a perfectly rational response to the circumstances in which she has found herself.'

Health was an outcome that crossed traditional departmental boundaries into education, welfare, environment and the economy. The understanding that we need to look at any outcome – sought not in isolation but in context – was something I wanted to put at the heart of my approach to city leadership. And that meant moving beyond seeing the local authority as a collection of services to using the mayoral platform to convene every lever in the city.

When I first became mayor, I said that if we were serious about running the city, then we had to recognize that people don't sit in

* Marmot, M., 'Fair society, healthy lives: the Marmot Review: strategic review of health inequalities in England post-2010' (January 2010): https://www. gov.uk/research-for-development-outputs/fair-society-healthy-lives-the-marmot-review-strategic-review-of-health-inequalities-in-england-post-2010

a linear relationship with a single service or decision: their lives sit at the intersection of the whole collection of decisions and non-decisions made by a whole range of organizations and departments that make up the city. If someone has mental health issues, they may well get fantastic support from a mental health facility. But if they leave that facility, and return to a situation in which they have no job, or have housing problems and are isolated, then they are still vulnerable.

Because of my background in public health, I wanted to make population health the pre-eminent outcome of my time in office. Population health isn't only an outcome, it is itself a determinant of social resilience, public service spending and educational performance. In my role in mental health we had grappled with the relationship between mental health and the criminal justice system. Police were reporting that as many as 30 per cent of their arrests were actually mental health issues – and as a result, Black people's mental health was effectively criminalized. After losing the 2012 election, I had written to the Local Enterprise Partnership about their skills strategy, stressing that it was essential, but adding that nowhere had they talked about health. There was no point in having a highly skilled workforce if it's sick at home with back pain and depression. I ended the letter asking them to 'Think through what it would mean to the West of England economy's ability to attract inward investment if we were able to boast of the most well workforce in Europe with the fewest number of workdays lost to sickness-related absence.' I raised it again that day.

In 2010, I had been the director of something called the Local Strategic Partnership. This was an initiative by the then Labour government, which wanted to build a framework of organizations within a particular area to help them work together for the city's common good. The job had been brought to my attention by Deborah Evans, my CEO at NHS Bristol. I arrived in the office one morning to an email from her with a job ad and a message saying 'you should go for this'. At the time, I was a bit of a surprise appointment for the role: at thirty-seven I was comparatively young for the council and hadn't had a senior role in local government. Now I was managing meetings with the Bristol police commander, leaders from local housing associations, businesses and schools.

While there were plenty of meetings, it struck me we were all having separate conversations. I wasn't the only one. A few of Bristol's biggest organizations had started to send substitutes rather than their most senior representatives, while others had stopped coming altogether. There was no overarching framework for a conversation – everyone was left to see their individual issues, rather than how they might impact other areas. Yet a budget cut in one area (say, for example, children's mental health services) might lead to repercussions elsewhere (issues for the police further down the line). But if these different groups could work together, then Bristol lives could be better and savings could be made: it pays for the police to help with the mental health budget, or the chamber of commerce to help ensure a more mentally well workforce.

But there was no framework for us to talk about such interdependencies as a city. I initiated a piece of work by a brilliant academic, Professor Leroy White. He was head of the University of Bristol Management School and was an expert in systems and partnerships. I asked all the organizations to give me three days, spaced over three months, with their lead strategist. For each of them, I wanted them to come up with a ten-year plan for their organizations and forecasts for where they thought the city could be. What did they think the city would look like in a decade's time? How would they like it to look? What would need to get done for their ideal vision of Bristol to be achieved?

That was on day one. Leroy took all the information away and a month later, at the second meeting, presented it back. Leroy is an engineer and management expert: what he was able to do with these plans was to match them up. He lined up the visions and highlighted where the different goals aligned, and where they clashed and contradicted one another.

Now the conversation was different. The various organizations could start discussing how to make their plans fit together. It became a conversation about what needed to be prioritized to create the change needed for other aims to succeed later. Leroy took the notes and suggestions away to pull together and begin the formulation of a ten-year plan.

At the time, that was as far as the discussions went. I was offered my place at Yale to go on the World Fellows Program, and when I came back, the discussions had stalled. The local authority had got cold feet about the project. I spoke to Leroy, who said it was the right thing to do, but 'they've let the air out of it'. Neither of us were happy.

Following that first City Gathering, we won the support of our city partners to take a look at the city's strategies. It showed the city I inherited in 2016 had its priorities all over the place. I had brought in management consultancy firm KPMG to look at how the city was run, and they did some amazing pro bono work for us. What they discovered was what I came to term the 'three chaoses'. We had a chaos of sovereignty with boards all over the city hosting conflicting strategies and overlapping decisions. There was a phalanx of boards and groups making decisions, and none of them were doing so in conjunction with anyone else. Any time somebody wanted something done, they just started another board. We had a chaos of metrics – there were around 1,500 separate measures spread across these boards and city partners of how we lived in the city. And we had a chaos of strategies. KPMG's work revealed over 500 strategies in the city, many of which didn't speak to one another and most of which would finish before 2021. That was partly due to the way the political cycle works, but there was more to it than that. It was also down to the way the city as a whole failed to work together. Anyone could have initiated a conversation to get the city better aligned. It wouldn't have been easy, but it could have been done. We had a city of nearly half a million people with few plans that went beyond the next five years.

I wanted to look at a wider canvas, but be more focused. I also wanted to challenge people to look as far ahead as 2050. What did we want that city to look like? How did we want to be able to describe Bristol? What are we pointing our city journey towards? I had in mind something John Savage, who ran Bristol West, a local business leadership group, and author of *Bristol 2050: High In Hope*, had once said. He described Bristol City Council as being like an old Victorian fairground machine. It had loads of cogs and chains and was phenomenally complex. It kept moving, consumed energy and needed maintenance. But it didn't actually have a purpose beyond keeping going. We needed to change that.

We needed a focus and came up with the One City Plan. We decided on six key areas – transport and connectivity, children, the economy, the environment, health and homes and communities – and plotted out a timeline of priorities to 2050, year by year, decade by decade. For each of the key areas, we set up a board, each co-chaired by a cabinet member and someone from the city. This was a city-wide project and it was important that representatives from across the city were part of it. Inclusion and involvement were important – I didn't just want everyone to feel as though they could be part of the process. I wanted them to own the process and the plan it produced.

We worked with the city to agree on how we wanted to be able to describe Bristol in 2050. I put together a blank timeline from 2050 back to the present day. How would we become that place? We started working through our boards and getting people in working groups, during which we asked them to identify the three things we could and should achieve each year to become the city we wanted to be.

Limiting the aims to three goals per year was crucial. We made everyone stick to three. To begin with, people suggested a mass of priorities for the first few years, and then nothing. But we needed to prioritize. One of Bristol's problems had been a lack of collective focus. And we had to sequence our different goals – some things create conditions that make the successful delivery of others more likely. We hadn't done that before, and we hadn't come together as a city to look that far ahead before.

The idea of a city plan is not new. New York has one, and it was my inspiration to try a similar project in Bristol. Chicago, too, famously had fifty-year plans. This also offered a collection of ideas as to how Bristol might look going forward, a plan that stretched far beyond the next electoral cycle.

Having a plan to work towards is crucial to any endeavour. An army officer friend, Maring Sturgeon, once said to me, 'Make a plan, any plan. Just make a bloody plan.' Plans can be changed. What we've published as the aims we want to achieve in, say, the 2040s, isn't set in stone. Situations change. But with a plan in place, you've got something to work with and, if need be, kick against. The plan is a live document and is continually refreshed. To begin with, we did it every year. Now it's every two years.

The opening sections set out what the plan is for. And what it's not. It's worth setting it out here:

The One City Plan is not . . .

- *A plan to usurp all plans; we recognize organizations will continue to have their own plans and strategies and this plan should enable those.*

- *Perfect; it will continue to become more sophisticated with every iteration and as we make demands of it and respond to it collaboratively.*

- *An instruction manual; it is up to partners to decide if, what and how they will change to achieve our shared overarching goals.*

- *A bureaucratic barrier; the plan should not stifle innovation and other work occurring in the city.*

- *Complete; there will be no such thing as a 'final version' because it will be in constant review.*

- *To be owned and/or run by Bristol City Council.*

The One City Plan is . . .

- *An attempt to describe 'what it will be like' to be in Bristol and to be Bristolian in the years to come.*

- *An attempt to focus the city on a sequence of key outcomes which we all agree to concentrate on and contribute towards and which take us to 2050.*

- *Something to grapple with; a tool to provoke and enable the wider city to engage in a meaningful way with the city's future.*

- *In constant review — it will be refreshed every year through the City Office and the One City Boards.*

- *Built on an understanding that what citizens receive from the city should be more than the sum of its parts. We are interdependent — no organization or sector can be all it can be whilst others struggle. We need to set out the future we want as a city with the powers we have.*

As mayor, I have always encouraged the boards to talk to each other. Say the housing board is planning for new homes and the environmental board wants to ensure those houses are net zero (carbon-neutral homes that produce as much energy as they use). They have to work together to ensure those targets are compatible. An early discussion between the environment and economy boards illustrated this. While the economy board was keen on exploring opportunities to expand tourism within the city, the environment board expressed concerns over the potential environmental impacts associated with increased air travel, particularly concerning the airport's operations and the resulting rise in passenger numbers. Under a different process, any conflict would have happened invisibly, with one group moaning about the other in their own forums and not engaging. Under the One City approach, these groups came together and attempted to find a solution that worked for both jobs and the environment.

What's been particularly exciting for me has been the response. At that first City Gathering, we had about seventy people. Now we have about 400 people requesting to be there. When Covid hit, and we were holding meetings online, we still had 400 people coming along. We have so many people applying to be on the different boards that we have to turn people down. Getting that many people engaged with city leadership, and wanting to participate, can only be a good thing.

9.

The Humility of Leadership

A plot of land in Bristol North wasn't the most auspicious place for a photo opportunity. It was run-down and overgrown – weeds and grass growing among the ruins of buildings, the whole area cordoned off behind lock and key. It reminded me of the sorts of places I used to visit as a kid with my cousins: we'd be scaling the gate, over the wall and exploring in no time.

Now, however, I was mayor. This was one of my first photo opportunities and I'd chosen it for a reason. Housing had been a big plank of my election campaign and was my biggest priority as mayor. I'd appointed Councillor Paul Smith as head of housing as my first cabinet appointment and now I was here to show what we were about. Developers had complained to me about the lack of political focus on housing and the impenetrability of council processes. I wanted a lead for housing who could cut through all that and drive delivery. This piece of land in Bristol North was an example of past failures. It was lying there, redundant, in a city with a growing housing crisis. It was a prime site for the first of the many new homes that I wanted to build.

We needed to tell people that Bristol was building homes. The communications team wanted a photo. I was full of enthusiasm and a plan of action, telling my team that we should scale the gate and get in that way. They looked horrified. I was talked down: we'll find a key, they said. Eventually, one was found, the padlocks and chains were undone, and the gate creaked open. The requisite hard hats and hi-vis jackets were found: the picture was taken. Our message was simple. 'We're going to build homes for people.'

Housing is one of those policy areas the importance and significance of which grows the more that you talk about it and engage with it. In fact, I'd argue now that it is the single most important policy tool we have – its role in terms of health, in terms of education, in terms of the economy and the environment, is fundamental. Having an affordable home (which includes the purchase price or rental level and the running costs) in a stable, mixed community (class, race, ethnicity, tenure) that allows residents to build the relationships that combat isolation and create a community is of major importance.

When people ask me now what my number-one policy priority was as mayor, my answer is always the same: to build more affordable homes. Whether we build them ourselves or create the conditions for them to be built, Bristol City Council has to be an organization that delivers homes. And not just any old homes but the right ones: good-quality homes that are affordable, in the right locations and that help to foster communities.

As a city, Bristol has had its fair share of slums. We had our slum clearance era, when houses in the city centre, around the districts of St Philips and Easton Way, were knocked down and people were given new homes, on new estates such as Hartcliffe, Lawrence Weston and Southmead. This happened to my nan's brothers and sisters. Some of them were among the first people to move from Easton to the newly built Hartcliffe estate in the 1950s. That shift created two challenges. First, a number of people were left behind in the slum-clearance areas. Some, like my father, were post-war migrants and part of the Windrush generation, and although these areas weren't majority Black – they were white working class as well – they continued to suffer from deprivation. Those who moved ended up in housing estates, which developed all sorts of problems – poor transport links and industrial transition, eventually leading to high unemployment, poor health outcomes and low educational attainment. The city's housing mapped the inequalities within Bristol, and the inequalities were mapped onto its housing.

Over the years, one of the biggest changes in terms of housing in Bristol, as in many parts of the country, has been the sale of council homes. The right to buy was a key policy introduced by Margaret Thatcher's Conservative government in the 1980s which, initially, led to a growth in home ownership. But it first disempowered then financially crippled local authorities' role as house builders and then failed to address the internal contradictions of the house-building market, which creates value for companies through increasing land values rather than housing delivery. It also failed to anticipate that people would come to see houses as investments rather than homes. The combination has left us with a reduced council-housing stock. The issue has now come full circle, compounding the housing shortage, making home ownership harder to achieve and seeing a proliferation of the rental market, which is also becoming increasingly unaffordable. The scale of renting in Bristol now is massive. As the population continues to grow, we simply don't have enough homes for the people who need them. At the time of writing, there are 20,000 people on our housing waiting list and another 1,000 who are living in temporary accommodation. For a city the size of Bristol, these numbers make the housing crisis our number one issue.

One in three Bristolians is now renting in the private sector. It is a shift in housing and living that local government has been given neither the power, policy support nor adequate finance to deal with. We have little control over private landlords. A rethink is needed, and, in my opinion, we should begin to recast housing, at least partly, as a public good. As it is, we have let the rental sector become too powerful in a way we would never countenance in health or education. We need more powers to be able to intervene, not only in the name of social justice and fairness but also for the benefit of the economy. A city needs all kinds of workers for it to function, but if people are priced out of the market, how are they going to live in the city where they work?

The government tried to step in on housing delivery by looking at planning and making it easier for developers to get permission. But that was solving only part of the problem. We have had a big problem with permissions for homes that weren't being built: land banking, where property developers buy up land to build houses on, but then don't build the houses. Developers are content to benefit from the increased value of land they have on their balance sheets. At the time of writing, we have 6,000 plots that have been given planning permission, but nothing has been built on them.

It's important to understand it's not all down to individual developers. The market itself works in a way that deters building – as soon as building starts, the land value is locked in. These challenges have been compounded over recent years by the inflationary effects coming out of Brexit, Covid and the war in Ukraine, which has increased materials costs and seen restricted labour.

But land, as you might imagine in a popular city like Bristol, is at a premium. We've got very limited space to build houses. The developers' efforts to minimize their risks and protect their profits come at the expense of building the homes we so desperately need. In an ideal world, we'd have the power, legal and financial resources and political cover needed to compulsorily purchase land and partner with developers who are ready to build. Alternatively, we should be able to tax land value directly to change the market drivers. It's incredibly frustrating.

This behaviour, coupled with the growth of the rental market, means that the available housing stock continues to be inadequate, which in turn pushes house prices out of reach for an increasing number of people. Not every landlord is a property baron, by any means. Many of them have bought a second house to rent instead of – or as well as – investing in a pension. But those individual decisions add up. It isn't only house prices that have gone up. While wages have increased in Bristol by 24 per cent over the last decade, rents have increased by 52 per cent, which has pushed the rental price well above the maximum local housing allowance. For a three-bedroom house, that allowance stands at £950 a month, but the average rental for a property that size is currently £1,350 – a difference of £400 a month. As of May 2021, only 2 per cent of private rentals in Bristol were at or below the applicable local housing allowance rate.

Bristol's land mass is about 42 square miles. If we want more houses, we either need to build in and up or sprawl out. The World Bank described this as a choice between pancakes and pyramids. Actually, there's a third option, which is to not build and take the hit in terms of increasing pressure on the local housing market. But the consequences – poorer members of society without homes, people paying extortionate rents, people delaying having children because they can't afford to buy their own homes and so forth – mean it's not an option at all.

Building out and building up both have their challenges. Building out means urban sprawl and building on greenfield sites. The land is easier to build on in practical terms but is often rich in wildlife. Building in and up on brownfield land relieves pressure on urban sprawl, but then 'Protect the Land' protests become 'Protect the Skyline'. Both come at a cost but both are better than letting the housing crisis get even worse. And of the two options, building in and up on previously used land is, for me, far more palatable. It makes more sense in terms of efficiency and in cutting car use by reducing the need to travel. It doesn't have to be the barren, concrete existence that we often imagine. Go to any of the major cities across Europe and you can see how communal living at a higher density can work, while still giving access to green spaces.

We need to change perceptions on this: it's curious that 'high-rise' has such negative connotations, while a penthouse flat is something people would pay a lot of money for. Some people can happily live in the sky, it seems, but not others. The bad press that high-rise buildings get is less to do with the buildings themselves than it is about how life in those buildings sometimes unfolds. If you put everyone suffering from deprivation in the same place, it's going to create a certain dynamic. But if developments are mixed, with a doctor living next to a key worker, who in turn lives next to a socially rented flat, then the atmosphere is different.

The Grenfell fire is a tragic example of where things can go horrifically wrong. It's a story of social injustice and poverty, and voicelessness. The residents had tried to raise the issue of fire risks on several occasions, but no one would listen to them (in his MacTaggart Lecture, Jon Snow of Channel 4 News pointed out that the media had ignored the residents, which led him to conclude that more diversity in the newsroom was very badly needed). If the residents of those flats had been rich and white, the tragedy would never have happened: the complaints would have been heard and the problems would have been resolved. The fire was not merely the result of people living in a high-rise building but about the inequality and the poverty they had to live with and the powerlessness that went with it.

One of the hardest things for me about housing is that most agree we want a solution, but few people are prepared to take on the challenge and cost of actually delivering the homes.

In 2019, I went to a community meeting at a church in Hotwells to discuss the Western Harbour regeneration plan, part of which involved the building of 2,000 new homes on the waterfront. Sometimes it is hard to drum up support for local politics and get anyone to turn up for such events. But set up a meeting about house-building in the area, and it will be packed. That was the case in that church. There must have been three to four hundred people there with others unable to get in. And onstage, to listen to their objections, was me.

Western Harbour was the name given to the potential redevelopment of the Cumberland Basin. It's at the end of the docks, with wonderful views of the suspension bridge. But it's an area dominated by a 1960s Spaghetti Junction-style flyover. Key to that flyover is a swing bridge, which opens to allow ships access to the docks. Soon after becoming mayor, I was presented with a list of city infrastructure that was in need of attention: I have sometimes compared taking over the city to buying a car and discovering it hadn't had an MOT or been serviced in years. High on the list presented to me was the swing bridge, which was nearing the end of its natural life, and requiring £40 million of repairs just to keep it functioning. When the quote came in, we thought, why spend all that money repairing the bridge and keep things as they are when we could use the money to start the regeneration of the area instead? It was an ideal opportunity. It's a brownfield site within active travel distance to the city centre: a ten-minute bike ride or twenty-five-minute walk, which helps with the challenge of car dependency. New homes would put new customers next to the city centre and North Street, which in turn would support businesses in those locations. We started sharing the potential opportunity to build up to 2,000 homes there, including a large number of affordable homes. They'd be built in blocks – high density but not high, six floors in total. It would allow us to put flood defences in at the same time, which we needed, and could be done aesthetically and sympathetically. And we could really open up the area. At the moment, no one goes down there because it's under a huge flyover.

It felt like a golden opportunity for the city, and I thought people would welcome the ambition and opportunity to transform the area from road-dominated to home- and community-dominated. We shared the ideas early to maximize the opportunity for people to shape what was to come, but residents disagreed. Some of the councillors in the area had seized on the disquiet and the discussion soon evolved from a conversation about housing to one about my character and leadership style: there were accusations that I didn't listen, that I just wanted to build tower blocks, had little respect for the local heritage and was destroying nature and local business.

I took my seat on stage at the local church. Two women were hosting the event but apart from that I was alone, and not just on stage – only Simon Cowley, deputy head of the Mayor's Office, had come with me and was sat in the audience. I didn't mind the dynamic. The meeting was due to last for ninety minutes: I had to finish on time because I was picking my nine-year-old son up from football practice. For the first hour, I would just listen to concerns, say nothing, then have the final half hour to interact and respond to comments.

Having listened and made detailed notes on the objections to the scheme, I made my case, and the challenges that Bristol faced as a city: 42 square miles of space; a population of 465,000 growing to 550,000 by 2050; a chronic housing shortage and entrenched inequalities that must be solved in the face of a climate and ecological emergency. That is the raw material of our city. 'What do we do?' I asked them. 'If you don't want to build, then own that and its consequences. But if you believe we should build, we have to build somewhere. The most environmentally responsible decision would be to build on brownfield sites within active travel distance of jobs, retail and entertainment.'

And there's the nub of the problem. You make the case for the bigger picture, and people get it, but very local politics can block the necessary changes happening in local places. 'Just don't build here' is always the response. But if you don't build anywhere, and wherever you suggest building there is opposition, then you are back to square one. Another frustrating thing is that the local councillors rarely help in these situations. Rather than bringing their communities with them, or even challenging them, they enjoy the easy political mileage they get from opposing the plans. I call it 'save our . . . politics'.

Some objections are simply unrealistic. Someone said to me, 'Well, I'll only support you if the development is 100 per cent affordable.' I tried to explain that it doesn't work like that. It sounds laudable in theory, but you don't want 100 per cent affordable housing in the same place, you want mixed developments to create a mixed community. The sale of homes at the market rate also effectively subsidizes affordable homes. The maths has to add up. Another person said, 'I'll only support the development if it is 100 per cent net zero homes.' Again, that would be amazing, but net zero homes are more expensive to build. There's a trade-off here: the number of net zero homes against the number of affordable properties in the development. That's where the serious part of the discussion happens – what you can achieve with the resources at your disposal. Blanket wish list demands isn't engaging with the real world. Then there were the people who said things like, 'You can't build down here. I've had my house down here for thirty years.' Good for you, I thought. I'm really pleased that you have a house in a place where the prices have grown exponentially. You've got a million-pound property out of it: Bristol has nearly 20,000 people on a housing waiting list with over 1,000 in temporary accommodation.

Community engagement is important. It's important to listen to the concerns of an area's residents. But at the same time, politicians also need to challenge people with the bigger picture. It's a delicate balance, and costly. It was Jean-Claude Juncker who said, 'We all know what to do, but we don't know how to get re-elected once we have done it.'

It's respectful to be able to have an argument and a proper, in-depth discussion with them. Local knowledge is essential, but local opposition can be built on misinformation and unfounded worries about the proposals. In this case, one of the issues that was raised was that we were planning to put a huge dual carriageway through the middle of the area. I pointed out: 'The area is already dominated by the road. I'm just trying to move it. And by doing so, we can reduce the amount of road in the area and open up the waterfront in the process.' I explained, too, that these properties would hopefully lead to a reduction in traffic pressure from the growing population: the people moving into them would not need cars to drive into the city. I stressed that we were exploring all options. We had even investigated plans to build a road tunnel, but there were engineering problems that would have made it impossible. And no firm decisions had been made. We were engaging very early.

I sat on the stage and listened. I could see councillors from the opposition parties in the audience; they didn't say anything, wouldn't venture an opinion. That's a deliberate strategy – keep your head down, don't make any decisions, then jump on a grievance: 'What are you angry about? Let me be a vehicle for your anger.'

The way both words and situations are twisted makes it difficult to have a proper conversation. One comment at the meeting was, 'You're going to ruin the view of the Gorge. That view *is* Bristol.' I replied, saying, 'I understand that. But at the same time, there are lots of people in Bristol who never come to the Gorge. They don't even get to see the bridge.' I tried to explain. 'When I was growing up, I wasn't far away, but the Gorge wasn't part of my Bristol.' And that's true: we never went to that part of the city. Since my days working for local Radio Bristol, I had often been frustrated by the 'Balloons, bridge and Brunel' definition of the city: a definition that felt very Clifton-oriented, and left out areas like Hartcliffe, St Pauls and Lawrence Weston. The spin on social media became 'Marvin hates the Gorge because he never went there as a child.' That's both untrue and misunderstands how cities work. For those living in poorer communities, the iconic landmarks that 'are' a city can be inaccessible. I was making very much the same kind of argument as I had when I pointed out boxing was more important to my journey than libraries – and I got the same kind of response. A few days after the meeting, I was walking through Hotwells and a woman came up to me and angrily said, 'Put them in Avonmouth.' Avonmouth is miles away and an area that has faced some of the biggest challenges in Bristol. Putting a development there would do nothing to help the environment – rather than a ten-minute bike ride to the centre, people would have to drive in, adding more traffic to the mix. *Put them in Avonmouth*. There was something so dismissive in that response – an out-of-sight, out-of-mind attitude, for those who would live in the new homes and for the people of Avonmouth, that I really didn't like.

The lack of understanding troubles me, too. I did an event more recently with some kids from Hartcliffe. 'When was the last time you went to Avon Gorge?' I asked. Their responses ranged from years ago to never. There's a legitimate story there about poverty and social mobility, but the press didn't pick up on it. The focus was on the 'conflict' between me and the community. But it is important to acknowledge the fragmentation of city life: don't assume that everyone has the same experience as you.

Another potential development was on the site of Bristol Zoo. The Bristol Zoological Society had made the decision to move to a site on the outskirts of the city. The Clifton site had become financially unsustainable. By moving, not only would they have a site that would become financially secure, safeguarding the zoo's important work in conservation, but the animals would have much more room with 'wild space' that was more than ten times the previous size. The old site and its accompanying car park were therefore available. From a housing and environmental point of view, its location was perfect: a brownfield site within active travel distance of the city centre. Yet local Green councillors and a campaign group opposed the plans. Another possible brownfield site was Baltic Wharf: to prevent that development, a group of local activists held a ceremony where they married the trees in the area. As with the Cumberland Basin, they didn't want a new development built near them. The question

remains the same though: if not there, then where? Kevin pointed out
we had opposition councillors who supported housing in concept but
not in practice. At an economic growth event in London a partici-
pant suggested we'd moved beyond NIMBY (not in my back yard) to
BANANA (build absolutely nothing anywhere near anyone).

This is politics at its most basic level. You can't have everything,
so what do you do with the limited resources that you've got? There
is a price to be paid for every solution. Pretending that you can
have it all without consequence is fantasy politics. Real politics is
about making choices: sometimes difficult choices, sometimes choices
you don't want to have to make. It's about working with limited
options and recognizing that although good things can have negative
consequences for some, inaction is worse. Choices have to be made.

Let me give you one more example which encapsulates this in
microcosm: I once found myself in a discussion about what to do
with some trees on Whiteladies Road, a key thoroughfare in the city.
Down the side are some big, old, long-established trees. These trees
have grown so much that the roots are ripping up the pavement. If
you're disabled or have sight issues, those pavements are a nightmare,
a real hazard.

So what do you do? One choice is to cut the trees down. The
environmentalists, unsurprisingly, are against that: the trees must be
saved. But in which case, what do you do about the pavement, which
is unwalkable for some of the most vulnerable people in the community? You can't just tarmac over the pavement: even if that doesn't kill
the trees in the process, it's a sticking-plaster solution that will only
last for a year or two at most. One option is to turn that pavement
into a green verge, which would be great for biodiversity. But you
still need somewhere for people to walk. That would mean extending
the pavement out onto the road. But the only way that you could do
that would be to remove the cycle lane to accommodate it. At which
point, the cycling lobby is up in arms.

What do you do? You've got three competing claims – the cyclists,
the environmentalists, the vulnerable. You've got to make a decision,
and whichever group you support it's going to upset the others. That's
real politics. This issue of the trees on an individual road might be a
small issue, but it's typical of the types of decisions that a leader has

to face day in, day out. It would be ideal if the different perspectives talked to one another, but the habit has become to just channel the 'demand' at the council.

One of the key elements of good housing policy, and one that is sometimes overlooked, is to think about the community that will grow up around any housing development. We need to build quality homes where people can live stable lives, develop relationships and get to know their neighbours. That sense of community came to the fore during the pandemic – people were looking out for one another and helping those who were more vulnerable. That sense of social resilience and togetherness was critical to our city's resilience and something we must foster throughout our cities.

One of the biggest threats to our sense of community is the process of gentrification. This isn't a challenge unique to Bristol by any means: it's one faced by cities across the world. It's an issue that is particularly acute here, though, because of the problems with our housing stock. Of all the major cities in the UK outside London, Bristol is currently the least affordable place to live, both in terms of properties to buy and properties to rent. It's a product of our city's success. We have a strong economy, two world-class universities, a plentiful supply of parks within the city and easy access to the countryside around. It makes us a very attractive place, especially to people moving out of London. But it reduces the number of houses available to buy, which in turn pushes the prices up for everyone else. Professionals like nurses and teachers, who should be able to afford properties, are commuting into the city instead. Just as people from London relocate to Bristol, so people in Bristol relocate to Chepstow or Newport.

You can see the shift in places like Greenbank, an area that used to be very mixed in terms of both race and class, but now feels increasingly middle class and white. And as the house prices go up, so that shift passes through to other areas. Often the first gentrifiers are people like artists, who move into cheaper areas where they can afford to live, then – because of the vibe they create – others are attracted to those areas. And then the coffee shops start opening up and the feel of the place changes completely. Ironically, it's the early gentrifiers who have been the most vocal opponents of the waves of gentrification that come after them.

Take Easton, where I grew up. My mum bought her house on a right-to-buy for £17,000. Today it's worth around £250,000. When I was sixteen, I was out with my friends and saw a group of white kids with skateboards. We shared this 'what's going on?' moment, as they looked so totally out of place. Around the same time, some girls gave me a lift back from a party and dropped me off near my house on Stapleton Road. As I was getting out of the car, they asked, 'Are you going to be OK?' To begin with, I wasn't sure what they meant, but then I realized. 'It's fine,' I said. 'I live here.'

At the time, there was a well-known stretch of Stapleton Road near where I lived. An ITN News report had once called it the most dangerous street in Britain. Today, there's a typical Bristol bike shop at the bottom of the road, a yoga studio and a cafe selling sourdough bread. It's becoming very different.

Too often, change imposed from outside can be a precursor to loss. Most people don't mind change, but they do fear loss. What's curious is that both the working-class communities and the middle-class communities, such as those I faced in that church meeting, may come from different places, but they do have something in common: the middle class don't want new houses built, while the working class don't want to lose their familiar communities.

But places change. People change. The make-up of where we live changes. It's an ongoing process that sometimes works out for the better, sometimes for the worse. But what you don't have the ability to do is press pause. Cities are organic, living, breathing things. The challenge is to manage the process of change so that it doesn't bring loss, and to ensure change is shaped and jointly led by existing residents.

Mayors all over the world are looking for the solution. We've tried to be creative when it comes to housing by working with innovative firms and ideas. BoKlok is a Scandinavian company owned by Skanska and IKEA that is building a development of 173 houses on Airport

Road. The houses are all built in a factory and manufactured off-site, then transported and put together on-site. The development was split so that 94 houses were sold to the public, 55 were affordable homes for people on our housing waiting list, and 24 were shared ownership. The houses for sale to the public were sold through the Bristol branch of IKEA, with over 1,800 people registering their interest. Of the 48 apartments in the development, 46 were sold in the first weekend.

The houses are built to a Nordic design and align with the sustainable development goals that we have as a city. They produce lower CO_2 emissions and cheaper running costs thanks to thermal insulation and airtightness. Being built with timber frames also reduces the carbon and energy costs in their construction. It's the sort of innovative approach we need more of, and the sort of collaboration I am always willing to explore.

Another scheme I am particularly proud of is the Zed Pods scheme, led by Jez Sweetland's Bristol Housing Festival, which we set up at St George's Park. These are properties that are built on steel-frame stilts. They're affordable and zero carbon, and like BoKlok, are built off-site and then brought in. They can also be built on hard spaces, such as car parks, as in this case. And the manufacturing and construction process is much faster than for traditional housing.

Thanks to this, we were able to get houses up quickly on a piece of land that otherwise wouldn't have been available for housing. There were eleven homes in total: a two-bed at each end, and nine one-bedroom properties in the middle. They're occupied by young people who would otherwise be at a high risk of homelessness, while adults who help them get their lives together live in the two-bed houses.

The development, fittingly, is called Hope Rise. Perhaps by using such innovative solutions, we can rise to the housing challenge and offer hope for everyone who wants and needs a home.

Late in my second term as mayor, I was in North Bristol, visiting one of our new children's homes, when I had a sudden sense of déjà vu. I didn't recognize the place, yet was convinced I'd been here before. Then, slowly, it came back to me: the gate, the photo op. This was the same piece of land I'd stood on and promised to build on. It had been transformed: covered with homes.

It's a success story, but it is not nearly enough. It would be great to sit here and tell you I have solved Bristol's housing crisis. But the truth is, despite our best efforts, despite making housing a priority for my administration, we haven't come close. The list of people waiting for housing grows. The growing population of Bristol puts increased pressure on housing stock. The number of people in temporary accommodation continues to rise.

The housing crisis is a problem bigger than Bristol and isn't going to be solved by any individual political leader. But a big part of any leadership role is to learn to understand your limitations and to be humble in the face of often intractable issues that you face, and know that you simply cannot solve them in a few short years in office.

That's not easy to admit. When I won that first election, I knew what we wanted to get done. I knew how we could go about it. I knew it would be difficult. I knew that many of the levers I needed to pull would not be available to me, and many of the determinants of success and failure would be outside of my control. Politics is the art of the possible, sometimes in impossible situations. I just wanted to be able to stand in front of the city at the end of my time and say, 'This is what I wanted to do. This is what I did to make it happen,' and for them to believe I did all I could with what I had, in the face of the opportunities and challenges we faced to deliver that, because that's all I could really do. I wanted to be judged against that.

Housing isn't the only issue where I haven't achieved what I wanted to when I took office. Our bus services have been decimated through Covid and a lack of finance. The mass transit system I worked for hasn't become a reality. We've still got Black boys being excluded from school at disproportionate levels. We still have a pay gap in terms of race and gender. Looking back and having to acknowledge these unsolved challenges is painful. But nor are any of these issues hopeless. I look at what we've tried to do, and I know that we've shifted the dial. Take that housing development in Bristol North – the people who lived there didn't have their own homes when I came into office, but now they do. Or the lives impacted through our welcoming spaces and the sanctuary we have offered to refugees making Bristol their home.

I was speaking at Christchurch Clifton at a graduation event for a programme supporting some of the most marginalized young adults back into employment. I shared with them an explanation of change I have since often repeated. Sometimes change is revolutionary and very visible. But more often, it's about nudging the compass just one degree. It can be barely perceptible at the time, but in ten years you'll be in a totally different place to the one you would have been otherwise. That goes for making change in individual lives and in our collective life in cities.

You can't solve everything. But if you go in promising the earth, you will only end up flat on your face, and with an electorate feeling that you've broken your promises. It's better to be honest, to be humble, enjoy the wins where you do succeed, and reflect on those times – and there will be many – where you don't.

10.

Helping the Next Generation

It starts with a handshake. First impressions count in life and the confidence of the greeting you give sends signals to the person you are meeting. When I applied to join the marines, I shook the commanding officer's hand. His first words to me were, 'That's a weak handshake you've got there, Mr Rees.' I was embarrassed, but no one had ever explained to me how to shake a hand properly, or what it meant. It's a small detail, but that bit of body language matters so much.

I don't want future generations to make the mistakes that I did. I wanted to help find the people who would lead Bristol in the future and give them the best possible chance of fulfilling their potential. I had been inspired by what I'd seen at Yale, the power of its networks and its boasts of educating four of the last five presidents of the United States. That led me to think: what if a city became intentional about leadership, doing it on purpose, rather than leaving everything to chance? And what if we targeted our efforts at young people from more challenging backgrounds, those under-represented in leadership? The result was the City Leadership Programme, which was founded in 2012 by a small group that included my close friend Tracie Jolliff, an executive coach I had met while working at the Black Development Agency. We select around a dozen candidates from a range of backgrounds and give them the tools that they need to achieve.

This begins on day one with teaching them how to shake hands. It's a session that Tracie and I have run for years. We get the young people to stand in a circle and one by one we go round and shake their hands. More often than not, their handshakes are the same as my teenage attempts. 'That's too limp,' I tell them. 'You need to squeeze harder.' Sometimes, the person is looking down at the ground as they shake hands. 'Don't do that, I tell them. Look me in the eye as you shake.' 'Own your space,' we tell them.

Throughout the course, we get them to practice. Every time a guest speaker comes in, we encourage them to go up, shake their hands and introduce themselves. They're often nervous at first, but there's always a moment when they get it. What's brilliant is that the guest speakers often tell us how impressed they were at the way the students welcomed them and presented themselves. I always ask them to feed that back to the students. It's great to see: once, over dinner, I watched the guest speaker tell a student that their firm handshake had made a real impression. The student was buzzing and told me afterwards that they had been shaking inside so it was an amazing response. And it gave them more confidence for the next time.

The programme identifies young people with high ability and aspirations who are under-represented in leadership roles: people from Black and Asian communities, the working class and others who may have struggled with homelessness or deprivation and disabilities or arrived as refugees. It's a two-week programme made up of personal coaching, skills-building, seminars with academics from the universities and dinner with a guest speaker.

We have an incredible range of speakers to get them thinking in all sorts of different ways. We have a philosopher talking about why we think the way we think, political scientists talking about the big questions of the moment and astronomers talking about reality and infinity. In the evenings, we invite different leaders in – local MPs, police commanders, NHS chief executives and university vice chancellors. We asked them to address the question: what kind of leaders does the world need?

We give these young people a lot of skills-building. There are sessions on CV writing and creating LinkedIn profiles, others on public speaking and how to present yourself. Some of the participants find it really difficult at first. At the beginning, when we ask everyone to stand up and introduce themselves, some of them simply can't do it. I remember one young woman in tears, unable to speak. By the end of the fortnight, she volunteered to stand up and give a three-minute presentation on her life goals.

Seeing the effect that the programme has had on these young people's lives is a privilege and one of the projects I've been involved with that gives me the most satisfaction. When I was campaigning in Hartcliffe in 2012, I was stopped by a woman who introduced herself as the mother of one of the participants. Claire (not her real name) was a young white girl from a working-class background.

'Are you Marvin?' the woman asked me. I thought she was going to give me a hard time about politicians. I said, 'Yes.'

'Well, I'm Claire's mum. I don't know what you've done,' her mother said. 'But you've changed my daughter.' From small things, like getting on the bus by herself, to big things like starting her own small business, her life had shifted gear. Ten years later, I was walking in the city centre when a taxi pulled up beside me. 'Oi, Marvin!' the driver shouted. He was a big old boy, tattoos up his arms. Again, I thought I was going to get a going over about the state of the roads, or the clean-air zone. But as I braced myself for a broadside, he gave me a big grin. 'I'm Claire's dad,' he said. 'Thank you so much for what you did for my daughter.'

One of my favourite parts of the programme is when we take the participants out shopping. When I applied to join the marines, I didn't have a suit, so I had to buy one. I didn't have enough money, so I bought the only one I could afford, which was a size too big for me, convincing myself that I could grow into it. I tried to look the part and thought I'd pulled it off, but I hadn't. I also wore white socks with it. It was an NCO who took me to one side and quietly said, 'Mr Rees, we don't wear white socks with a black suit.'

Tracie and I had been thinking about whether we'd need to get the participants clothes to go with the skills. The deal was sealed when one of our first interviewees for the programme came into the room. He was a Polish-heritage kid, his mum a first-generation migrant. They were obviously having financial difficulties, but he had done his best to look smart: even so, his trousers were unstitched up the inside seam by about four inches. Everything else was pristine – shirt ironed, shoes polished. We knew we needed these guys to have 'the kit' to go into any interview with confidence.

Just like handshakes, appearances matter. One of the skills-building sessions we run is called 'The unwritten rules of the game'. One of the speakers is a fantastic guy, a barrister called Darren Lewis. Darren came from a working-class background in Neath, South Wales. He talked to the young people about how, when he first joined chambers, he was taken aside by an older barrister, who gave him the once-over and said, 'No one's going to tell you this, but let me tell you how it works.' He told him what kinds of shoes and socks to get, and where to get them, what kinds of shirts to buy, as well as little details like not to do up the bottom button on his suit jacket. He was given the lessons that money and private schools give their students as a matter of course.

Tracie and I decided to go shopping. She takes the young women, I take the young men, and we buy them suits, shirts, cufflinks, ties and shoes. They come in the next day in their new gear and they all seem about a foot taller. Now they are ready for any university or job interviews, or wherever they are going to go next. They are ready to fulfil their potential and flourish.

As I've said, I've long been inspired by the sessions I attended at Yale with the theologian Miroslav Volf. To me, the word 'flourish' captures the fullness of academic, emotional and physical excellence, living life to the full. That, in essence, is what education should be about. It must deliver the basics, the grades the students will need to give them options and make their lives easier. But we are increasingly aware of the need for the curriculum to be more comprehensive and include personal and social skills, and an awareness of the world and of polit-ics so that our young people leave school able to flourish.

The second element that is key to a good educational journey is to teach our children resilience. Everyone faces difficult times and failures in life. But a good start in life reduces the chances of these challenges and failures having a destructive impact. Instead, they can become growth opportunities. I once heard the head of Eton give a talk in which he said that one of the best things that Eton teaches its students is the ability to overcome failure – although it is important to recognize the part a wealthy parental safety net plays in creating a safe space for young people to develop the habit of taking risks and bouncing back from failures.

A third element of a good education system is to recognize that it does not exist in the abstract. Housing, transport, health, employment, parental health – all contribute to the shaping of the educational journey. The head teacher of one of Bristol's primary schools told me: 'For all the educational interventions we have, if there was one thing I could do, it would be to ensure every child had a kitchen table.' A kitchen table was symbolic of a stable home. We need schools to open up and reach out to influence the wider determinants of education. And we need the public and private sector throughout the country to step up to their collective responsibility in creating the right conditions for pupils to thrive.

If our schools can teach our children to flourish, build their resilience and understand community, then we'll have done our job.

Because it is a key city outcome, education falls under the mayor's remit. Yet, changes in governance over the years mean that many schools have become academies, putting them outside the local education authority's control. As a result, though the city has full responsibility for a high percentage of Bristol's primary schools, at secondary level, the situation is split, with fewer local authority schools, and academies and private schools in the mix too.

Although the mayor does not have direct power over how Bristol's schools operate, they do have soft power. The fact that I'm a local kid from a working-class background and went to local schools also helps. We talk to the schools about what they need from us, and what we want from them. Exclusion policy is a case in point.

The statistics are bleak. Students who are excluded are more likely to end up in court or in hospital with long-term sickness. And unfortunately, exclusions still disproportionately affect Black boys. In one of our City Office meetings, Steve Chalke, founder of Oasis Academy Schools, said: 'We exclude Black students, poor students and students with special educational needs and then fifteen years later, we send them to prison.' Irrespective of the effect on the individual children, that has social, political and financial implications for us as a city.

It was our seventeen-year-old youth mayors who, having reviewed the evidence around a series of stabbings in the city, asked me to work with them to make Bristol a zero-exclusion city. I don't have the power to direct schools to become zero exclusion, and I wouldn't approach it like that if I did. But it was important to share the vision and a goal that we could all agree on even though we know it would be difficult. We can only have a city-wide policy with the support of the academies and their head teachers. We don't command and control, we convene around a shared goal. After all, as the African proverb says 'It takes a village to raise a child'.

The racial fractures I navigated growing up in Bristol were evident in my own education. When I was at secondary school, there were three entry gates to school, and each served different geographical communities with different racial and class make-ups.

I walked through the gate closest to Easton and St Pauls. It was the gate most of the Black, mixed-race and Asian kids walked through. At the other end of Russell Town Avenue was the gate closest to Barton Hill, which at the time was still very white working class. At the back of the school was the gate closest to St George. That was where the rich kids entered – or at least that's the way I saw them, because they paid for their school dinners.

At school, we'd hang out in the same groups. Mendip Hall tended to be the place we hung out, while Severn Hall was where most of the white boys would spend their breaks. We'd come together to play football in the tennis courts or on the bottom field. The teams would be picked by saying 'Black against white'. Those splits were partly about race but it was also a reflection of geography and class. Our Black team had one or two white kids on it and that was because they went to our junior school. It would have been odder to everyone if they hadn't been on our team.

These fractures played into the teaching sets. I was the only Black boy in the top set and I found it hard. I thought I had the brain but, at the same time, that I should not be there. Part of it was down to the fact that when I went into the top set I left my social circle behind and stepped across the racial boundaries into the world of the other kids.

But it wasn't only the world around that shaped our approach to belonging and not belonging in our teaching sets. Our school was originally split over three sites, but falling pupil numbers meant the school was merging everyone onto the Redfield site. Kids from the Rose Green site were merged first, then we had a year waiting for those from the Park to join us. Park served the more affluent pupils – as we then saw them. During that year, when I was thirteen, there were four or five Black boys in the top set. My RE teacher focused on us and clearly didn't like us. 'You wait till they come down from Park. None of you will be in this top set.' This went on all year. The more she said it, the more we acted up, the more she foretold our demise.

Thirty years on, diversity in the teaching workforce remains remarkably low: the number of teachers from Black and Asian backgrounds in Bristol is less than 2 per cent. We've tried to turn that around, but it isn't easy. I've spoken to Black and Asian teachers at teaching union events to encourage them to come to Bristol and offering support by giving people a 'cash landing' to try to offset the lack of affordable housing. And I've been out in the communities, too, telling leaders that they need to encourage people to come forward for teacher training.

Not having enough Black and Asian teachers in our schools affects the learning experience of Black and Asian kids. I was asked to intervene in a case involving a number of Black and mixed-race kids at a Bristol school who said that they were being treated unfairly and getting detentions and punishments. The teacher was white. That's an important detail because of what was happening. The evidence shows that if a Black school child gets told off on a Monday and a different Black kid gets told off on a Wednesday, the Wednesday child will be punished as though they had also done something wrong on the Monday. The burden is carried forwards. I went into the school to discuss – to be fair, they were really responsive. They were going to move the boys to a different class but when I asked why, they ended up moving the teacher. The school looked at the record of disciplinary points given out and saw that they had been directed at these boys. They looked at the boys' record in other classes and their academic performance and both were good. The anomaly was this class. It wasn't overt hostility, just the daily attrition of small negativities and unfairness. It was like my RE teacher all over again. I had warned the school that mishandling the situation could lead to the children feeling aggrieved, and they would start to frame their relationship with education and the school through that grievance. I am pleased to say they took it seriously and took appropriate action. But I am left wondering what would have happened if I hadn't been there to intervene.

The lack of diversity in the staffroom has an effect on a school's culture, too – on a number of levels. Apart from anything else, a Black teacher would be less vulnerable to, and more likely to spot, the racial tropes such as finding a Black student threatening. There's a great sketch by the American comedian Bill Burr, in which he talks about how racial stereotypes work: racism doesn't work by coming up and shouting at you, it sneaks up in all sorts of smaller ways, tapping you on the shoulder and saying hey. So rather than a teacher saying 'I find them threatening', it's rephrased as, 'I don't feel comfortable with these boys'.

I've taught my children to speak up. I've told them that if a teacher does something to them that they don't feel is fair, go to them after class and respectfully ask them about it. That's not talking back. That's the mature, responsible thing to do. But with my boys, I found myself having to talk to them about what might happen in their lives. Some days, people are going to find you threatening, I explained, and talked them through how they would have to deal with it. That's a ridiculous conversation to be having in the 2020s and I hated having to do it, especially at their age. I expect that when they grow up and have kids they will still have to have the same conversation with their children.

As I said earlier, I've been trying to push Bristol towards a zero-exclusion policy. Exclusion is tough on the kids and there are too many cases where there is no justification for such a drastic decision. I can't help but notice that exclusions disproportionately affect the Black community, which suggests that the problem isn't the kids, but the system around them, and some of the people in it.

Thinking back to my own childhood, I only ever had two Black teachers, and they were both important to me. Miss Griffiths had a reputation at school because she once said to one of the kids, 'You're cruising for a bruising.' We thought that was the best line ever and automatically felt affinity to her. She was seen as cool. Then there was Miss Viera: when I had problems in my fourth year – Year Ten in today's terminology – I used to go and see her. She would take the time to sit and talk to me about what I was trying to do with my life.

More diversity in the classroom isn't a quick fix, but it is part of the long-term solution to the problem. You can't change the staffroom overnight. Once you're a teacher in a school, you can be there for fifteen, twenty, thirty years. Apart from the lack of openings, there's getting enough Black and Asian candidates to train to be teachers. It's a vicious circle: people from Black and Asian communities often get unequal education outcomes; fewer people from those communities apply to be teachers; this, in turn, reinforces the unequal outcomes and the whole cycle starts again.

It's not easy to break that cycle. I do what I can: I try to get out there and talk to people. Recently, I went to a mosque to talk to community leaders about what they could do. I pointed out that there is never going to be a time when everything is perfect: if you wait for a perfect invitation to come from a perfect system, it's never going to happen. At some point you have to make a plan, even if you aren't invited. I asked them if they would make a five-year plan to encourage members of their community to become teachers.

It's up to them. I can drive and support and encourage, but change also has to be community driven. I've seen how we've managed to change the make-up of Bristol's magistrates, and the effect it has had. A more diverse magistracy means more community support for the system, which in turn encourages more people to come forward and apply. The education workforce is bigger, but if we have changed things in one area, why not here?

Ultimately, education should be about giving our children the best preparation for life. I'm acutely aware of this as a politician, but also as a father, and I continue to teach my kids how to navigate a world that still has a long way to go in terms of equality.

In August 2016, just after I became mayor, we were in New York to see Kirsten's parents. Although it was a family holiday, not a work trip, I took a couple of days to do some city stuff. I wanted to raise the profile of Bristol and other British cities and talk about trade. It made sense to do that while I was already there, rather than charging Bristol for an overseas trip.

I had an appointment at the British Consulate, which is in midtown, on 2nd Avenue. I was in my suit and tie, ready to do business. But when I got there, I couldn't find the building. I was wandering around, lost, when I saw a reverse-parked police car, pointing out into the road. It was parked diagonally, facing away from the pavement. I thought, if anyone's going to know where the consulate is, it'll be these guys. I was on the other side of the street, so I walked over to speak to them.

As I walked over, I had a thought: I didn't want them to see me as a threat. I was approaching the police car from the front, and saying to myself, I've got to get in front of him so he can see my tie, hear my English accent, and know that I'm OK. I wanted him to know that I was British, not African American. The driver was your classic New York cop. He had his window down, arm out, a huge cigar dropping ash on the pavement. As I asked him where the British Consulate was in my best English accent, he shifted, nodded and pointed down the street. As I walked away towards the Consulate, I felt a burning sense of shame.

My natural affinity in the United States is with African Americans. But I had just walked over to the officer with the knowledge that once he heard me speak and realized I wasn't African American, he would not find me a threat. I felt like I'd abandoned my people, as it were. Later, after the meeting, I spoke to Kirsten about it. 'Is that what it means to be white?' I asked. 'That you can walk down the street without having to make all of these calculations?' It's something most white people would take for granted, wouldn't think twice about.

I tell my children that they need to develop three assets: intellectual strength, physical fitness and good character. If you've got those, then you're going to be safer on the street, including in those moments when you come into contact with the police. Don't get me wrong, there are plenty of decent, hard-working police officers out there, but there are also others who'll look for an excuse to cause trouble. If you have the ability to put your case forward and string a sentence together and deal with unexpected situations then you can stand up for yourself. I advise my kids not to get emotional. If you get emotional and start to shout, it doesn't take long for someone to use that against you. In 2009, my younger brother got pulled over by a police officer in Easton. The officer had been going up and down the street, talking to the older Black kids in a mock-Jamaican accent, waiting for someone to react. I'd talked to my brother about this before and warned him that if he ever found himself in such a situation, he should not respond. Instead, he was to get their number and call me.

My brother came home and told me what had happened. Together, we went to Trinity Police Station. I wasn't in a position of power. I wasn't dressed up: I turned up at the station in my T-shirt. But I went up to the counter and spoke to the officers on duty. At first they were dismissive, but within a couple of sentences they started to take me seriously. They realized that this guy in a T-shirt could string a sentence together. He wasn't shouting or ranting, and he knew what he was talking about. I wanted to take my brother to see that, to show that it could work. We walked out of there with an apology.

Keeping fit is about discipline and taking control of yourself. I am sure it's a legacy from my childhood, but I am also aware of there being physical threat out there and fitness is a good defence. My eldest boy boxes, like I did. They both do their weights. My little girl does her Ju-Jitsu. God forbid they ever find themselves in a situation where they need to use any of that, but if they did, I want them to be able to handle themselves. Fathers of daughters will know this feeling.

You're going to find yourself challenged in other ways, too, not just physically, which is why being of good character is so important. When I worked for the council, my deputy was badmouthing me to my own line manager. My manager brought the charges, as it were, to me. I just looked at him and said, 'That's not true.' He nodded, saying, 'No, I believe you.' He trusted me, he knew my character and took me at my word. There is great power in people knowing that you tell the truth and mean what you say, even if they disagree or don't like you.

Behaviour isn't only checked when you come up against a police officer on the street: it's in the corridors of power as well. I might be the mayor, but there are plenty of moments where people perceive me as the bad guy, the threat. I have to make calculations about my behaviour every single day, always mindful of how I present myself.

What starts as an exchange of views with an opposition politician becomes a letter to the head of legal alleging that I've been physically threatening towards them. I can be robust when talking politics, but physically threatening? That, I'm afraid, says more about their prejudices and indulgence of racial tropes about Black men than about my behaviour.

Towards the start of my time as mayor, I had a meeting with the leader of the Greens in my office. I used to try to have one-to-one meetings with the different party leaders to talk over things. On this occasion, the Green leader had written an article in the paper criticizing me. She said that I wasn't working hard enough to tackle austerity, that I was weak and needed to work more closely with the Core Cities grouping to oppose government. (Bristol is part of the Core Cities group – a network of the eleven largest cities in the UK outside of London. As well as Bristol, the group consists of Belfast, Birmingham, Cardiff, Glasgow, Leeds, Liverpool, Manchester, Newcastle, Nottingham and Sheffield.)

I'm not a fan of people who criticize me in public and then want to be friendly in private. So when she came in, I was cool towards her. I told her I'd seen her article about Core Cities and started asking questions about it. As the conversation went on, it quickly became clear that she didn't really understand the work of Core Cities at all. She didn't know which cities were involved, nor who the chair was. She thought it was Andy Burnham.

We sat there in silence for a few seconds while I allowed the leader of my main opposition to reflect on this. And then she started to tear up. At this point, the calculations started: I was alone in the office with a white woman. And rather than being able to have a robust conversation, I was compromised and panicking and apologizing. She had been attacking me, but I was now the bad guy and had to back down. I told a Black friend about the incident afterwards. She shrugged, saying, 'That's just white tears.' But it was a lesson learned for me. After that, I was far more circumspect about how meetings were set up.

Not long after I became mayor, I was driving from the office to a meeting. My route took me past the Empire Boxing Club in Easton where cars are parked on both sides of the road. It means that the traffic is down to a single lane there and drivers take their turn from each end to pass through. I'd flashed three cars through, and their drivers all drove past with their hands raised to say thank you. But when it was my turn, a police van suddenly pulled out from the other end and drove straight towards me.

The officer driving wasn't on a call, and didn't have his siren on or anything. He just drove straight towards me, so fast that I had to stop. We ended up nose to nose. He then gestured at me through the windscreen, a sort of backhand wave, meaning I should get out of his way. There was a space on my side, so I reversed back down the road and nodded to suggest he pull in to it to let me pass. He did so and I drove slowly past. We were right up close, windows down.

The police officer looked over and said, 'What's up, buddy? You seem a bit agitated.'

I had to catch myself. I'm the mayor, I thought. And I thought about the right and responsibility I have to fight for the best for the city. 'Do you talk to all members of the public like that?'

'What's your problem, buddy?' he asked. 'I think you need to calm down.'

At this point, there was all sorts going on in my head. One of which was that I was mayor. I'd been elected to speak for the people of Bristol and this is the way our police officers were talking to the public.

'OK,' I said calmly. 'What's your badge number?'

That got a look. He gave me his number slowly, then sat back in his seat staring at me, as if he didn't give a shit.

'And what's the registration of your van?' I asked.

'I don't know.' He shrugged, and looked at me in silence.

'Well, today's not your lucky day,' I replied. 'I'm going for dinner with your chief constable next week.'

I could see the cogs beginning to whirr, his clocking the fact I was in a suit. By now, a small crowd had gathered, watching the exchange.

Then I think he got it. He started to say he was just being friendly in calling me buddy. 'Not the way you were using it,' I said.

This was Easton and the crowd knew who I was. As I drove past them, they shouted over.

'What did he say?' they asked.

'I don't think he recognized me,' I replied, to bursts of laughter. And I know why: this was an overturning of power.

It's because of stories like this that I tell my children they've got to be smart. Because even if you're mayor, you're still going to be subjected to racial profiling. It would be nice to think that one day this might change, but until it does, the next generation needs to know how the world works and the best way to navigate it.

Leadership is a Team Effort

Temple Meads Station is the largest and oldest railway station in Bristol and one of the oldest in the country. It was built in 1840 by Isambard Kingdom Brunel and for over 180 years has been the entry point for people visiting the city. When the train pulls in to the impressive sweep of Victorian curves, it immediately makes me feel like I'm at home.

But impressive as it is, the station's history is not enough for the modern city Bristol has become, and for the city we want it to be in the future. Bristol is the only one of the UK's core cities that lacks a modern railway station. The station and its surroundings have lacked investment for decades. A building that once housed a postal sorting offices stood there derelict for twenty-five years. It looked like it had been bombed out: not a great first sight for people visiting the city. The station forecourt, too, was tiny. Compare the sweep and the shops and cafes of any other station in a major city: Bristol has a small WH Smith and a ticket office. Then there's the fact that you can only access the station from one side.

Transport links in a city are important for so many reasons. A railway station is not just about first impressions: it's about mobility, about business, about encouraging people to use public transport. And so, on becoming mayor, Temple Meads and its surrounding area were high up on the agenda. I also knew that it was the sort of project that politicians often shy away from: it needs a long-term plan, so you're unlikely to see the final outcome while you're in office. It falls firmly under the 'hard yards and no credit' category. But it was something I wanted to tackle, to see what we could achieve.

As intrinsic as Temple Meads might be to the city, it's not actually owned by us, but by Network Rail. The only way that we can change anything is to get them involved. By a turn of good fortune, Peter Hendy, the current chair of Network Rail, lives in nearby Bath, so I went to see him and told him that I wanted to modernize the station. He'd carried the same ambition for years and so we shared a commitment to get Bristol the modern station it needed, and agreed to work together.

If the city didn't own the station, what it could bring to the table were plans for the surrounding land. So rather than just modernizing the station, the project developed into a plan to regenerate the whole area. This involved bringing others on board as well and we started talking to the University of Bristol, who had bought a site behind the station and wanted to build a new enterprise campus there. We talked to Homes England about building houses. For years, there had been talk of building an arena in the area, but housing seemed a more natural fit. Once the plans were pulled together, the regeneration had the capacity to deliver 10,000 homes, 22,000 jobs and £1.5 billion to the local economy.

The station is the gateway to all of this. Modernizing the station means that we can add new entrances, so it can be accessed from opposite sides. We can rebuild the forecourt to give people a proper welcome to the city. We can turn a historic site into a forward-looking transport hub for Bristol. That's a complicated job: much of the station is a Grade I listed building and so requires protection. We therefore brought in Heritage England to talk about how we could protect the history of Temple Meads, as well as celebrate Brunel and his legacy in the redeveloped station. We then looked at how we could use a combination of tunnels and bridges to create the accessibility we needed.

As I say, it was a lengthy process. The first time we sat down to talk about the project was in September 2017. One by one, we gathered the people we needed to get the finance and green light from national government. It was quite the coalition: Network Rail, Homes

England, the Bristol universities, the Department for Transport. The promises from government started coming in: I could see that there was support for the plans; that people understood the size and scope of the investment potential for the area. But getting government funding is a tricky business: there are quite strict funding pots that you apply for, and if your project doesn't match up with them, or overlaps with other projects, then it risks being overlooked. At one point the Temple Meads plan linked with a combined authorities application to do some work on the A4, one of the key roads that comes into the area. The two projects running in tandem made everything too complicated, and we lost out on the funding.

Even so, I knew we had champions in government. And once we separated out the schemes, the way became clear. There would be money from the Treasury for the modernization of Temple Meads: the university raised their funds from a mixture of public and private money. Some parts of the development came from private funds; others were a private/public combination. All these funds were coming from different sources, and they all relied on each of the other sources of income to make it work. It's a bit like being involved in a chain when buying a house, where all the separate agreements have to be coordinated for the whole thing to come off.

One of the first pieces of advice I got when I was running for mayor was from Sir Richard Leese, the long-serving and very successful leader of Manchester. It was quite simple: 'Don't make yourself annoying to government departments. Because if you do that, you'll end up missing out on money.' Although there are funding pots that might be available if you fulfil all the criteria, there's still a political judgement made as to whether to sign things off or not. I've lost count of the number of times I've been told, 'It's on the minister's desk.' Sometimes I wonder how overloaded that desk is with documents like mine waiting for a signature. I try to follow the advice of that northern leader, but it's not always easy. And sometimes, too, you can be as nice as you like to the minister of the relevant department, but if they don't have the necessary influence, you're not going to get your project through. There was a point in the process when the project ended up on Robert Jenrick's desk, then the local government minister. But we were told that he didn't have the traction needed with the Treasury to get the funds signed off.

The project dragged on. There were moments when I thought it might never happen, that the coalition of partners we'd put together would peel away and the funding would unravel. But I persisted. I sidestepped the minister and rang up a very senior figure at Downing Street, who has always been supportive of me.

'Can you tell me what's going on with Temple Meads? Is there anyone there who could just flick the switch? Because as soon as you say we can crack on, we'll crack on with it. We can start looking at the supply chain. The economy starts moving.'

'Everyone wants it to happen,' he told me. It was a Friday and I was told it would get sorted on the Monday. But Monday came and I didn't hear anything. Am I not wearing the right ties? I wondered. Is there a funny handshake I need to offer up? After previous false starts, I was worried that the plug might be pulled at the last minute yet again. But whether it was my contact in Downing Street or the minister making a call, the sign-off came. Six years after the first meeting, we were granted £95 million, which will fund the first stage of the project, and unlock the full development.

This isn't a short-term plan – it will take fifteen years for the regeneration of the area to be completed. And it had taken almost six years to secure this funding. But just as the Temple Meads regeneration unlocks the funding for the rest of the project, so public transport, more widely, unlocks so many of the issues that a modern city faces. It's intrinsic to the environmental policies we want to pursue, for example, in so many different ways. It's not just about getting people out of cars and onto trains: if you regenerate the area, then people moving there won't have the same transport needs that have been required hitherto. They'll be able to walk or cycle to where they want to go. In the jargon, it's what is called an active travel zone.

A leader is nothing without his team. The more you can surround yourself with people who are smarter than you, and have confidence to both do that and give those people the space to do their stuff, the better a leader you'll be. It's not always easy to get those people in the public sector. Pay in the public sector can be a real challenge, which means you can't always compete to hire who you want to hire. But when you can bring them in, you do so.

The Bristol Housing Festival is an example of this. It was founded by Jez Sweetland. He was someone who'd come from a corporate role – he was a lawyer and chief executive of a barristers' chambers by his early thirties. Super-smart guy. Phenomenally intelligent. And he gave all of that up because he was passionate about housing.

Jez was developing expertise in modern methods of construction and came up with the idea for a housing festival involving an exhibition of modular homes on the waterfront. I spent some time with him and I could sense immediately he was a ball of energy, talent and integrity. He had big ideas and he needed backing. The scheme he proposed to me needed to be underwritten to the tune of a hundred thousand pounds. Right away, my officers were nervous. It was a big sum of money, but I had absolute faith in Jez. I knew that he would go away and raise the money. And as good as his scheme was, it was Jez I was underwriting. This was leadership as team action all over: find someone smarter than you, let them run with their ideas, and back them to deliver. I provided the backing, and Jez did the rest.

The money we got for the regeneration around Bristol Temple Meads station is a good example of this. This sort of project and the funding required is only achievable through a team effort. To succeed, we needed Homes England, Network Rail, the University of Bristol, the Department of Transport and more on board. I could facilitate that, and play my part in bringing a coalition together, but the success of the bid was a team effort through and through. We could only achieve what we managed to achieve by working together.

I wasn't any sort of technical expert on the engineering, or on ground management, or on the finances. But I could bring in people who were. And I could hold that group together, go out to bat for the project and serve as the voice and the face of the scheme. It's in moments like this, when I am surrounded by people who are much more expert than me and I am holding on to the subject matter by my fingernails, that I face my biggest leadership challenges. But I think that's maybe what I offer: the willingness to have such people around me, without asking them to be anything less than their best.

There's a TED talk by Nancy Duarte that has always resonated with me. She gives an account of the great talks of history, the secret structure of great talks. And when she analyses the likes of Martin Luther King Jr and JFK, the reason those speeches are successful is because they're not about the person doing the speaking. They're pointing to the listener and asking something of them. And that, in essence, is how I see leadership: it's not about me, it's about empowering and helping others to fulfil their potential.

The Temple Meads development is a great example of what good leadership can do. I can't run a city – or any single project – on my own. A leader is nothing without a good team around him. With a strong team, you can bring people on board and really get things done. And that's what we did with the campaign to bring Channel 4 to the city.

The first I knew that Channel 4 was looking to relocate from London was when I read about it in one of the daily bulletins I get from the Local Government Information Unit. One newsletter mentioned that Coventry was pitching for the TV channel to move their base to the city.

I went straight through to an officer in the council. 'Did anyone know about Channel 4 relocating? Coventry is applying?'

'Yeah, we knew that was happening, but we didn't think we'd get it, so we didn't raise it,' they replied.

I was irritated, not only for not having been in the loop but also for the lack of ambition it showed for Bristol. *We didn't think we'd get it, so we didn't raise it.* 'You don't get to make that decision,' I told them, and asked them to get me more information.

As I read through the briefing notes, I became convinced that Bristol was a good fit for Channel 4. We already had a high media presence in the city thanks to the BBC Wildlife Unit being based here, as well as a number of independent TV production companies. Then there was Aardman Animations, the makers of *Wallace and Gromit* and *Shaun the Sheep*. Ever since its first broadcast in 1982,

Channel 4 has built a reputation for offering an alternative worldview than those of the other terrestrial TV stations. It could be provocative and controversial, but it was also ground-breaking and innovative. It was the sort of TV that seemed to chime with a lot of what the city was about.

Not surprisingly, with the news now out there that Channel 4 was looking to move, a few other cities were throwing their hats into the ring. Manchester and Birmingham made public pronouncements about how they were the natural home for the channel. I was told that one mayor even claimed they had already been chosen and that it was 'in the bag'.

I wanted to go about things a different way. Rather than voicing our interest publicly, I asked for a meeting to be set up with the chief executive of Channel 4: I wanted to speak to him face to face and find out what the situation really was. Did Channel 4 actually want to move out of London? The news about the moving had come from a politician rather than the channel itself. Was it government policy to relocate people out of London, or was it a process driven by the channel itself?

I spoke to Grant Mansfield, founder and chief executive of Bristol-based Plimsoll Productions, at the time the UK's largest independent production company outside of London. When I asked him what he thought of the bid, his advice was that we should focus on the commissioning side – Channel 4 were looking for a site for both a national HQ and also a Creative Hub, with commissioning focus. I liked Grant and knew that, like me, he was passionate about the city. So when the meeting with Channel 4's chief executive, David Abraham, was set up, I asked him to come with me. I also took along Fiona Francombe, director of the Bottle Yard Studios and another key figure in the local media set-up.

The three of us met David in Channel 4's London office. I opened by asking, 'Everyone is talking about you, but what do you think of the proposed move?'

'You know, you're the first person to even ask me what I think,' David replied, then paused before adding, 'We're not that keen.'

At that point, I knew that we understood each other. When I'd talked to Grant beforehand, we'd come to the conclusion that the real win in the situation was not necessarily to get Channel 4 out into the regions: it was about getting them to spend more money outside the M25.

I then said: 'Look, if you are going to move, obviously we'd want to have you come to Bristol, but what I will also say is that we understand. And what we really want is to encourage you to get the spend up outside of London.'

Not long afterwards, David left Channel 4 and was replaced as CEO by Alex Mahon. We went back up to London, this time with Lynn Barlow from the University of the West of England, to see her and again put the case for Bristol. After the meeting, there was a lot of stuff in the press about our bid. I don't know where it came from but it wasn't from us, which I explained to Alex. We still weren't saying anything publicly about the bid. Again, I think they appreciated our approach.

When it came to sending in the formal pitch, we made it clear that we weren't interested in Channel 4 coming as a piece of city jewellery. We wanted it because we wanted to use our leverage and location to help increase diversity within the creative sector, which was pretty low.

Our pitch also made clear that it wasn't just the council bidding, but that we had the support of the media industry in the city firmly behind us. Before I had requested the meeting with David, we held a meeting at City Hall to get their input and representatives from about fifty production companies came. I asked them at the meeting whether they wanted us as a city to go ahead with the bid.

'It can't just come from the council, but from all of us,' I said. 'I'll only front a drive to get Channel 4 here if it is something that you want to happen.' But I also had something else to ask them: a commitment to greater inclusion. A number of us had long been frustrated with a media sector that was full of politically progressive people and yet remained one of the most race- and class-elitist sectors in the city. 'It's not just something that we want as a political administration,' I added, 'it's what Channel 4 wants to see as well.'

There was a great atmosphere in the room – a real buzz about what we were trying to do, and people were keen to help. Paul Appleby, director of Bristol Media, launched a film competition for young filmmakers in the city, aimed at getting Bristol's story out there. We had been very struck by the fact that when the Channel 4 relocation was first talked about, no one had mentioned Bristol. We needed to change that. We needed to show the channel and the wider world the skills and talents that we had here.

Our bid made it through to the next stage, at which point Channel 4 started to set up site visits, to get a sense of the cities in the running and see where they might work. When it was Bristol's turn, we pushed the boat out – literally. When they arrived at Temple Meads, we took them down to the river to board a boat we had borrowed and cruised along the Avon to the wharf by Gas Ferry Road, where Aardman have their studios and where we were holding a big reception. Apart from people from all the local production companies, we had also invited the local community radio stations: Ujima and BCFM. We invited a lot of Black and Asian community leaders, as well as those from the disabled community. We wanted to show that our relationships with diversity were real, and not just for show. I was really proud of the turnout we had that day. It felt properly representative of the place I knew Bristol to be. The community element created a real warmth to proceedings. 'We're really excited about you coming here,' Channel 4 were told, which was very different from the business leaders and investors who had been lined up to meet them elsewhere.

We then took them to Ujima Radio to get a sense of how a community radio station works. The station manager there had no childcare, so brought her two-year-old to work with her. We sat on well-worn sofas in their meeting area, with a pool table in the corner. The station manager's child wandered around us while we talked, rolling a pool ball loudly across the wooden floor.

'This is for real,' I told Channel 4. 'If you come here, you're going to have the chance to meet potential talent who can run a community station without childcare.'

When the phone call came through with the decision, I was really nervous. I was away on a retreat in Hastings at the time. I was in the stairwell of the dormitory accommodation we were staying in when I took the call. I can still remember my heart pounding as I waited for their answer – just like I was waiting for exam results.

If I hadn't seen that initial piece in the newsletter, we would never have gone for it. But it proved to me – and I hoped to Bristol – what we had here and what we were capable of when we came together. No one thought we had a chance, yet we succeeded over cities that had spent a lot more money on their bids. I know this is true because at one point we talked to the consultancy KPMG about helping out with our bid – they declined, saying they were already representing other people in the process. Those other cities spent a quarter of a million pounds on wooing Channel 4. We spent a tenth of that – just £25,000 – and we won.

Building and growing a local economy is hard work on several fronts. At a city level, you don't survive unless you have big economic players. These are the anchor institutions around which everything revolves: the size of their workforce, the scale, skills and contributions that their presence brings to the city. They are companies that also give the city a national and international profile. In turn, they encourage other businesses to set up in the city, connecting it to the wider world.

At the same time, less high-profile but equally important, are the small- and medium-size businesses. This is where new ideas and creativity happen, and where the local communities get their chance to shine. A city economy is about stitching these different elements together, so businesses of all sizes can feed off one another and grow together, rather than at the expense of one another.

It's very easy for local businesses to feel left behind when bigger organizations move in. But we want to see benefits for the local supply chains and local skills. I am unashamedly ambitious for the city, but it has to be the right kind of ambition – unashamed but not unqualified – and not inequitable. At its heart is the desire to have an inclusive economy.

That desire goes back to my childhood. As a kid growing up in Bristol, I sometimes felt as though I was watching the city happen around me. Life, and hope, seemed to happen in places like Clifton, literally on top of the hill, whereas I was down in the valley, in Easton. There were opportunities available in the city that were so close geographically, but also felt as though they were half a world away.

A split and unequal city isn't firing on all cylinders nor fulfilling its potential. And Bristol has, historically, been a city of entrenched inequalities. We have some of the most deprived wards in the country, but also the fastest rising house prices. A recent survey showed that men in the most deprived areas of Bristol have a life expectancy that is ten years lower than those who live in the wealthiest areas.* The wealthiest are expected to live sixteen years of more healthy life than the poorest.

When I was growing up in the 1980s, Bristol was a city of high unemployment. There had been inequality before that, but the policies of Margaret Thatcher's Conservative government ensured inequality became entrenched and gathered pace. And just as Covid impacted the poorest most, so unemployment hit specific areas of the city the hardest. Those areas still bear the scars today.

When we put contracts out to tender, we make sure that we incorporate social value into them. And when bids for a project come in, we don't just take the lowest offer, but the one we feel is genuine about offering help and support to the local economy. I sometimes feel a bit self-conscious doing this: I'm aware that I'm the Black kid from the local comp in the room. But it does filter through and we find willing partners. I was at a meeting recently about the Temple Meads regeneration and a senior white male member of staff from Network Rail brought up the issue quite naturally – stressing that we had to make sure that we were including local people in the project and sharing the benefits. I thanked him afterwards – I really appreciated that the suggestion had come from someone other than me.

Sometimes my role in these situations is to help firms to do this. Strip away the business acumen and there can be good people underneath who want to do their bit for the common good but don't know how to go about it. And why would they? If their career is making television programmes or property development, why would their expertise be in community development and engagement? That sharing of knowledge and experience is exciting: everyone benefits and if I can help to facilitate that, I'll have done my job.

Part of my role as mayor is to encourage businesses to come and

* https://www.bbc.co.uk/news/uk-england-bristol-62888093

set up in Bristol. But we don't just want any business to turn up: we want companies who will fit into our vision for the city. That's where something like our One City Plan comes in – we can show investors a vision of how we want Bristol to grow and develop over the next few decades. If you're bringing your business to the city, you're going to be part of that: we want your input for our economy board. We want you to look at what we're doing with our children and students – how can you help invest in their skills now so that you'll have the work-force you need in ten years' time?

Channel 4 is a good example of how this process can work. We're constantly on the lookout for firms who are thinking about relocating and might be interested in moving, or an American company who might be building a headquarters in the UK. Sometimes we hear about these from a source in government. Sometimes they come via a group we co-fund called Invest in Bristol and Bath. Sometimes they come via the universities.

Early in my time in office, I went to Guangzhou in China. Bristol has been twinned with Guangzhou since 2001, so the visit hoped to deepen ties between the two cities. Coincidentally, Dr Erik Lithander, who was part of the senior leadership team at the University of Bristol, was also there to encourage Chinese students to come to Bristol. We got talking and I told him that this sort of meeting shouldn't be happening by chance: everyone doing international work for the city should be working together.

As a result, when I got back, I wanted to bring greater coordination to the international work happening out of Bristol. And so, we brought together organizations from across the city who were operating around the world. Bristol has a global population with 180 countries of origin: we wanted to take advantage of this global connectivity and drew in members of the diaspora communities who are not always represented on our formal bodies. Our local Pakistani community was doing good business with Pakistan, for example, but without Bristol's chamber of commerce being involved. We brought all these different groups together and mapped out everywhere Bristol was connected to. I'd always known that Bristol was a global city, but when you actually pull everything together like this, it's a remarkable sight.

From this, we started to draw up an international strategy for the city. But what should we focus on? We had the links to build economic relationships across the world, but where was the best place to begin? We decided to start with the US. We talked to the Department of International Trade, who were very supportive: not all international trade deals have to be done through national government; a cumulative place-by-place approach can be just as successful.

I took a Bristol delegation to Boston and Chicago. As well as myself, we had the universities, the Metro Mayor Tim Bowles and representatives from some of our tech companies. In Boston, we met with the tech industry there, and with Marty Walsh, who was the mayor of Boston at the time. We travelled on to Chicago, to the university, and visited the business incubators set up in the city. The law firm Womble Bond Dickinson hosted an event for us, at which we also met people from law firms and construction companies. Our main focus, though, was on tech and university-related businesses. We had a good pitch – we could tell these firms that the University of the West of England has some of the most advanced robotic labs in the world and that the University of Bristol has a business incubator that was voted the world's number-one incubator for two years in a row. We talked about opportunities for collaboration, innovation and access to markets.

Part of the purpose of these trips is, of course, to do deals – one of the companies we went out with signed a deal while we were there. But they're also about opening up channels and creating possibilities. You hope that in two years' time, you'll get the call from someone thinking about moving who has remembered that they met you and liked what you had to say. Certainly, we've increased our profile massively over the years. Bristol exists on the world stage in a way it didn't two decades ago.

Over the years, Bristol has shifted from a manufacturing base to more of a service-based economy. Aerospace has long been important for us, but also banking and insurance: that's a legacy of our shipping past. Tech, media and science are key areas for us and align with where we think the economy will grow in the future. All economies evolve – if you don't lay the foundations for change, then you're in danger of being left behind.

At the same time, building the economy for the future is a balancing act. We didn't want an economy that only had jobs for people with a PhD. Creating an economic strategy is about the entry-level jobs as well. We still need an economy where, if someone goes to prison at eighteen and comes out at twenty-five, there are jobs there that they are equipped to apply for. A strong, inclusive economy is a mixed economy, made up of jobs ranging from high-tech to retail and construction.

There are always areas that we would like to grow further. One sector I'd love for the city to expand into, because it links to our plans to tackle the housing crisis, is to bring some off-site manufacturing industry to the city for houses. As we look at new technologies for building homes, I want the Bristol city region to have factories producing the composite parts we need for those homes.

Predicting the city's future is difficult. One of the effects of Covid has been a shift in working patterns and an increase in people working from home. Will this be a short-term phenomenon or a permanent shift in how we work? And if it does result in a long-term change, what effect does it have on the need for office space in the city? At the moment, the demand seems quite resilient and strong, but it could change.

There is a danger that office space could go the same way as retail. Whether they are losing out to out-of-town retail parks, or to online shopping, British high streets are now full of empty shops. Bristol is no exception and the situation here has been exacerbated through having too much retail space. Compared to other comparable cities, we have about 40 per cent more shops. In the centre, we've got Broadmead and Cabot Circus right next to each other. I remember The Galleries in Broadmead being built on the site of Fairfax House, an iconic department store. I watched the new shopping centre rise, brick by brick. I was at university by the time it opened and I remember coming back and walking around, thinking, Wow, this is like America. It seemed like the future had arrived in Bristol.

That shift from department store to shopping mall encapsulates how retail was shifting thirty years ago. Now it has shifted again, but the shopping centres haven't caught up. There's an ongoing challenge to reinvent these spaces, to stop the centres of the city feeling empty and deserted. Bristol has too many shops but even if we had the 'right' number, we'd still be struggling to cope.

Like so many cities, Bristol's transport challenge is not merely how to service today's population, but how to deal with the demands of a fast-growing population that will be at least 550,000 by 2050, on an infrastructure that was built for simpler, less complicated, less populous times. Bristol's main railway station might be old, but that's nothing compared to the origins of the road network, which goes all the way back to Roman times. Over the years, as the city has grown, the city has become more and more car-dependent, a process that accelerated as people moved out to the suburbs from the inner city. Some of the planning decisions made by previous generations are barely fathomable. When the M32 was built, the original plan was to bring it right through the centre of Bristol, spanning the top of the harbour and carrying on south to the M5.

For much of the twentieth century, the car was seen as the vehicle of the future, offering people freedom and independence. But as with any freedom, it comes with costs and responsibilities and, by the end of the twentieth century, the philosophy behind road-building had shifted. Rather than dealing with more cars by building more roads, we now realized that those new roads would be full as soon as you'd finished building them. The New Labour government of the late 1990s offered a moratorium on road-building and the emphasis shifted: the way forward was not to build more roads, but to get people out of their cars and offer alternative ways to travel around. And all the time, as the population grows, so does the pressure to find a solution. It's not just about dealing with the problem today but laying the groundwork for transport in thirty years' time – so that future generations don't curse the leaders of today as we do the town planners of the 1960s.

Historically, Bristol has taken a patch-and-mend approach to transport. It hasn't worked. We need a better solution – and that is to go underground. With limited space, it frees up the surface space for everything else that makes demands on it.

One of the projects I have worked to get off the ground is the construction of a mass transit system that tunnels under the densest parts of Bristol. Buses play an important role in getting a city moving, but in a meeting about Bristol's bus network, as we looked at the numbers of the growing population, it seemed that we were trying to fix today's problem with yesterday's solution.

At the very start of my tenure, the city transport team was having a really good, open discussion about transit policy. I asked a question about tunnelling, expecting to be swiftly knocked back. Instead, one of the team said to me, 'Actually, the technology around that has moved on a lot in recent years. It's a lot cheaper than it used to be.'

I was taken aback by this. 'So can we go under the city? Is that a possibility?'

Again, the answer was positive. 'Why isn't anyone telling us this?' I asked. 'Let's get working on it.'

We started to look into what building a mass transit system might entail. We looked at other cities with undergrounds, like London and Newcastle, to see how those set-ups worked. The proposal we worked up was a sort of 'hub-and-spoke' system. It involves a central base with four lines from different sides of Bristol feeding into it. They would start above ground in the outskirts and go underground in the city centre. One line, which financially would be the banker, would go out to Bristol Airport. The airport is notoriously difficult to get to: it is the only airport in the country that isn't connected by a railway line or dual carriageway. Other lines would go up north to Cribbs Causeway, out to Lyde Green and Longwell Green, while the fourth would go to the Hicks Gate roundabout and ideally on to Keynsham and Bath. To give you a sense of numbers, every day that roundabout is used by about 35,000 cars, with people driving into Bristol along the A4. If we could build a park-and-ride there and get people onto a mass transit system, it would have a transformative effect on our transport system.

The opposition parties have been negative about the proposal. They've called it a vanity project, a pie-in-the-sky idea. To me those criticisms show a lack of ambition, allowing yesterday's failures to rob us of today's possibilities. With that sort of attitude, would Bristol ever have built the suspension bridge, the SS Great Britain, the Great Western Railway? Decarbonizing a city is a big challenge and a big solution is required to deal with it.

It also shows a lack of understanding of how such a project works. As with the regeneration of Temple Meads, such projects demand a coalition-building, brick-by-brick approach to get the green light. You don't just write a cheque for £4 billion and get started. Instead, there are a series of gateways you go through to get there – at each one you have to check that it is financially and technologically possible for the project to go ahead. And if, at one of those points, it isn't practical, then you stop. But if it is possible, then you go on to the next gateway in the process and see what happens next.

Some of the criticisms come from a different angle. *It's all very well talking about transport problems in ten years' time*, runs the argument, *but we need a solution now.* To which I'd counter, why can't you think about transport now *and* in the future? Immediate solutions tend to be short-term by nature. I know that my successors won't thank me if all I thought about was Bristol's needs today, and not the needs of future generations.

1 2 .

A City is a Collective Act

Sandy Park Depot in Brislington is not somewhere you'd normally take a second glance at. It's where the council runs its repairs and maintenance services, keeping our fleet of vehicles in check. But in April 2020, the site took on a darker purpose.

The skies were leaden on the day I went to visit. Everything about the site was monochrome, the only splash of colour the mid-blue of the depot gates as I drove in. Inside, a series of huge white gazebos had been erected, their entrances screened off by further fencing, also decked out in clinical white. As I walked in, I caught my first glimpse of what was within: refrigerated storage containers, rows and rows of them.

This was Bristol's temporary mortuary facility. It was the beginning of the Coronavirus pandemic, and no one had any idea how it would unfold. The overriding concern was that services would be overwhelmed. As a result, a Nightingale Hospital was built at the University of West England, to deal with the potential influx of patients. The site at Sandy Park was more sinister though – what if so many people died that we didn't have the facilities to deal with all the bodies? The phrase 'excess deaths' is a misleadingly dry term – it belies every single human story and tragedy contained within it. We had to navigate this difficult, sensitive situation while maintaining the dignity of those who would lose their lives, alongside the practicalities of coping with unprecedented numbers of deaths.

It was a sobering sight, seeing those containers – and it put the scale of the challenge that we faced as a community into sharp relief. Sandy Park was ready to take hundreds of bodies that our regular mortuaries would be unable to cope with. That overcast day marked its formal opening. I was joined by other city and faith leaders – some present but socially distanced on-site, others joining via Zoom. Both social distancing and online meetings were quickly becoming part of the new normal. People I'd known and worked with for years were now being awkwardly greeted elbow to elbow. The ceremony was short but poignant – each of us offered thoughts, prayers and blessings for the new site in an attempt to reassure Bristol's communities that this was a place of peace, comfort and dignity.

It was a powerful moment, this coming together of all the city's faith leaders. It was a time when faith was both going to be tested, and needed, too. As I drove back to City Hall, through the silence of empty streets, the skies seemed to hang that little bit heavier. On a normal working day, these roads would have been bursting with life, bumper to bumper with cars and bikes and public transport, people trying to go about their business: but as I drove through to City Hall without stopping, I almost missed their presence. Much like the storage containers, regular life was frozen that day. The thought of what might happen in the days and weeks ahead sent a shiver down my spine.

In October 2018, Bristol played host to the Global Parliament of Mayors. This is a gathering of mayors from across the world, getting together to discuss the different challenges that we face as communities, and looking at how we share ideas and solutions to deal with them. I was really proud that we had been chosen to host that year's event and I was able to showcase Bristol to over a hundred city mayors.

During the summit, we discussed three key issues, which led to a final declaration of global aims, voted for by the majority of those participating. The first was migration; the second was urban security;

and the third was health, and more specifically how we would deal with a possible pandemic. When I first saw the proposals about what we were discussing, I remember pulling a face.

'Why are we talking about a pandemic?' I asked. 'It doesn't really seem an issue for us. Should we not be spending the time talking about more relevant priorities, such as climate change, or housing?'

If I'm being completely honest, I was irritated to see it on the agenda. It felt like a wasted opportunity. Pandemic preparation didn't feel urgent, or at least not in the UK. I could see it would be an issue for a gathering of mayors from the global south, but not for cities like Bristol in the global north. Sharper minds than mine, thankfully, had read the signs. In 2015 Bill Gates had given a TED talk about the international response to the 2014 Ebola outbreak in which he concluded that the world had been lucky and urged global leaders to plan for when the next outbreak came along: 'We're not ready,' he said. In 2016, the UK government had undertaken Exercise Cygnus, a three-day simulation to test responses to a serious flu pandemic. Though that did lead to a series of recommendations, four years later many of them had yet to be implemented.

I'd be lying if I said the Global Parliament of Mayors summit was a Damascene moment for my understanding of pandemics. But I listened to the debates and committed to our intention to prioritize pandemic preparedness as a key component of urban planning. As the summit came to a close, though, it was the agreements we'd reached on migration and refugees that were – for me – the key breakthroughs and would, I thought, be what the summit would be remembered for.

Fast forward eighteen months, however, and those conversations about pandemics suddenly took on a new urgency. Those who'd pushed for the debate had been proved right – another example of cities being on the front foot while national governments were left behind. I was fortunate that those conversations were so recent. I was fortunate, too, in having worked in public health before I became mayor. It gave me a little bit of insight to build on and long-established relationships to draw on. Taken together, I at least had a starting point in how the city would deal with Coronavirus.

Like most people, I watched the beginnings of the pandemic in early 2020 with a feeling of concern, but also reassurance that Wuhan was a long way away. However, the globalization of the modern world meant that it wasn't long before the virus spread beyond China, to Asia, to Europe and on to the UK. It was only a matter of time before it would be on our doorstep.

By early March we were organizing ourselves to respond. At this point, we didn't know whether the country would go into lockdown or not, but either way, we knew that as a city we needed to be ready to react. I ran a weekly meeting of city leaders – the health service, the police, fire brigade, businesses, the voluntary sector. It was our One City approach in action – if we hadn't already had that in place, we would have had to invent it. Everyone coming together to connect was so important.

A further stroke of good fortune was that my director of public health, Christina Gray, had been my manager when I had worked for the NHS. She was the one who had seen my potential and encouraged me to 'catch my star', as she put it. I couldn't think of anyone I'd rather have at my side to tackle the crisis.

Those weekly meetings were Christina's floor-space. She'd give the truth, unvarnished, as to what the situation was like on the ground in Bristol. Rather than wading through the headlines, companies and organizations could come to us to find out what was happening first-hand. Everyone's workforce was impacted, but business and community leaders could hear directly from Christina and Bristol's hospital bosses, who gave them precise figures on how many people were being admitted.

The challenges we – and every city in the country – faced were unprecedented. Lockdown led to a multiplicity of knock-on effects. We anticipated increases in domestic violence and Jonathan Downing in my office led a project pulling together the organizations in Bristol supporting victims of such abuse. Digital exclusion was also something we anticipated right from the start: what happened to those people who couldn't work from home, or whose children couldn't study at home because they didn't have a computer? Hunger was another huge concern: how could we ensure that the most vulnerable would continue to get food? Even before lockdown started, we were asking questions about how we would re-open schools. What would we need to put in place so that they would be Covid-ready when students returned?

We already had a project to combat child hunger up and running, led by Andy Street, a member of the City Leadership Group. We were able to redirect and expand the project to reach all those we knew would be vulnerable. By the time the government announced that they would be sending out boxes of food for distribution, we were already on the case. Just as well – the promised national supplies arrived days late. Fortunately, we already had food to send out and organized a fleet of taxis to get it to those in need.

It often seemed that there was quite a contrast between what was happening on the ground and the help that was coming from the government. Parts of the response were chaotic. The government would announce money for this or that, but without explaining how the various schemes would be put into practice. We would watch the Number 10 press conferences like everyone else, then spend the evening working out how to implement the latest announcement.

Robert Jenrick, who was the secretary of state for housing, communities and local government, organized a number of webinars for city leaders. Unfortunately, the sessions were really poor. To begin with, the message was 'get done what you need to get done, we have you'. He told us that he was our man in government, that he was on our side. But it didn't take long for the messaging to subtly change in a way that pushed more of the burden onto local government's shoulders at local government cost. The government line shifted to, 'It's down to local government now. We've given them the money.' That felt like a shifting of responsibility. Then the message changed again: 'spend what you need to spend' became 'spend on what we've agreed as critical areas'. That didn't go down well, and begged a question or two. If any of us had followed his earlier advice but had spent on something now not considered to be critical, would that mean funds were not going to be forthcoming?

I think Jenrick lost the trust of many leaders across the country, of all political parties, as his position shifted. The credibility he had at the start of the process quickly drained away. One of the reasons, I would guess (and which had been hinted at by people in Whitehall in regard to other funding issues), is that he didn't have the necessary traction with the Treasury to get the cash local government needed.

This was compounded by a distinct lack of leadership skills. Jenrick didn't seem to understand how to build relationships, and both misunderstood and underestimated who he was dealing with. He certainly wasn't the first or last government minister to do that, I should add. Sometimes, once someone becomes a minister, they seem to think that they can turn up at a meeting with people they see as lower in the political hierarchy than they are and the gift of their presence will see them through. Whereas I look at them and think, you might have the title of minister, but you're not owning the job: we are the people actually delivering.

There's also an attitude I've come across a number of times, which is that ministers believe that because we're local government, we should be grateful that they are spending their time talking to us. Whereas I'm thinking, we're the ones here doing the real work. We're the ones with the budget and a population in need. I didn't see any traction with the Treasury, and I didn't see him deliver any big wins for local government.

Some city leaders went more public than me. Andy Burnham, for example, notably clashed with the government over the levels of funding being offered. I would hope that, at some level, one outcome of the pandemic might be that the government got a sense of how much we do at a local level. That's where the real organization of policy happens. Announcing a big pot of money might make headlines, but unless you've got someone to deliver it on the ground, it's nothing but an empty news story.

As lockdown started, I quickly became acutely aware of the responsibility resting on my shoulders. City Hall became a hub for food distribution. I'd walk in and the first thing I'd see were piles and piles of boxes waiting to be delivered. While the vast majority of the City Hall staff relocated to work from home, I made a point of going in every day. One of my concerns in those early days of lockdown was that Bristol could end up looking like the disaster movie *28 Days Later*. I didn't want people to think that with the world collapsing, there was no one at the steering wheel. So I felt it important to come in, to keep the City Hall lights on, to reassure people that we were there. Even when 'we' was sometimes singular – there were days when it felt as though I was the only person in the building: just me and the piles of emergency rations, trying to keep everything afloat.

In 1832, cholera killed 584 Bristolians out of a population of 96,000. Of those who died, it was the poorest who were the hardest hit: overcrowded slums and unsanitary conditions made them far more susceptible to contracting the disease. It might have been water that transmitted it, but it was poverty that exacerbated its impact.

Nearly 200 years later and although cholera is now – in this country at least – confined to school history lessons, the underlying factors that amplified the disease remain. In 2010, as I mentioned earlier, the government published the Marmot Review, which looked at health inequalities in the UK. This was followed by another, more practical report: 'If You Could Do One Thing – Nine Local Actions to Reduce Health Inequalities'.

Both reports are underpinned by the same argument: that socio-economic inequalities affect health outcomes. The numbers quoted in them have stayed with me: only 20 per cent of health outcomes are connected to health services and the quality of care received. Health behaviours (30 per cent) and environmental factors (10 per cent) are important, but by far the greatest impact (40 per cent) is from socio-economic factors.

It was when I was working in public health that I'd got to really understand that, at its heart, understanding health is about understanding the underlying conditions. And when Coronavirus hit, I was acutely aware of how this might play out.

I wasn't the only one. Richard Horton, the influential editor-in-chief of *The Lancet*, argued that what we were facing was not a pandemic, but a syndemic, in which two separate diseases were combining: the communicable disease, Covid itself, and then a second cluster of non-communicable diseases, in which poverty and inequality played a fundamental part.

'The most important consequence of seeing Covid-19 as a syndemic is to underline its social origins,' he wrote in *The Lancet* in

September 2020. 'The vulnerability of older citizens: Black, Asian and minority ethnic communities; and the key workers who are commonly poorly paid with fewer welfare provisions, points to a truth so far barely acknowledged [. . .] that unless governments devise policies and programmes to reverse profound disparities, our societies will never be truly Covid secure.'*

That's true on a national level, but it's worth adding that it's also true internationally: until everyone is vaccinated globally, the risk of new mutations and variants remain. It's not enough for the richer countries to protect themselves: helping vaccinate poorer countries is critical to getting the disease under control.

On a local level, tackling a syndemic involves what Richard Horton describes as 'a larger vision, one encompassing education, employment, housing, food and environment.' Reading his comments was wholly in line with what I learned from my time at Public Health. Finding a vaccine was going to be fundamental in dealing with the virus, of course, but purely focusing on that leaves out the fullness of the picture. The virus was being given strength and agency by the social conditions in which it was landing – if you didn't do anything to deal with those, the problems weren't going to go away. For all its success, Bristol still has some of the most deprived neighbourhoods in the country. I knew that they would be hit particularly hard.

From early in the pandemic, I started to stress how important it was to recognize the lessons we would learn from it. It's hard to think in that way when you're in the thick of a crisis, but once you find yourself in such a position, you know that you don't want to end up there again. It's a bit like the financial crash in 2008 – how do you stop yourself from dealing with the immediate situation and just going back to the way things were, setting yourself up for the same scenario to play out repeatedly?

Horton's syndemic theory is a key point for me. It confirms that poor social conditions generate health vulnerabilities, which create conditions for pandemics to flourish. It also confirms that population health is a major economic issue. Everyone gets hit by it. Building

* https://www.thelancet.com/journals/lancet/article/PIIS0140-6736(20)32000-6/fulltext

social resilience with better social policy is a vital economic tool, not just some sort of fluffy, left-of-centre, woke thing to do. The pandemic showed us so clearly that, at a fundamental level, we are interdependent as a society.

In our weekly Wednesday call with the director of public health, Christina held the floor for the first twenty-five minutes or so to fill everyone in on what was happening. The numbers were terrifying. To begin with, cases in Bristol were in prevalence rates that were single digits per 100,000. I remember a conversation early on when we were seriously concerned about the number of cases approaching 15 to 20 per 100,000. Compared to other cities — Swindon at the same time had 40 to 50 cases — we were lagging behind. But that meant that when the cases did come, we leapfrogged everyone else's numbers and the rate started to rise incredibly quickly.

Where we'd previously worried about 20 cases per 100,000, we were suddenly at 500 cases. Week by week, the figures continued to rise: 500 became 600, became 800, became 900. We were bracing for the wave to hit. Had we done enough? We had our temporary mortuaries, our Nightingale Hospital. Thankfully, we never needed to use them and we survived the threat of being overwhelmed.

The city's response also showed me yet again the power of what we can achieve when we come together as a community. To give just one example, at our weekly meetings we looked at what would happen when university students started returning to the city. The universities obviously wanted, and needed, to get their students back, but at the same time, doing so presented a major risk for the city. But by discussing it well in advance, when they did start to come back — and in serious numbers — we were ready.

We also talked at length about what companies could do to make their workplaces Covid secure and we set up weekly Zoom meetings between Christina, Business West and trade unions to talk them through all the latest guidance. We wanted to help businesses to get back up and running, as well as making sure it was safe for people to return to work, and to give them the confidence to do so.

I did a video every day, which was broadcast on YouTube and Facebook. I'd talk through the numbers, try to reassure people about the situation, and what they could do. Again, I felt accessibility was really important. And as mayor, I had a role to play, to remind people that we were there, and we were looking out for them.

In one of the videos, I talked about the campaign that we set up called We Are Bristol. Our message was very straightforward and simple: be kind to each other. Look out for your neighbours, especially those that are vulnerable. Check that they're OK: call in help if they're not. We set up free phone numbers for people to call – if someone hadn't got food, even if they didn't qualify for a government scheme, we still wanted to know.

Even when lockdown was over, we continued to push this message of kindness. We knew there might be problems with face coverings, with some people wanting to wear them and others refusing to do so. There would be situations where social distancing would break down with people saying, 'Do you mind not standing so close to me?' As we learned to interact with each other again, there'd be all these mini-flashpoints. It was going to be important to remember that people would be making these requests not out of rudeness, but because they felt vulnerable or scared. If everyone could take a deep breath before responding, then we'd be in a far better space.

We set up another scheme, too, Can Do Bristol. If you were able to volunteer and help out, we wanted to hear from you. In the first instance, this was a valve to release the pressure coming from people who wanted to do something. It was a way of coordinating volunteering and also of getting ahead of criminal predators who started offering to help vulnerable people in order to get access to their lives. People registered in their thousands. It was heart-warming to see that even in the city's darkest moments, there was a light of support that never went out. Just as we all discovered something about ourselves as individuals during the pandemic, so I felt that we learned something, too, about the character of the city that we lived in.

I firmly believe that a city is a collective act. It is only by working and pulling together, by everyone contributing, that you can achieve the true potential of a place. And your personal leadership style reflects back on those you work for and with. I was talking to an audience of young people recently and I said, 'Listen, I'm the mayor but I'm not going to tie your shoelaces up for you. I create the conditions but the shoelace tying, as it were, is not down to me.' That's my idea of political leadership. Don't come to me with an ask, come to me with an offer.

This idea was formed before I was mayor, when I was involved in the city's strategic partnership. At the time, these meetings took place once a quarter, with all the city's big agencies involved: the police, public health, the universities, and so on. The meetings weren't great: they didn't have much energy to them, and some people simply stopped attending.

I went to see everyone individually and asked them, 'What do you want from me, from the meetings?' Then I pooled their answers and created a set-up that suited their agendas. As a result, they felt they were being listened to, and started to get more involved.

When I first stood for mayor, I did the same thing. I identified seven prominent people in Bristol, each of whom I thought was significant in the city in their different ways. I asked for forty minutes with each of them. And when we sat down, the questions I asked them were, 'What's the job? What do you think the mayor's role is?' At this point, Bristol had never had a directly elected mayor, so there was space to define what the role was. I wanted to know what these individuals thought it should encompass. And when I ran, their responses infused my campaign in 2012, then again in 2016. And to this, they were an important part of how I led things at City Hall.

Once I was elected, as I've described elsewhere, the One City approach was central. It's been at the heart of everything we've done – that vision and strategy across different areas, encouraging everyone to work together for shared and common goals.

When the Covid vaccines became available, the relief was palpable. The response to the pandemic had showed something about the character of the communities that we lived in. The discovery of a vaccine displayed human ingenuity at its best. It was a remarkable achievement.

On the ground, we were involved in the more prosaic challenge of rolling out the jabs to as many people as possible as quickly as possible. Behind the scenes, there was a lot of preparatory work to make sure that we would be able to deliver it. The work put in by those involved was relatively unsung but it was incredible. And again, national government took the credit, while those of us on the ground were doing the hard work.

We had sites all over the city but the main focus was on the football stadium at Ashton Gate, which was the first mass vaccination centre in the country. In just over six months, we managed to vaccinate over 235,000 Bristolians. Again, that's an extraordinary achievement and was only possible through a combination of hard work, detailed planning and dedicated volunteers. Everyone who was involved in that operation should be hugely proud of having played their part.

I waited my turn for a jab like everyone else, but when my time came, I booked mine in a community hall in South Bristol. Having sat in all these meetings about putting the process together, it was great to finally experience it for myself. The hall was full of medical students and volunteers helping out. A local pharmacist, Addy, jabbed me and I got someone to take a photo of the injection and had it posted on social media.

One of the challenges with the vaccine rollout was ensuring that everyone who was eligible for a jab got one. But in some communities, the Black community particularly, there was not only hesitation but suspicion about it. It's a historical reaction, a consequence of decades of mistrust of public institutions. These are communities that have been lied to, whose poverty has been ignored, who have been the victims of racial stereotyping. At the precise point when you needed people to trust in the government, and trust that the vaccine didn't contain some sort of tracking chip and didn't have a whole range of side effects, these communities didn't believe what they were being told. For me, it's a classic example of how important it is to invest in people. If you don't, then something that might seem inconsequential now will have repercussions further down the line. It may not be immediately obvious, but one of the lessons we must learn from Covid and Brexit is to think about how to rebuild trust between communities and government. It's so important – for all sides. People mistrust the vaccine, but without the jab, they are more likely to end up in ICU, which has huge financial consequences, quite apart from the health of the individual concerned.

The second challenge we had with the jabs was in making them convenient. It's a bit like if you find a lump that you think you should probably get checked out: if it's easy, you'll do it. If it isn't convenient, you put it off. For some people, the vaccine became an 'Oh, I'll get round to it' sort of thing, rather than being something to do urgently.

We did what we could to counter these attitudes. That's why I shared that photograph of me getting the vaccine – to show it was safe and easy to arrange. We looked for local champions in our communities – people who would go out and advocate for getting it done. I remember in our Somali community we found this brilliant, proactive group of women, who spoke to everyone, reassuring them and persuading them to get jabbed. Some people might be suspicious of government messaging – and with good reason – but they would listen to and trust leaders in their local communities. One thing we asked them to stress was that getting a jab wasn't just about individuals: it was about helping to protect your family and those around you as well.

The consequences of Covid were everywhere. The health issues aside, there wasn't a part of the city that wasn't touched in some way and the effort to keep Bristol running was immense.

Social care was a huge challenge, with care-staff numbers dropping and people needing to take time off and isolate if they tested positive. Transport was an issue, too: you can't run the buses without bus drivers. Then there was waste – people were still generating waste, and plenty of it what with being at home all day every day. It all needed collecting.

There were other major consequences of people being stuck at home, too. We knew schooling and access to online teaching were going to be a problem for many families, but we also knew that if schools locked down, it would inevitably lead to an increase in domestic violence and child abuse. We set up a big campaign around domestic violence at the start – we wanted people to know that they could reach out to us.

At times, it felt as though everything you knew about governance had been thrown up in the air. It wasn't only reduced numbers of staff, but reduced revenue as well. Like any council, Bristol makes money through people coming into the city and parking in their car parks. If people are forced to stay at home, that stream of revenue dries up.

The criminal justice system was another area that was under pressure. One of those attending our regular meetings was Peter Blair, the city's honorary recorder, or most senior judge. With the courts closed, all trial dates were postponed. This might seem to be a matter of logistics, but it causes deeply personal problems for the people involved – every one of those cases was someone waiting for a trial, or a release date from prison. For each of those families, the stress they were living under, waiting for that day in court, was being stretched.

There were other repercussions from Covid, too, in terms of the shape of the city. Bristol has always been a popular city, but the pandemic led to more families making the move from London. It accelerated a growing trend that has had financial repercussions as it put more pressure on the affordability of house prices. In the city centre, meanwhile, the ongoing trend of people buying goods online rather than in person also grew. It has been a tough time for retail anyway, but getting people back in the shops after Covid was doubly hard. Then there's the issue of empty office spaces as a result of more people working from home. The consequences of lockdown will ripple through for years to come.

Covid also amplified other economic trends, albeit in different ways. As well as keeping a regular eye on the number of cases, another key statistic was the number of families needing emergency support. We had an emergency fund for those families needing food or financial support and there was also a government scheme in place. But we went further in Bristol, making support available for more people. But each week, I saw the number of families applying for emergency funds ticking up. The disparity in income between the haves and have-nots was painful to witness.

Looking forward, my concern is whether we will learn our lessons from having lived through the pandemic. There's that Winston Churchill quote, 'never let a good crisis go to waste'. In the aftermath of the Second World War, it was the Atlee government that rebuilt Britain, laying the foundations of the NHS and the welfare state.

Covid tested every system we depend on: education, food, transport, and our democratic and economic systems, too. And while we have heroes who fought to keep things going, those systems have been found wanting: exams were missed; jobs were lost; people went hungry; transport ground to a halt. The question now is, how do we build back better? If we just shrug it off, think to ourselves 'thank goodness that is over', then we will have learned nothing to protect ourselves going forward, and missed our chance to change things for the better.

Covid was a global shock. But there are potentially bigger ones down the line, climate change in particular. Even at the height of the Covid crisis, there was a sense of being able to see a way out: our services are stretched, but there'll be a vaccine, we'll get through this. But climate shock will be more open-ended. There's no vaccine to get society out of that.

Even without Covid and its ongoing repercussions, the dilemmas we face in public health are immense. They start with simple demographics. As people live longer and our population gets older, there is an ever-increasing demand on resources, and at a time when there is continued government pressure to cut back on those services. It's not just an ageing population, but an increasingly sick one, too, whether from the consequences of higher levels of obesity or an explosion in mental health issues.

There are two elements at play here. The first is to ensure there are good services for people who are in crisis. The second is to look at how we can prevent these crises in the first place. This involves looking at how we can enable people to have longer, healthier lives. One of the metrics I use when it comes to health issues is not just the difference in how long people live, it's how many healthy years those people enjoy. It's well known that there is a difference in life expectancy between the richest and poorest in our society: in Bristol, the differential is about ten years. But the difference in healthy years life expectancy is wider still: around sixteen years.

That's a huge number – over a decade and a half. And the challenges – and costs – of those extra years are immense. If we're being blunt about it, when you die, you die. But if you become ill, the associated costs quickly stack up. It might be that you can't work and require support, that you're socially isolated, that you need to rely on local services, that your family may need to change their lives to take care of you. The costs of looking after you, both for local services and also for those around you, are immense.

Political leadership on this must mature and shift to public health in local government. It's all well and good – and important – to ringfence NHS spending. But, as I mentioned earlier, just 20 per cent of health outcomes in this country have to do with the NHS. The NHS does an amazing job in terms of treating heart attacks, cancer or broken legs, or dealing with disease. I'm not saying this isn't important – of course it is. But in terms of prevention, once people are in hospital, it's too late. Prevention starts with public health, but while the NHS funding is ringfenced, the money for public health is pared back time and again.

We spend a disproportionate amount of political time talking about serving sickness, serving for health. We need to take a more mature approach. We need to move the national approach to health beyond treating sickness, beyond even the prevention of sickness to the delivery of well-being. How do we create the social, economic and political systems to encourage and enable people to eat well and maintain physically and mentally healthier lives? How do we cope with people who struggle with social isolation, which statistics show is as bad for health as smoking? There are no resources to tackle it.

Historically, public health has played second fiddle to the NHS. The NHS has a higher profile politically and it says something about priorities that public health has ended up being a bit of pass-the-parcel between government departments. It was part of the NHS, then it was moved to local government. Following Covid, the government abolished Public Health England and created a new UK Health Security Agency: public health is now one of this agency's remits, alongside the Joint Biosecurity Centre and future pandemic planning.

I was working for Public Health when it was moved from the NHS to the aegis of local government. It created difficulties for me personally because, as I've said, I'd lost the mayoral election to

George Ferguson in 2012, but found myself working for him. That said, though, on a practical level public health sits better under local government than under the health umbrella. It needs to be properly resourced, and because of the way that health is determined by so many different factors – housing, educational experience, access to nutrition, the way we put communities together – it sits better in a place from which it can reach and influence those wider determinants.

During the Conservative leadership election in summer 2022, Liz Truss talked about putting the NHS back into the hands of people on the frontline. I'm not even sure what that means. This is the sort of soundbite approach to the nation's health that is repeated by national politicians and repeatedly lets us down. If we are going to talk about redistributing power and leadership, the priority must be to elevate directors of public health and give them more authority and resources. If they had the power to be involved in all sorts of decision-making – the impact of house-building, for example – then the effect could be transformational.

This is yet another area where the short-term political cycle works against the long-term solutions needed. Health outcomes begin before birth. Although people often start showing vulnerabilities and appearing in doctors' surgeries in their late forties and fifties, those vulnerabilities are a result of the resilience, or the lack of it, that has built up over that person's lifetime. It's down to parental relationships, educational experience, exposure to poverty and so forth. What GPs see in a ten-minute surgery appointment are the outcomes for the previous forty-five years. However, there is no immediate political mileage in tackling this. In terms of short-term election advantage, there's little to show for enacting public health policies that won't reap any rewards for decades to come. But that doesn't mean it isn't the right thing to do.

In Bristol, we've tried to approach things differently. The One City Plan allows us to think about and plot health outcomes in the decades ahead. I've also tried to give Christina, our director of public health, a more prominent role in decision-making. She is on leadership calls and asked for advice on all sorts of issues. Even before I was mayor, I approached our local enterprise partnership and challenged them over their economic strategy: 'You talk about skills', I told them, 'but nowhere have you talked about health. Yet health is an economic issue.' A healthier, more robust workforce leads to fewer days of absenteeism. If Bristol can go out there and say we have the healthiest workforce in Europe, what might that do for inward investment? And that cuts to the core of public health – whatever area of government you look at, it plays an important but overlooked and underfunded role.

One of the biggest challenges of recent years has been the rise in mental health issues. Although the increase can, in part, be explained by greater awareness – in the past many people went undiagnosed or simply did not come forward – we have also seen an increase in many of the main drivers. Economic insecurity and inequality have risen, and this is without the effects of isolation and other issues that have arisen since the pandemic.

It's difficult not to respond to the world around you without feeling some anxiety. As a kid growing up in the 1980s, I spent several years obsessing about the threat of nuclear war. I had a whole routine worked out about what would happen if we got the four-minute warning. I would make sure I was with my mum, and we'd run round to my nan and grandad's. It was family I wanted to see, to offer them my support and reassurance.

The other day I was thinking about what my children think about climate change. Does their generation look at the world burning and wonder if it's still going to be there when they grow up? We have begun to talk about the stress of living with climate change, especially the fears of our young people, and it's something that we will need to be more aware of. For them, it's another cause for anxiety on top of the many economic problems they face. They're looking at a future, wondering if they'll ever be able to own their own home, living in flat shares for years, or having to live with their parents into their thirties and forties. All this risks stunting their development as adults and being able to live fulfilled lives.

At the same time, there is an additional layer of pressure that comes with social media. The perfect life portrayed in people's posts on Facebook or Instagram may be artificial but it's difficult not to respond to them, comparing them with the difficulties we face in the real world. That's not only social media, of course. It's reinforced by TV programmes from *Love Island* to *Cribs*. And the way that much of the online narrative, particularly on Twitter, is often laced with bile, binary options and extremism.

If you're a public figure, it's impossible to get away from this stuff. I've had my fair share of abuse online – if there is such a thing as a 'fair' share. But nine times out of ten the trolls are hiding their own sadness and struggle behind the aggression they publish online. It's a front to mask whatever is going on underneath.

When it first started happening, I was quite sensitive to it. In 2008, in the early days of social media, when I was working in public health, someone wrote about me in an online blog, claiming some sort of collusion between the health service, the government and the Black Development Agency, which I had previously worked for. The claims were spurious but what shocked me was finding my name out there. I was furious: I didn't know this person, they didn't know me, and here they were making all sorts of nonsense tying me and the Black-led organization I worked for to some conspiracy. I got their email address and replied, firmly pointing out their privileged position, among other things. I now know it's not the best way to deal with this.

One thing I find most confusing is online attacks from people who should be allies. When I first ran for mayor in 2012, it was the Greens who attacked first. I was very new to the world of Twitter at the time and so this seemingly came from nowhere. It gave me reason to pause. Why are they attacking me at the cost of potential allyship? I wondered. I wasn't a party product-line candidate. I'm a mixed-race kid from the inner city focused on poverty: I've worked in the voluntary sector, I've worked for charities, I've worked on the Jubilee 2000 campaign. Yet there they were, taking lumps out of me.

Over the years, I have learned through experience that some of the most vicious attacks can come from those who could be politically closest to you – driven by a pursuit for purity or their fight to own what would otherwise be a shared political space. When I worked for Sojourners in the US, which had come out of the civil rights movement, a member of staff told me about an incident where someone was chastised for their attitude. 'It's OK to live in line with the values that you profess to be fighting for,' they were told. When people are fighting for a good cause, it sometimes makes them feel that they have a free pass on how they behave towards others. There's an element of this in all activism, perhaps particularly in progressive left circles where we (and I include myself in this) are inclined to believe we occupy the high point of political rightness.

It's easy to criticize from the sidelines. Touchline prophets I call them. It's a phrase I made up for the speech I gave when I introduced Ed Miliband to the 2012 Labour Party conference. They are people who watch and criticize and tell everyone how they should do things, without ever having played the game themselves. On the wall of my office, I have a poster of Theodore Roosevelt's 'The Man in the Arena' speech: 'It is not the critic who counts,' he said, 'not the man who points out how the strong man stumbles, or where the doer of deeds could have done them better. The credit belongs to the man who is actually in the arena, whose face is marred by dust and sweat and blood . . . who errs, who comes short again and again, because there is no effort without error and shortcoming . . .' It's there to remind me, and others, when the negative comments come in. I have given the poster to my son.

When the critics go after people I work with, rather than me, it's particularly hard. There was an incident when Christina made a comment that was quickly misinterpreted, whether accidentally or deliberately, and social media descended on her. I was really upset for her. Christina is such a good person, phenomenally competent, and these were people making mischief at her expense. She offered to resign, a sign of her integrity. I dismissed that out of hand – 'It hasn't even crossed my mind.' And it hadn't. To me it was the usual background noise and was insignificant. But it's another reminder that trolls don't always think about the consequences of what they say to others online, and the ensuing stress it puts people under.

It has an effect on our ability to run the city, too, not least since it has consequences for recruitment. There have been occasions where people we've wanted to bring in have seen some of the abuse and comments online directed at city employees and have then had second thoughts about coming to work for us. We've lost people we wanted to hire. A recruiter told us it put several thousand pounds on the salary we'd need to pay to get people here.

We get more Freedom of Information requests, FOIs, than any of the other core cities in the UK, by quite some margin. Some of those requests are genuine: others are from individuals and groups promoting their particular political brand. It gives them a sense of significance for a moment, but for us, it's costly and time-consuming – time and money that could be spent on more important things. It's got to the point where people have even put in an FOI over the number of FOIs that we have responded to. It would be funny if it wasn't so costly.

All of this is part and parcel of the job and I've learned to deal with it. If I hadn't, I wouldn't be able to function.

I was talking about social media abuse with someone recently and they said, 'It must be really hard.' So I told them it wasn't really, not compared to what we'd experienced growing up in Bristol. In comparison, mean comments from activists and commentators who, more often than not, come from privileged, white, middle-class backgrounds, mean very little.

I have taken to blocking people online. I started doing it to set an example to young people in particular. If someone is being foolish or bringing toxicity into your life, block them! If the mayor is doing it, you can too. A number of opposition councillors were very angry about this and said I was being anti-democratic. But I'm not stopping anyone from posting. I am just not engaging. One councillor who had been particularly mischievous over the years was making particular hay over this in a full council meeting. So I blocked him as he spoke. It was quite amusing to some, but it remained very serious for my children and others.

Being mayor, even if I didn't have to deal with such abuse, is still a highly pressured and stressful job. Like anyone, there are moments when I find things difficult, but I'm fortunate that I can generally cope with what's thrown at me. My faith helps. I've found the logic in the Serenity Prayer especially helpful: 'God, grant me the serenity to accept the things I can't change, courage to change the things I can, and wisdom to know the difference.'

Having good people around me is really important, too. I've got a great team. I've mentioned Kevin but I also had Simon Cowley from day one. When I came in, he was a very junior member of the mayor's admin team. Over the years, he has grown into one of the most trustworthy and dependable people in my world. I know that not everything is on my shoulders, that we're in this together, and Kevin and Simon have got talents I don't have that I can draw on when needed. I'm there for them, and they're there for me. I've found over the years that the more stressed other people are, the less stressed I get. I'm not sure how much of that is down to my own resilience and how much of it is down to them taking the stress on my behalf. But I do know that if I can portray a sense of calm, then hopefully it filters down through the organization.

Good mental health is important for everyone. None of us is immune to the consequences of poor mental health. And I know all too well how important it is, because of what happened to my brother.

I was in my morning meeting at work when I found out about Martin. I was with Kevin, our chief exec, and other members of the executive team. It was a key meeting to work through the financial difficulties that faced us and their consequences for service provision. It was quite full-on, so when I heard my phone vibrate, I ignored it. It buzzed again. I ignored it once more. Then it buzzed a third time. I still didn't answer, but I did begin to think that I needed to take this. I discreetly looked at my phone and saw the missed calls were from my sister Dionne in Switzerland. As I did so a message pinged up: 'Call me.'

I apologized to the others and stepped outside, heading for the CEO's office. I'd pressed call as I left so Dionne had already picked up by the time I got into the room.

'Marvin, Martin tried to take his own life and he's in hospital.'

'What?' I struggled to process what she was saying. 'What's happened?'

My mind was racing. I started thinking about Pauline, Martin's mum, Leon, our and Martin's brother, and Martin's son and his mum, and wondering how they were feeling. Even though I had worked in mental health, I still didn't really understand what it all meant. I assumed that Martin had tried to take his own life, survived and was now safe in hospital, in good hands and on the way to recovery. I started thinking about the conversation we would have once he had fully recovered. We would all share our relief, pain, love and anger with him and ask him what he had been thinking and how he could have put us through this and how we could now support him.

But at that moment, I didn't know what to do. I like to think of myself as a fixer. I'm not necessarily effective, but it's where I find my value. In this situation, I felt useless. I returned to the meeting and waited to hear more. 'Everything OK?' the CEO asked.

'Yeah, fine,' I replied. Of course, I wasn't. I was in a parallel reality. I might not always be the most emotionally expressive person, but that doesn't mean my emotions don't run deep. Here, they were swirling in opposite directions. One part of me was rooting for my brother, willing him to be OK. But another part was seriously angry with him for what he'd tried to do, and what he was putting everyone else through, and because he didn't know we loved him.

That might sound harsh, but I always remember my friend and political agent Kelvin telling me about the hospital unit he was in after he broke his back in a motorcycle accident. The unit was full of people who'd tried and failed to take their lives by jumping from a high place. They all had back injuries – some of them would be in wheelchairs for the rest of their lives, while others needed permanent care. They'd suffered life-altering consequences, consequences that they and those around them would have to live with for ever.

Martin had always been a mix. He was emotional and expressive, a loving brother. He was phenomenally creative, a gifted artist who could draw, design and rap. I'll always remember the first time I heard him. I was walking with Mum and Dionne up Stapleton Road, and we bumped into him. He had a mini tape player on him, told us he'd got into music and had some on tape. We took it in turns to put the headphones on and listen. When it was my turn, what I heard blew me away. It was one of those moments when the non-verbal communication has to kick in because words aren't enough. I looked him square in the eyes and said, 'No, I mean that's really good.'

Martin grew into a hugely influential MC – he performed as Sirplus, and those in the know knew how good he was. Have a look on

YouTube and you'll see what the fuss was about. His music always gave me a bit of street cred – I'd tell people I was Sirplus's brother, and they'd look at me in disbelief and say, 'You're Plus's brother?' And I'd have to say, 'Yeah, Martin,' just to establish that our relationship was pre-Sirplus. Sadly, he didn't really appreciate this, and once told me he didn't want to do anything that caused me problems. I tried to reassure him, telling him again and again that that was far from the case. He was a source of pride for me.

Martin's career was one always on the cusp and it finally seemed that it was about to take off. At the time of his suicide attempt, he was signed up to go on tour across Europe with a national artist.

He was so gifted, but he could also be what we saw as moody. It seemed to be the flip side of his creativity. In my limited under-standing, I came to see it as a trait that came with his talent in the way some creative people in the public eye seem to carry emotional burdens along with their gifts. He'd disappear, going off the radar for weeks at a time. As with anyone, there could be tensions. But he remained one of the most loving, kindest, gentlest souls you could hope to meet. Sometimes I wish I had more of that. My need to be useful has its positives, but engaging through actions and plans means I don't just sit in the moment with people, which can leave me with an awareness that I'm missing out.

My sister told me that Martin was at Southmead Hospital. After our budget meeting, I told Kevin what had happened and in the afternoon I went up there, my head swirling with different thoughts and emotions all the way. When I arrived, the family was all there: my mum, Pauline, Leon, Ellie, my other brothers and sisters and members of the wider family. Dionne was booking flights from Switzerland and would be with us within days. And that's the way it would be throughout his stay, a visitor's room full of family.

It was so good to have them there. Seeing him was a shock. He lay on the bed, unconscious, wired up to all the hospital machinery. The doctor explained that he'd suffered traumatic brain injury because he had been starved of oxygen. At one point, his heart had stopped as well. The doctor said they didn't know what would happen but I remained convinced he would pull through. Of course, that wasn't based on any medical evidence but simply on the impossibility of the situation we found ourselves in. It just didn't seem possible that Martin could cease to be. And it didn't seem possible that something as big as suicide could find its way into our family. One week, two weeks, then he'd be back. I was certain of it.

I sat at his bedside and talked to him. 'Martin, it's Marvin. What happened? Everyone is here waiting for you. Come on, we need you back.' We didn't know if he could hear us because the medics didn't yet know the full extent of the brain damage. They told us he might be deaf and blind or he might be able to hear and see us but unable to respond.

One week became two weeks, became a month, became two months. They moved him down to a hospital in Plymouth and we'd travelled down there to see him – me, Leon, Pauline, the whole family – but his condition didn't improve. Months turned into a year. I was very conscious of the toll this was taking on Pauline, Leon, Ellie and Marley. Eventually, he was moved again, this time to The Dean in Gloucester, a specialist rehab unit. Martin and I were a similar build as young men, but he built up his muscles with years of training. Two hundred push-ups a day was one of his routines. Years earlier, at Dionne's wedding in Switzerland, we were all at a swimming lake. As he emerged from the water, my sister Dionne started everyone singing 'Mysterious Girl' by Peter Andre – Martin's muscular physique was every bit as impressive as Peter Andre's in the video. Now, though, after months in a hospital bed, his body was changing. Each time we visited, he was thinner and thinner, older and older. It was brutal to watch. Whether he knew we were there or not, I don't know. His eyes would drift around the room, but we were never sure if he was looking at anything, taking us in.

After fifteen long months, the end came quite abruptly. The family got a call telling us that Martin's condition had deteriorated and we should come to Gloucester immediately. We all dropped what we were doing and drove up: there must have been about fifteen or twenty of us who made the trip, a mixture of family and close friends. When we got there, we sat and waited for news, talking about life and talking about Martin. We were together. We were in one unreal reality, and about to enter another.

After we'd been there a couple of hours, the nurse took Pauline and

Leon in. Then she came back and said Leon had asked for me. The nurse took me to the room next door and told me Martin had died. I felt numb. I went to look for Pauline and Leon. He was sitting on the floor, leaning up against the wall with his head in his hands. He's a big guy, fifteen stone or so at the time. He might have been the younger brother but he had always looked after Martin. When I saw him there like that, that was the moment it hit me. I went back into the waiting room with all the family and tried to tell them what happened.

The police later said that when they went to his flat, they found reams and reams of lyrics all written out. If you listen to him perform you can hear how articulately he could capture and express the pain he felt inside.

> It's cold on the road and I'm old and I dunno my worth no more . . .
> Because in life I been hurt so many times that it don't even hurt no
> more . . .
> Spent so many nights on the floor that I don't wanna lie in the dirt
> no more . . .

In real life, though, he found it much more difficult to talk. As did I. I wish I had talked more, wish that I'd tried at least. I wish I had told him more often how proud I was of him, how much I loved him, how incredible it was for me to have him as a brother.

The press, to give them their due, were careful and respectful in the way they reported it. I decided I would only say something when Pauline and Leon said it was OK. Rather than speak to the media, though, I've only really discussed what happened in talks when I thought it might help. If a mental health charity asks me about Martin, for example, I'm happy to speak and share my experiences.

It means a lot, too, to see how he was remembered by the community: in the Mina Road tunnel in St Werburgh's, there was an amazing mural that celebrated his work. Someone made the mistake of painting over it but that was quickly put right, and a new mural was painted next to Mina Road Park.

When I think about Martin now, my memory always goes back to when we were children. I'd have been about twelve and he was five. He and Leon would come and stay at Mum's, so I'd go over to Pauline's to collect them. On the way back, I made the pushchair do wheelies. He loved that. When they got older and were too big for that, they'd have to walk. I was already dreaming about joining the army, even back then, so I'd challenge myself to give them a piggyback all the way home. It was just over half a mile or so and those boys weren't small. The nearer I got to home, the heavier they'd become. But I'd always carry them as far as I could. If only I could have found a way to do the same as an adult.

1 3 .

Race and Class

When I was growing up in Bristol, I didn't know who Edward Colston was. Colston was just a word, a place name scattered across the city. If you went to one of the schools associated with him, then you would have been told about him. But at my school, in my circles, he wasn't mentioned. I took no notice of the eighteen-foot bronze statue of him in the middle of the city centre.

If I had gone to one of the various schools that Colston had helped to found and fund, the story I would have been taught is what I'd call the philanthropist version. Colston was born in Bristol in 1636 into a wealthy merchant family. They subsequently moved to London, where he went to school, and although he would later become Conservative MP for Bristol, he never returned to live in the city as an adult.

Like his father, Colston became a merchant, originally trading in textiles and wool, and amassed a considerable fortune. He gave a significant amount of money to charity, both during his lifetime and, via various legacies, after his death in 1721. He donated more than £70,000 to charitable institutions, the equivalent of £5.5 million today. He also founded alms-houses and schools, and gave money to churches, including Bristol Cathedral, although his munificence was confined to institutions that were in some way connected with the Church of England. In the mid-eighteenth century, the Colston Society was set up to commemorate and celebrate his work. The Society established an annual church service to give thanks for his generosity. At the end of every service, large, sugar-sprinkled buns were handed out to the children in the congregation. Inevitably, these were called Colston Buns.

The bulk of Colston's fortune, however, came from the kidnapping, enslavement and trafficking of African people. In the 1670s, a number of members of his family became involved with the Royal African Company and in 1680 Colston himself joined the company as a shareholder, rising to become its deputy governor a decade later. Founded by Charles II, the company's governor was the king, which was an honorary role. The power, therefore, lay in the hands of the sub-governor and the deputy governor.

The Royal African Company traded in enslaved Africans. It took them from the west coast of Africa to the Americas, primarily to provide labour for plantations in North America and the Caribbean. From 1672 to 1698, the Royal African Company had a monopoly in this trade.

During Colston's tenure, it is estimated that almost 85,000 enslaved Africans were transported by the company. There were appalling conditions on board, with the enslaved shackled together and lying in their own filth. A combination of disease, murder and suicide led to between 10 and 20 per cent of the slaves dying before reaching shore. Sharks learned to follow the ships, waiting for the bodies of the sick and the dead that were thrown overboard. These 'losses' were claimed on insurance.

Precisely how much of his fortune Colston made from his involvement with the Royal African Company is disputed. Many accounts suggest that he made the equivalent of millions, if not tens of millions, from his 'investment'. Whatever the sum, that Colston made money from the company and was heavily involved in its decision-making is clear. His benevolence to the city of Bristol, therefore, is based at least partly on earnings from the slave trade.

None of his complexity was traditionally taught: that he gave money, but only to certain types of people and institutions – he didn't like Catholics for example – nor that the money was made from this slavery. Those who went to his schools were only taught about his charity. The stories of his philanthropy were then passed down through the generations. Over the years, they were embellished. One tale even suggests that a dolphin stopped one of his ships from sinking by plugging a hole in the hull with its body. There was something almost spiritual in the way that people spoke about him, not unlike the way in which America honours its founding fathers. It's almost blasphemous to question their morality: founding fathers could be – and indeed were – slave owners, but it is still somehow acceptable. Founding fathers, it seems, transcend the ability to sin.

The Colston myth is thought to have been created to quell the political unrest that was building across Bristol's working classes. Lionizing Colston gave them and the city a founding father figure to revere.

In 2007, I stood in front of the Colston statue, microphone in hand, looking to the cameraman for my cue. I was in the middle of making a film, *Unfinished Business*, for *Inside Out*, the BBC's regional TV documentary strand.

It was the 200th anniversary of the act of parliament that abolished the slave trade (although it would be another twenty-six years before those who were already enslaved would be given their freedom). For Bristol, the anniversary was of particular significance. In the century between Edward Colston's stewardship of the Royal African Company and abolition, Bristol had played a major role in the transatlantic slave trade: more than 2,000 slave ships were fitted out in the city, which carried half a million people from West Africa to the Americas. Under the banner Abolition 200, Bristol was spending a quarter of a million pounds on commemorative events, including Breaking The Chains, a two-year-long exhibition at the British Empire and Commonwealth Museum, education projects through which secondary schools were sent boxes of shackles and other artefacts, and what was billed as a 'People's Service' at Bristol Cathedral.

But was Bristol equipped to have this conversation about this aspect of its history? Local filmmakers Rob Mitchell, Shawn Sobers and I weren't sure. We didn't feel the city was ready to discuss the issues properly, and so we pitched a film to the BBC which would look at the history and legacy of Bristol's relationship with the slave trade. The commissioning editor, a guy called Roger Farrant, looked at the proposal and promptly rejected it. 'I don't think there's a story in it,' he told us.

Six months later, Farrant came back, apparently having had a change of heart. 'We've got nothing in the pipeline for next year,' he explained. 'Can you do that documentary idea for us, after all?'

At the same time as the BBC were deliberating over whether there was a story in our proposal, discussions continued as to whether Bristol should apologize for its role in the slave trade. In 1994, the city of Liverpool – like Bristol, heavily involved in slavery – had offered a public apology. By contrast, Bristol's 1996 Festival of the Sea made no mention of slavery. In May 2006, Dr Gareth Griffiths, then director of the British Empire and Commonwealth Museum, set up an Apology Debate, bringing together a panel of experts to discuss the issue. Opinions in the city were sharply divided. The front-page headline of the *Bristol Evening Post* read 'It's time the city said sorry', but the philosopher Professor Anthony Grayling, chairing the debate, dismissed the idea as 'a rather empty gesture however sincere it might be'. Those at the meeting voted overwhelmingly in favour of a formal apology. By contrast, in a subsequent telephone poll for BBC Points West, 91.7 per cent of 10,000 viewers voted against an apology. In the end, the then Lord Mayor of Bristol, together with other political, business and religious leaders, signed a 'Statement of Regret' over Bristol's role. Regret, of course, is distinct from an apology, avoiding any potential liability. And this was a course followed on a national level, too, with the then Prime Minister Tony Blair offering an expression of 'deep sorrow' over the country's role in the slave trade.

That was the background to the documentary we were making. Here I was, a mixed-race man, trying to come to terms with a city that was fractured by race in the present, and had a complex and distasteful (to put it mildly) relationship with race in the past. As someone with a white mother and a Black father, how did I make sense of that? Over the filming of the documentary, I got to speak to a whole range of people on the subject – young and old, rich and poor, Black and white.

For me, it was both a fascinating opportunity to get a sense of the different opinions on the issue and also one that allowed me to reconnect with the city I grew up in. When I left Bristol to go to university in Swansea, I wasn't engaged with the city and its politics. I was escaping it and, politically, I was more interested in global issues: I was passionate about world poverty and in the behaviour of multi-nationals. When I came back to Bristol in the mid-1990s, it was initially to work for Tearfund, whose work resonated with the things that drove me: poverty, injustice, international development, Jubilee 2000 and the cancellation of third-world debt, landmines, unfair trade. I then went back to the US and my mind was elsewhere.

It was only when I returned from America that I started to engage properly on a local level. I got a job working for Radio Bristol and immediately I found myself tuning in to the city a lot more. It was then that I became properly conscious of Bristol's particular political dynamic. And that was when I first became properly aware of Edward Colston and his legacy.

It was fitting, therefore, for the documentary to feature me standing next to the statue. Designed by the sculptor John Cassidy, it was made of bronze on a pedestal of Portland stone. It depicts Colston leaning thoughtfully on a stick, with a bronze dolphin on each corner, both a nod to his family crest and the story about his sinking ship. There are plaques depicting Colston at the harbour, handing out money to the poor, and one of them carries the legend: 'Erected by citizens of Bristol as a memorial of one of the most virtuous and wise sons of their city AD 1895.' Yet most people who passed it, as I had when I was growing up in the city, didn't give the statue a second glance.

How significant were Bristol's statements of regret? As a rule, I'm generally wary of apologies of this kind: there is, as suggested by Anthony Grayling, a danger that they are no more than empty gestures. Bristol churches had first attempted a reconciliation process a decade before, starting the conversation about the city's slaving history. They had argued that there was a spiritual aspect of the history that impacted on our ability to live together and become whole. The churches had got together, held a joint prayer service and apologized. Then the members of Bristol's Black churches walked back down the hill to second-class schools while the white churches stayed on the top of the hill.

For me, this is the salient issue. I am wary of symbolic apologies that aren't attached to real policies and real economics. If I'm given a choice between walking down Colston Street to a well-paid job that enables me to feed my family and serve the rest of my community, or walking down Smith Street to unemployment, I'll walk down Colston Street. At the end of the day, it's about the reality.

The churches getting together might have made for an emotional service, but the life chances of Bristol's children according to the colour of their skin didn't change after the apology. And they didn't change after the city's statement of regret, either. A lack of change leads to frustration, which in turn leads to a feeling of resentment from the white establishment. *We apologized and still people aren't happy. What more can we do?* When that becomes the prevailing sentiment, you're in a worse position at the end than you were at the beginning. And all the while the underlying issues remain unresolved, with dormant feelings ready to emerge again at a later date.

On 25 May 2020, at the Cup Foods grocery store in Minneapolis, Minnesota, George Floyd bought a packet of cigarettes with a $20 bill. Floyd had lived in Minneapolis for a number of years, having moved there from Houston, Texas. He had been working as a bouncer before being made unemployed due to the Coronavirus pandemic. He was a regular customer at the store, and although known to the owner, it was a teenage employee working that night.

That teenage employee thought that Floyd's $20 bill might be counterfeit. He called the police at 20.01 local time. At 20.08, two police officers arrived. One, Thomas Lane, drew his gun and pulled Floyd out of the parked car that he was sitting in round the corner from the store. Floyd was handcuffed. When the police officers tried to put Floyd in a police car, he refused. More officers arrived, among them police officer Derek Chauvin. Another failed attempt at getting Floyd in the car ended with Chauvin pulling Floyd onto the ground. As Floyd was restrained, Chauvin put his knee between Floyd's head and neck. As passers-by filmed the incident on their phones, Chauvin kept his knee there for nearly nine minutes. More than twenty times, Floyd said he couldn't breathe. Six minutes in, Floyd became unresponsive. At 20.27, Chauvin removed his knee. Floyd was taken to the Hennepin County Medical Center, where he was pronounced dead an hour later.

I was at home when I heard the news. I didn't watch the video. I still haven't. Some incidents are just too painful to witness. Tragically, the murder of George Floyd is just one of a long line of such instances and injustices. Breonna Taylor. Tony McDade. Ahmaud Arbery. Eric Garner. Trayvon Martin. Recently, the US TV series *When They See Us*, about the 1989 Central Park jogger case, was broadcast in the UK. Again, I couldn't watch it. I find that sort of thing incredibly difficult to view.

I'm still not completely sure why the George Floyd case blew up while that of Eric Garner or Trayvon Martin or the countless other deaths failed to do so. The fact that it was captured on camera is part of it. Maybe it was primed by the American footballer Colin Kaepernick taking the knee and losing his career. Maybe it was the fact the Black Lives Matter movement had built up more of a presence. Looking back to the example of Rosa Parks, she refused to stand up on the bus on a number of occasions. Then, one day, it took off. It wasn't the first time it had happened, but it was the moment that caught. It was the same with the death of George Floyd. For whatever reason, when the elements align, it becomes a moment.

Once that had happened, it was clear that the inevitable protests would not be confined to the US but would ripple out across the world. In Bristol, as mayor, I found myself trying to balance people's right to protest alongside the fact that we were in the middle of the worst pandemic that the country had faced for over a hundred years. I worried that if 10,000 people in close proximity turned up to protest, there might be a big surge in Covid cases. There was a dark irony there, too. People would be protesting for Black Lives Matter while the statistics showed that it was Black lives that were being disproportionately taken by the virus. The question that we struggled with in the days leading up to the protests was how to manage the situation. The protests were going to happen. How could we allow people to make their voices heard, but do so in a way that didn't create health risks for all and disproportionately for the Black community?

I wanted to make sure that my own voice as mayor was clear on the issue. On behalf of the Core Cities group, I wrote and coordinated a joint letter to the African American Mayors Association. In it, we pledged our support to the American Mayors and criticized the then President Donald Trump's approach to race and democracy in general and his response to the Black Lives Matter protests in particular.

'We in the UK have faced our own racial inequalities from entrenched economic and political inequalities to the Windrush Scandal and deaths in custody,' the letter stated. 'Racism scars our nation as well; we recognize your story, which is why what happens in your country and cities matters here.' The letter quoted Dr King's 1963 statement that 'we are caught in an inescapable network of mutuality, tied in a single garment of destiny. Whatever affects one directly affects all indirectly.' The letter concluded that, 'we want to thank you for the stand you have taken in the face of the President, and for being a source of political hope in a country that to the outside world appears to be losing its way and losing its hope. Your leadership today holds a new level of global significance, and we want you to know that we want to stand by you, however we can.'

The letter was a big deal. It was unusual for the group to come out with such an overtly political letter. But, not for the first time, an initiative led by regional rather than national politicians didn't get the media coverage it should have done. The same was true of the decision to change the name of Colston Hall. The hall, which has been a music venue in the city since 1867, was in need of refurbishment, and though owned by Bristol City Council, it is managed by the Bristol Music Trust. The refurbishment required funding, and when it came up for discussion I made my view clear that the name would need to change. The Trust did a great job consulting with people across the city and made the decision to change the name to Bristol Beacon in February 2020 with plans to announce this with a big ceremony in April. But then the pandemic and lockdown happened, so the announcement was postponed.

The renaming of the hall had been part of the ongoing debate about Edward Colston's role in the city's past and present. In 2017, Colston's Girls' School went through a similar consultation process as to whether to change its name. At the time, the conclusion was

that a name change would be of 'no benefit' to the school. A letter
to parents and former pupils explained the rationale: 'After much
discussion, it has been agreed that it would not be appropriate to
rename the school. There is no doubt that Colston's Girls' School
exists today as an outstanding school for girls, nationally known for
its academic excellence and well respected for its inclusivity and
diversity – because of the financial endowment given by Edward
Colston, but we see no benefit in denying the school's financial origin
and obscuring history itself.' (In 2020, the school was subsequently
renamed as Montpelier High School, to 'allow the school to forge a
new identity that represents its diverse and inclusive community'.)

In the same year, there'd been a debate about the Colston statue
as well. It was suggested that we add a second plaque. As well as the
one saying Colston was a wise and virtuous son of the city, this would
refer to his activities in the slave trade. But the negotiations over the
wording were tortuous. The interested parties met in my office. The
historian Dr Madge Dresser, who had done a lot to tell the story of
Black Bristolians, pushed for a radical rewrite laying bare Colston's
slaving history. A member of the Society of Merchant Venturers (the
society that had originally contributed to the funding of the statue),
rejected the wording on the grounds that the claims about Colston
and slavery were unverifiable. In the end, the agreed wording was so
watered down I said the city wasn't going to pay for it. There was a
belief that I was under pressure to get something done, and I was. But
I said I'd rather let the city contend with the fact that we still couldn't
reach agreement than put up meaningless wording.

The growing interest in Colston was down to the work of a campaigning group who wanted Bristol to acknowledge his full legacy. I
knew people in the group and I supported what they were doing. It
was horrific and a personal affront to have a statue commemorating
a person who had committed so much evil. But removing it needed
proper discussion, which would have meant expending a huge amount
of political capital, time and money. That would have limited our ability to tackle the issues that underpin racism – housing, hunger, work
experience, health and education. So, despite my personal views on the
statue, removing it was not top of the list of things I needed to do for
Bristol as mayor. Politics is a careful mix of the symbolic and practical.

Yes, symbolic acts can be launchpads for change. But they can also become means of safeguarding the status quo and sources of cynicism if they are detached from practical changes. I am wary that symbolic acts detached from practical policy can be more about feeding the emotional needs of the privileged than they are about the status of people disadvantaged by historical injustices. Removing the statue would have undermined my ability to drive those changes through.

The position of a Black politician when it comes to race is a difficult one. On the one hand, more is expected of you, but, in some ways, you have less latitude to act because everything you do on race is amplified. That amplification can be used and misinterpreted as showing a lack of interest in white people. I was once asked by a group of young Black people if I felt restricted on talking about race. My answer was that I wouldn't use the word *restricted*, but I would say that you have to be smart. If I'm dealing with opposition politicians describing me as an inner-city mayor, as the Conservatives have done, then we all know what that really means. You have to know how to respond.

I've learned over the years that it's broadly damned if you do, damned if you don't. On one side, there's pressure for immediate action and results: you've been elected, now solve racism! At the same time, there's pressure not to talk about matters of race – and not only from those on the right. One leading Black politician, who I won't name, once said to me, 'The left will never forgive you if you talk about their racism.' When I have spoken on the subject, even some who would describe themselves as being on the left have accused me of playing 'the race card', particularly if it exposes how white middle-class activists have held me and Asher to account for the system that supported their private education. When the argument highlights their privilege and challenges their activist status, they have been quick to echo right-wing claims that I'm only putting race forward at the expense of the many other challenges we face as a society.

In the run-up to the Black Lives Matter protests in Bristol – and elsewhere – despite a few stories in the press, there was nothing to indicate what was about to happen. My focus was trying to manage the right for people to protest while doing so in a way that was safe. One suggestion was for Bristolians to take the knee and send a photograph showing them doing so to President Trump. We set up a hashtag, so that people who wanted to protest but didn't feel comfortable in a crowd still had the opportunity to do so. For those planning to attend the protest in person, we put out messages about social distancing, the importance of wearing masks and carrying hand sanitizer.

The crowds who turned up did all that. But they did a lot more besides.

On the day of the protest, I was out with my three kids, on a riverside walk in the Avon Valley. It had been a hectic week and it was good to get some fresh air and spend time with my children. They are conscious of my job and my constant itch to check my phone and they call me out when they catch me looking. 'Put your phone down, Daddy' is their immediate response every time I reach for it. It's a balancing act to give them the attention they deserve while trying to keep up to date with what's going on.

On this particular Sunday, it was clear that something really was going on. I remember standing down by the side of a small riverside lake, my children playing on the edge of the water while my phone vibrated constantly. It was a peaceful, natural scene but the real world kept breaking in. The head of my comms team, Saskia Konyenburg, was giving me a running commentary on how the protest was unfolding. *There's 2,000 people. There's 5,000 people. There's 10,000 people*, she texted. Wow. I was worried about the Covid implications. But I was worried, too, about who those 10,000 people were. I was concerned there might be people down there hijacking the event for their own ends, less interested in the politics of race equality than the opportunity to confront the system. I was particularly concerned about self-declared activists from middle-class backgrounds who had spent the previous four years suggesting that I shouldn't talk about race because when I did it divided the working class.

Saskia texted again. *There are ropes around the statue.*

'Daddy! You're on your phone again!'

'Daddy! Put your phone away . . .'

They are trying to pull the statue down . . .

The statue's down.

It was surreal, as if normal reality had been suspended. At the same time, it was exciting. I won't deny that was how I felt. I could feel the adrenaline coursing through. As events continued to unfold and the statue was carried along and dumped in the docks, it felt like a piece of historical poetry was being played out. Essentially, it was a lynching. The statue being hauled down, kicked and rolled through the streets, the use of ropes. Then there was the fact that Colston's slave ships were moored down at the docks. The DNA of enslaved Africans forcibly carried away in those ships would have filtered out into that water.

This is now a situation, I told myself. It was scary, to be honest. There's a famous quote from Mike Tyson about how everyone has a plan until they get punched in the face. That was pretty much where I was at. Saskia texted me to say that Channel 4 wanted to do a TV interview. I explained to the children what was happening, called my wife and we headed home. On the way back, I tried to figure out what I was going to say. I was aware of the atmosphere and that emotions were running high and I didn't want to inflame things further. I could see them asking the kinds of question that would pitch law and order against the hauling down of a slaver's statue. In the end, I decided I would simply tell them what I thought. I stopped trying to find the right words and settled on telling it straight.

'Mr Rees,' the Channel 4 presenter Krishnan Guru-Murthy began, 'do you support the police in their search for those responsible for criminal damage, or do you support the tearing down of the statue?'

'Putting up those binary options really doesn't help us navigate a complicated world,' I replied. 'What I cannot do as an elected politician is support criminal damage or social disorder like this. But I would never pretend that the statue of a slaver in the middle of Bristol, the city in which I grew up, as someone who may have owned one of my ancestors, is anything other than a personal affront to me.'

'Why was the statue still up?' Guru-Murthy asked. 'Is that a failure of democratic politics or is it the result of democratic politics?'

'It's been a point of debate for the city and tension in the city for some time.' I then explained how Bristol had only recently started to talk about its slaving history in any meaningful way. 'Dare I say politicians and journalists as well did not cover this in a mature way . . . the city has not been equipped to have the debate about what the statue is and the place it holds in giving meaning today.'

'Who has done more criminality?' Guru-Murphy asked. 'Is it the protesters or is it Colston?'

'If you weigh up the two,' I said, 'Colston would clearly be a bigger criminal than the protesters. But again, that offers us a debate that isn't very helpful.' I tried to explain what I felt my role in the situation was. 'As a politician, one of your jobs is to understand your country. In 1967, Martin Luther King Jr said, "I walked the streets of Chicago and looked at people rioting and urged them to be non-violent." And they said to him, but what about our government? They are using massive doses of violence to solve their problems. And King said, "Never again will I speak to the violence of the oppressed and the marginalized without speaking to the biggest purveyors of violence in the world, my own government." Now we have a government that through ten years of austerity and the reduction of services, the loss of hope to many people at the margins of our community, through the Windrush scandal, through the hostile environment, have perhaps created a context within which the frustrations of our people have built up. That's not to justify the violence and the criminal damage, but if you're going to lead, you need to understand the material you're working with.'

It was a good interview. I've always liked the way Krishan Guru-Murthy goes about his business and he pushed me as I'd expected him to do, but as I came off air, I felt happy that I'd made my case. And when calls and texts started coming in, telling me I'd done well, it meant a lot. What I couldn't have known was that would be the first of numerous interviews. Over the next couple of days, as the story and the accompanying images reverberated around the world, I found myself on every show known to humanity. I did interviews with the BBC, ITV, Sky News, Australian TV, BBC World Service, not to mention all the American networks, including NPR, CNN and ABC. I sat at my desk all day, joining and leaving one video call after another. Saskia and her team did an incredible job coordinating it all and I was aware of what a privilege it was to be afforded such a platform. When we totted up the viewing figures over those few days, we estimated that I had spoken to the best part of a quarter of a billion people on the subject.

I found the whole thing exhilarating. You can't do this job unless you like speaking and enjoy being in front of people, but I was still surprised that I didn't feel nervous or overwhelmed by it all. Finding a truth is a great comfort, though. I approached it as I had that first Channel 4 interview, and just shared what I thought. It felt genuine – genuine in my responses and genuine in terms of the politics and honest about the complexity and contradictions. And though the interview schedule seemed daunting, dealing with the media ended up being one of the easier aspects of the aftermath of the statue coming down.

A week later, in St Mary's Churchyard, the headstone of Scipio Africanus, an African man who had been enslaved in the eighteenth century, was vandalized and smashed. 'Now look what you made me do,' the perpetrator had scrawled on the ground in chalk. 'Put Colston's statue back or things will really heat up.'

It was sadly inevitable that there would be a backlash to the statue being toppled. Whether those who desecrated the headstone were local or from a national organization is unclear. But the hate messages had started to arrive: someone sent me a golliwog pin, another a child's mathematics book that used racist imagery and language. Some people just sent threats. To give some sort of sense of the volume we receive at such moments, when Bristol Council passed an 'atonement and reparations' plan in March 2021, my deputy Asher Craig received 2,000 hate mails in a week. I got 4,500.

The week after the statue came down, there were plans for a counter-protest. The word was that a number of 'firms', hardcore supporters of different football teams, along with the Hell's Angels and other biker gangs such as the Wiltshire Force and the Sodbury Crew, were going to be in the city. Their aim was to 'protect the Cenotaph', the war monument which rests just a few metres from the plinth where Colston's statue had stood. As with the Black Lives Matter protest, my instinctive concern was safety: I hoped the protests wouldn't become violent – and while the organizers were planning a peaceful process, that other groups wouldn't hijack the original protests.

I wanted to speak to the organizers personally, to try to get a sense of where they were coming from. I had a city to hold together and having a dialogue with everyone was essential. Some were portraying the organizers as leading a racist reaction to BLM, but I knew it wasn't that simple. I knew a couple of Black people who'd attended, and I was also sensitive to the way in which white middle-class activists condemned white working-class people for racism while ignoring their own. My cousin had some contacts, so I asked if he could connect me with the organizer. One of the leaders agreed to speak to me. He was quite clear that he didn't want it to become a media stunt, but I stressed that I wasn't interested in headlines. I wanted to understand their position. 'Listen, I'm not far right,' the organizer said, at pains to emphasize that.

Kevin, my cousin and I went to his house to see him. He handed me a paper he'd written, which was very race and class literate. It focused on working-class struggles, the history of the football team their firm supported, and their resistance to the far right trying to infiltrate them. It talked about work they were doing to get food out to older, vulnerable members. I'm sure these guys weren't saints, and no doubt they'd had their moments on the terraces, but this man was keen to stress that they were 'not what a number of people are trying to label us as'.

To be frank, I felt good about the three of us who went: Kevin, my chief of staff, who's from a white working-class background; me, mixed-race, Black; and my white, working-class cousin. I don't think there are many political leaders who could have done that. And to be perfectly frank, I felt more at home, more connected with this man than I do with many of the white middle-class activists I come across.

'So what's going on for you guys?' I asked.

He looked at me and said, 'Marv, it feels like we're losing our city.' He spoke about the seeming lawlessness, the feeling that the city was getting out of control and that the space for the working class was getting smaller. He mentioned his suspicions that anarchists were going to move on from the statue to the Cenotaph.

This took me back to the question of what the purpose of Colston

was. The idea that he was something of a founding father was important to a lot of people. If you believed in the stories, then Colston
was part of the soul of the city. He said he didn't actually care about
the statue, but what was clear was that hauling the statue down and
taking his name away became symbolic of another loss of identity, a
loss of belonging, and a loss of control.

'You are losing your city,' I told him. 'But it's not to do with this. It's
to do with house prices and gentrification.'

We talked about what they were seeing and what we were doing.
These were working-class people watching house prices rise to half
a million, pricing them out of parts of the city they had grown up in.
I talked about our housing schemes, and our attempts to build more
homes.

'We've seen that,' the organizer said. 'You need to build more.'

I explained that I also wanted to build a more diverse economy and
again, there was a connection. He understood what I was trying to
do, and what the issues really were.

I'd heard that some of those protesting the counter-rally had been
calling the participants racist scum, to which someone had responded,
'Don't tell my wife I'm racist, she won't be happy.' I worked out that
day who it was when his wife brought us a cup of tea. She was Black.
Then, as we were leaving, he pulled his phone out, and started flick-
ing through his photos, saying, 'Marv, let me show you this.' There, on
his phone, was a picture of me stood with his wife. 'I took this of you
when you were elected,' he explained.

Like I say, it's complicated.

Bringing all sides with you on such issues isn't easy. The key to doing
so is respect.

I don't want a statue of a slaver representing the city, but we
do have to respect the fact that some people now feel that they've
lost a piece of their soul. I have to build a city in which those who
are happy at the statue coming down and the way it happened feel
respected. To ensure that people who are sympathetic to its removal,
but dismayed at the way it happened, feel respected. And that people
who are annoyed at it coming down at all, and horrified at the way

it happened, know that this is a fair city and that they too will be respected. For me, as mayor, though, it seemed that I would need the wisdom of Solomon to navigate this, and take everyone with me, but without having to go so slowly as to lose momentum.

This meant a number of things going forward. First, that the law had to apply and that those who hauled the statue down had to go before the law. Second, we had to get the statue out of the harbour. Leaving it there would have sent its own message.

This, of course, created complications of its own. We didn't want some sort of Jesuslike resurrection ceremony, with crowds standing on the harbourside cheering and clapping as Colston was pulled out of the water. So we left it there for a couple of days while emotions calmed down, then sent the cranes in at five in the morning with no advance notice. Sky News, if I remember rightly, was there, having camped out for days, and a couple of other people turned up. But apart from that, we successfully retrieved the statue and took it to the M Shed, a museum on the harbourside. There, they started work to ensure that it didn't deteriorate any further, but leaving the paint thrown by the protesters and the dents where the statue had been kicked.

Funnily enough, the statue itself isn't worth very much. Rather than being solid, it's actually hollow. The Bristol City Poet, Vanessa Kisuule, wrote a wonderful poem, called 'Hollow', after it came down, which ends as follows:

> Countless times I passed that plinth
> its heavy threat of metal and marble.
> But as you landed a piece of you fell off
> broke away
> and inside
> nothing but air.
> This whole time
> You were hollow.

As the discussions about how to display the statue continued, the more immediate question was what to do with the empty plinth. A couple of days after the statue got pulled down, Saskia told me that the artist Marc Quinn was on the phone. 'He's a really famous sculptor and he wants to make an offer for the plinth,' she said. I didn't know who he was but I took her word for it and took the call, interested to hear what he was proposing. Marc explained that he wanted to make and put a statue of a Black woman there. He said he wanted to provoke a debate.

'That's a really great offer,' I replied, 'and at some point in the future, it would be fantastic to do that. But now is not the time. We've got a really delicately balanced city here. I've got people feeling that a piece of Bristol's soul has been ripped out, that we are on the edge of anarchy. We need orderly processes right now. If we replace the Colston statue with that of a Black woman, you're going to get a reaction. For those insulated from a physical reaction, that's fine. It will just be a heated conversation. But for the isolated Black regional family who become the focal point of people's reactions, that's a problem. We're talking smashed windows, verbal abuse, faeces, even possibly physical abuse. Now isn't the time to stoke that. Right now, the city needs time to breathe.'

I pointed out that images showing the statue of a dead rich white man being rolled through the streets was one thing. But if there was a reaction to Quin's replacement and people pulled down the statue of a living Black woman, it could have very dangerous repercussions. The city couldn't cope with that.

At the end of the call, I thought Marc had got where I was coming from and didn't expect to hear from him again for a while. I certainly didn't expect to hear from him one morning at 5 a.m., when he sent me a text. *Just to let you know, I've put a statue up on the plinth.* I've got to be honest, Marc might be famous in the art world, but I didn't know who he was. When I got the text, I wasn't sure who it was. But when I worked it out, I was shocked. The statue was of Jen Reid, one of the Black Lives Matter protesters, who had climbed onto the statue during the protests and raised her fist in a Black Power salute.

I phoned Marc back as I was walking into work. I was calm personified, even though I was fuming inside.

'What have you done?'

'I've put it up. *The Guardian* are down there right now.'

'And how do they know about it?' I asked.

'Because I phoned them up.'

This was the detail that sealed it for me. This wasn't about what had happened in Bristol. It was all about him. He saw the plinth as a global stage where he could display his work to the world. When I spoke to him later that day, he elaborated, sharing his own insights into racism. 'The arts,' he said, 'is a place where Black people struggle to break in because the wages are low.' I asked him how many local Black artists he had involved in the work. He hadn't included any. I would have had a little bit of respect if he had used the project to give locals a bit of a break. I'd read up on him by then and knew he was a wealthy white guy with aristocratic connections.

'Why don't you take some of your money and set up a scholarship to support Black artists with some of your artistic friends?' I suggested. I explained to him the importance of connecting symbolic acts with real policy and money. I thought that at least we could redeem some of the profile and money he would gain from this and direct it to the practical challenge of tackling racism. He seemed really into the idea but I haven't heard from him since. What made the episode all the more galling is that it played out as I'd predicted: he got his free publicity and the hate crime charity Stand Against Racism and Inequality reported an uptick in hate crime against the people he said he was trying to support.

What should go on that plinth? It's not for me to decide. And it certainly shouldn't be at the behest of another rich white guy. The plinth has to be about – and for – the people of Bristol. I've set up the Bristol History Commission to look into it, a group made up of historians rather than campaigners. The starting point has to be an agreement on what the history we want to celebrate might be. When we've agreed on that, then we can go forward as a city and make it happen.

Until then, the plinth remains empty. I like that. It's the best representation of the fact that we're looking for answers that are not easy to find. Until we find them, that's how the plinth should stay.

A couple of weeks after the Colston Four – the four activists charged with taking the statue down – were cleared, I was meeting a friend at a pub in St Pauls. By chance, the activists were also there. Despite silly stories in the local press about how the meeting was set up, or that the artist Banksy was somehow involved in putting us together, we simply happened to be in the same place – The Star and Garter pub – at the same time.

The Star and Garter is a wonderful community pub, and one with a real history if you know your local music. When I got there, I was stopped by a shout from four older Black guys, first-generation Jamaican Windrush, in their late sixties and seventies, who were standing outside having a smoke.

'Hey Marvin,' they said. 'How's your dad doing?'

I stopped to reminisce about old times. 'We've known you since you was little,' they told me.

I love this sort of interaction. For all the noise, these men took pride in my becoming mayor. And I took pride in them. This was the generation who literally had to fight to make the streets safe for kids like me to walk down.

As we were talking, the person I was there to meet came out and said, 'Hey Marvin, just to let you know the Colston Four are in there, sat inside having a drink.'

OK, I thought. This could get interesting.

'Do you want to go somewhere else?' she asked.

I shook my head. 'This is my area,' I replied. 'This is where I grew up. These guys' – I nodded at the friends I was talking to – 'are my people. Why would I go somewhere else?'

I stayed there for a bit longer, talking about my childhood and my family, and then went inside. I didn't know what the Four looked like, so found myself walking straight past them and sat down to talk with my colleague. After ten minutes, one of the Four's dads came over.

'I thought I'd just say hello,' he said.

'Sure,' I said. 'How are you doing?'

We got talking and then, one by one, each of the four activists came over too. This was a couple of weeks after the court case in which they'd been acquitted of pulling down the statue and, of course, we got talking about it. A report appeared in a magazine later claiming that 'voices were raised'. That was just untrue. We just talked, and truth be told, I was very happy to have the opportunity to speak with them directly. They were in the full flush of victory and probably didn't want to hear what I had to say about it, anyway.

One of the central arguments of their defence was their claim that Asher Craig, my deputy, and I had done nothing for Black people in the city. Meeting them for the first time in that pub, I could at least try to refute that.

'You're four white kids,' I told them. 'How would you know what we've done for Black people?' Whether it's recruiting magistrates, feeding children or building affordable housing, we had a strong record. Beyond taking the statue down, I wasn't sure what they were suggesting we should be doing. But what we had done was important: the difference between symbolism and change of real substance. 'Did I want the statue there?' I asked. 'Of course I didn't. But taking the statue down in itself doesn't improve the lives of the Black community. And building your case on me and Asher not doing anything, that's throwing the Black leadership in the city under the bus.'

I talked to them about racism, too. I asked them if they thought racism was real and whether there was any area of our world it didn't reach? They agreed it was real and that it touched all areas of society. So I asked them if they thought Asher and I had escaped racism by being elected, and whether there were additional challenges faced by Asher and me that a white politician wouldn't face? They seemed to recognize that there were. So they were judging Asher and me against a freedom to act that would be available to them as white politicians but not us as Black politicians?

'You are four white kids that did this,' I said. 'Do you think Black people would have done what you did? To turn up with ropes, then in front of police and on camera pull the statue down and throw it in the harbour? And then have the confidence to request a jury trial and build a case on the offence that the statue gave them?' They seemed to recognize the dynamic. 'Maybe,' I spoke as gently as I could, 'you were indulging in an exercise of white power and privilege, in that you believed you could make this system work for you in a way no Black person ever could?'

It was a frank conversation, but certainly not the argument that the newspaper reports suggested. In fact, the meeting finished on pretty good terms. They asked me to sign one of the T-shirts Banksy had

designed and sold to raise money for their legal fees. I invited them
to City Hall to talk about some practical things that could be done to
tackle racism – housing, employment, mental health and education.
They seemed to welcome the offer but then a few weeks later they
emailed me. They didn't want to come in, they said, as they would
feel compromised if they did so. They wanted to focus on grassroots
activism within the community, where they said real politics took
place.

I don't doubt their good intentions, even if I disagree with what
they consider to be 'real politics'. Proper politics, politics that makes
a difference, involves compromise, negotiations, limited resources and
difficult decisions. The Colston Four had their headlines and their
moment in the sun: but in terms of changing the lives of the Black
community, I'm not sure their actions ever went beyond the symbolic.

Sometimes anti-racist activism perceives Black people as vulnerable. It's easier for them and their campaigns for Black people to be
seen as victims. And when Black people assert themselves against
that, it creates tension. This is a dynamic that is centuries old. In
nineteenth-century America, Frederick Douglass escaped from slavery to become one of the leading abolitionists in the US. William
Lloyd Garrison, one of the leaders of the anti-slavery movement,
was a huge influence on Douglass and inspired him to step up. But
Garrison wanted Douglass to speak about what it was like to be a
slave, and would then explain why slavery should be abolished. When
Douglass began to assert his own agency, and speak for himself about
abolition, their relationship never recovered.

Some of the activists going to BLM rallies are like Garrison. They
want the T-shirt but not the deeper conversation. If they're challenged about their own prejudices and privileges, they feel threatened
and react badly. At the same time, when I talk about the subject, I'm
accused of playing the race card. I have rarely found a healthy space
to talk about race in Bristol Labour Party circles unless I am talking
about racism in the wider world. That's not to say the other parties
are better – they really aren't. But Labour is the place where we
should be able to talk about race and class without fear or favour.
I've never really understood their logic. It's fine for white activists to
speak about race and the racism of others, but not me? And when

I do bring it up, it isn't long before the classic tropes are brought out. I start speaking about race and I'm at risk of being received as aggressive and divisive.

One of my biggest challenges is to show that Black leadership is credible leadership. I like to think that my handling of the Colston statue is proof of that. Even though there was a lot of tension, unlike other cities, there was no violence. We kept our communities onside and together. I tried to be respectful and empathetic to all sides, which opened a space for us to have a conversation about race and class and history that will prove invaluable for the city going forward.

People need to know the history of the place they live in, but it's amazing how many people don't. During the 2021 elections, I had a conversation with an older white woman in Lawrence Weston. She was lovely and told me that with the Colston statue coming down, I was changing history and taking her history away from her. It was a good-natured conversation (they aren't always), so I asked her about the Bristol Dockers Strike of 1889, one of the key events in gaining rights for the working class in Bristol's history. She looked blank and couldn't tell me what happened. I said to her, 'You've already had your history taken away from you. If you don't know about the working-class history of the city, who will?'

14.

The Age of the City

When Extinction Rebellion first launched in Bristol, I was invited to one of their meetings. It was being held at the Malcolm X Centre in St Pauls and wasn't quite what I expected. To begin with, someone banged a gong, and we were invited to sit there in silence, reflecting on life and purpose. It was an interesting way to begin, more like a religious event than a political one. And when the discussion got underway, it didn't really talk about the environment. People spoke about what motivated them, but not what they were planning to do.

'We are an example to the world,' a speaker told the room to applause. 'We are the future.'

At the end of the meeting, one of the organizers came up and asked me what I thought.

'Do you want me to tell you the truth, or do you want me to make you feel good?'

'Tell me the truth,' she replied.

There were 130 people there and only three, including myself, were not white. 'You're in a centre named after Malcolm X, in one of the most diverse wards, in one of the more diverse constituencies in the UK, an area where we've had some of the most famous rebellions in recent history. You're saying you're the future, but this —' I waved my hand around the room — 'is a bit of an issue.'

I talked with other members. A group from Extinction Rebellion

Youth crowded round me. I wanted their input: I was serious about seeing what ideas they could bring to the table.

'Do you want to take action?' I asked.

They all nodded.

I had with me a copy of our One City Plan. In the middle there are three fold-outs that stretch out the timeline of our six key targets. Each fold-out charts the ambition for the city for each decade. Bang in the middle, in purple, sits the Environment strand. As with the other strands, there are three aims for each year. It's a serious document, but it isn't set in stone. It's something to work towards, but it can be adapted and challenged – which is easier with a plan than without one.

I spread the document out and showed it to the XR members. Then I flicked through to the back where the contact details were.

'Here's the email address for the environment board. Why don't you contact them with your ideas and recommendations on what they've written? I'm sure we can sort out a meeting between you and representatives of the board. This is a live document,' I said, handing it over. 'It's there to be challenged and changed. If you want to take action, this is the place to start.'

A few weeks later, I asked the environment board what Extinction Rebellion had written to them about. I wasn't completely surprised, but I was still disappointed that they hadn't been in touch.

This wasn't the only time I'd tried to talk to them. When they first took action in Bristol and blocked the M32, I was careful not to take an adversarial approach. I simply said that while the concerns were right, they had made a strategic error blocking the main commuter road into the city. I invited them into City Hall. Five came in, and again all of them were white. I was ready to take them seriously – I wanted to take them seriously. The environment is such an important issue, how can you not be serious about it?

So I'd come prepared. Extinction Rebellion had three key goals: they wanted a citizens' assembly; they wanted political leaders to tell the truth about the environmental situation; and they wanted action now. It was the third of these that I decided to focus on. The idea of having a citizens' assembly has its advantages and disadvantages, but from an environmental position it seemed to be a bit of a red herring:

if the situation is as serious as they say it is, then you're better off with someone in charge taking action, rather than everyone talking about it and getting nothing done.

Being mayor is a practical job. Mayors must deliver. I wanted to flesh XR's Act Now aims out into, well, action. I had an A3 sheet of paper with me, on which I'd printed out a table. Down the left-hand side, I'd jotted down numbers from one to ten. Across the top, I'd marked out two columns: the first was titled Action, the second Lead. Not all the environmental actions were the responsibility of the council – if we could divide that list up into responsibilities, then we could make a plan of who should be doing what. I laid the piece of paper down on the table and talked it through.

'You say your goal is to act now,' I said. 'So where do we start? What should we do?'

The activists looked at one another. I passed them the pen. 'Let's fill out this table with the top ten actions we must do now.' And waited. Nothing practical was coming back. I found it painful. I tried to help. I took the pen to facilitate. In the end, one of them said, 'We want you to tell the truth.'

'OK,' I said, biting my tongue. 'So how could we do that?'

'You could put up billboards,' one of them suggested. 'To tell people about the climate emergency.'

I wrote 'Billboards' down on the action plan. 'OK,' I said. 'What else?'

But they didn't want to talk about action. Instead, they kept on talking about other things. When I tried to bring it back to action, one of them said, 'One of the problems is that I just don't think you really care about the environment.'

I paused at that. 'How do you know what I care about?'

'Well, you don't seem very angry about what is happening,' the activist replied with a shrug.

This is a phrase I've heard before. It came up in an interview I did on Channel 4 with the presenter Matt Frei, around environmental action. There was a group of us being interviewed, including a young climate activist. 'You don't seem very angry,' he told me. My response to him was, 'What, you've got some sort of superpower that you can see into my soul?'

I turned back to the XR representative. 'You don't know how I express my emotions,' I told her. There was a racial dynamic here that either she didn't appear to get, or didn't want to acknowledge: as a Black man, I simply didn't have the license to express my anger in the way that she did.

At this point, one of the other activists, a student, started to cry. I didn't have any patience with that. You're a Russell Group university student, I thought. Get a grip. You want to know about crying? Let me take you to meet some of the people I know, people who are hungry, cutting out meals so that they can pay their bills. I didn't say any of this, of course. But I hoped he would be able to work it out for himself. As the meeting broke up, one of them said, 'Did you know that Friends of the Earth have put out a list of thirty-three actions that local authorities should be doing on the environment? That's what you should put in your action plan.'

I went back to my office with my all-but-blank piece of paper. I asked the team to work through the Friends of the Earth action points. By the time we finished, we reckoned we were already enacting thirty-one of their thirty-three recommendations: the only ones we weren't enacting were plans for rolling out electric buses (we were aiming for biogas) and on parking (we'd introduced residents' parking zones instead). It was incredibly frustrating. If the activists had done their research, then they'd have known that we were doing all of this stuff already. If they were serious about what they were saying, then they'd be holding Bristol up as an example of a city that was taking action, not knocking us. But it was easier to get the emotional satisfaction of accusing others of doing nothing and calling for revolution instead.

So many people trade off politicians. They use them as a canvas on which they can paint a picture of the person they wish they were. Some activists dream of being Greta Thunberg facing down Donald Trump, but they don't have a world stage, just their home city. The only organization they can get to is the city council and the only person they can get to is me, as the mayor. So they sidestep the action we're taking and attack us for not doing enough.

The next time I saw Extinction Rebellion, they were on the roof. They'd scaled City Hall early in the morning to campaign about clean-air zones. When they saw me, they started shouting down, challenging me to have a meeting with them. I shouted back up at them. 'Have you phoned the office to ask for a meeting?'

'We're asking you now,' came the reply.

'So rather than contacting my office, you decided to climb up on to the roof?' I shook my head and told them, 'I don't respond to tantrums. If you want a meeting, just email my office.'

I went into work with their shouts ringing in my ears. It might not surprise you to know that they didn't get in touch. Instead, they stayed up there for three days of torrential rain. It must have been miserable.

In the summer of 2022, the UK experienced record temperatures, passing 40 degrees for the first time. It was brutal. Bristol itself didn't quite reach those peaks and was spared the outbreaks of fire elsewhere in the country, but that was pure luck. When record temperatures return, and they will, the city is as vulnerable as anywhere else. I once heard a CNN report that summed up our environmental situation: it's like we're living in a Hollywood disaster movie, going in slow motion; we can see it coming and we're not dealing with it.

As that summer's heatwave unfolded, I found two particular ideas stuck in my mind. As hot as it might be in the UK as a result of climate change, the people really bearing the brunt are in the global south: it is people in Africa, Asia and South America who are going to die disproportionately, who are going to see their livelihoods disappear and be displaced. There's nothing very new about this.

My second thought was for my children. I'm sure I wasn't alone in looking at them and wondering what kind of world they would be living in. When I was younger, I used to say I wouldn't have children as it would be bad for the planet and bad for them. I'm glad, personally, that I changed my mind: I wouldn't change having my children for anything. But the worry of bringing them up in a disintegrating world continues to nag at me.

The government response to the record temperatures was pitiful. There were COBRA meetings to discuss the crisis, but the prime minister didn't turn up for them, which suggests how seriously the issue was being taken. On a city level, we discussed our immediate concerns about the health effects. Bristol's director of public health was being given guidance by the UK Health Security Agency and we were monitoring the hospitals to keep an eye on what the effects of the heat were and to check that we could cope. But this was just fire-fighting. The important work that needs to be done is to tackle the underlying issues to try to bring a halt to global warming and the terrible effects it has on the planet.

One of the most important books I've read on the environment is Benjamin Barber's *Cool Cities*. Barber makes lots of brilliant points, but the one that really resonates with me is his argument that climate change is primarily a political problem. By which he means that the technology is there to deal with the crisis: it's about making the decisions and finding the money to achieve the outcomes we need to deliver. That analysis is full of hope. And I'm a hopeful person, which is not to say that I'm an optimist. I always think optimism is a little shallow – it's one of those buzzwords that politicians trot out, without any meaning behind it. Hope, though, is real.

Barber argues for the importance of cities tackling the environment. To use a football analogy, it's as if we've got the eleven players we need to win the match, but they're playing in the wrong formation. At the moment, decision-making and leadership are being held tightly by national governments, when the way that the world has developed and the challenges we face have outgrown that model. That doesn't mean that we don't need national governments – but the energy and directness that a network of cities can call on should be brought into play. A collective act of leadership – cities and countries together – is central to solving this crisis.

There's an oft-quoted line from Mario Cuomo, who said of politics that you campaign in poetry, but you govern in prose. Nowhere is this truer than in environmental politics. Tackling climate change is not about banners and T-shirts: it's about Excel spreadsheets and project managers. It's about the slog, not the slogans. I think that's why I so often find myself frustrated with elements of the environmental movement. I don't doubt their passion about the issue, but I do question their seriousness in getting things done.

I mentioned Extinction Rebellion earlier in this chapter, but I've had similar dealings with the Green Party. As mayor, they were the main opposition to Labour, so I've had plenty of opportunities to see them close-up. Some of what they've done smacks of symbolism: one of their leaders brought forward a motion to full council to declare a climate emergency. I struggled to sign it. Not because I don't think that there is a climate emergency, but because the motion offered nothing of substance as to how the emergency would be dealt with.

Instead, it echoes a phrase used in Parliament: that all that is needed to solve the crisis is the political will. I loathe that phrase. It's such a naive thing to say. Political will, yes, but also billions of pounds. To suggest that political will alone will solve the crisis is fairytale stuff, and feeds straight into their political strategy, which is to imply they are the only ones who really care about the issues, the only ones with the magical will to deliver the goods with the charge that all others are greenwashing.

Politics is easy on the margins. You can espouse all the platitudes that you want, without ever having your priorities properly put to the test. The minute ideals come into contact with reality, the situation changes. Look at Brighton, where the Greens have been in charge. For all the progressive projection, they've had a series of ongoing strikes with their waste collectors. You'd have thought Brighton Council's record on the environment would be leading the country.

The closer the Green Party gets to power, the more you get the sense that instead of serving the environment, they are using the issue as a springboard to power. At which point, they're no longer an environmental movement, but just the same as any other party.

The task ahead of us, to tackle the rise in global temperatures and to keep them within a range that won't cause irreversible damage to our planet and wildlife, is momentous. Key to it is decarbonization: at a national level, the UK government is, in theory at least, committed to a strategy of net zero for all sectors of the economy by 2050. At a city level, we want to go further and faster. In the One City Plan, Bristol committed to becoming carbon neutral and climate resilient by 2030.

It's one thing to make this sort of claim. It's quite another to go about doing it. I'm aware that as a city leader, there are only so many levers I can pull and some of the changes needed to achieve this goal are beyond our control: it will partly depend on the actions undertaken by national government, and the investment they put in. The capital cost for reshaping Bristol's heat and transport infrastructure is around £9 billion – a massive sum.

At one of the recent meetings for the UK's Core Cities, we were joined by the chief executive of Siemens Europe, who told us that we already have the technology to solve 80 per cent of the climate crisis. The problem is in deploying the technology, for which you need finance.

To give one example, when the building of offshore wind farms was in its early years, the government used public money to de-risk the market, to help the nascent sector to develop. Once the market was established, investors came through and that level of support was no longer necessary. That cycle of investment is one of the places where governments can help. And not just at a national level: it can be done on a city level as well.

One of the headline projects I'm proudest of is Bristol's City Leap Programme. We've done a deal with two huge companies: Ameresco, a leading renewable energy asset developer, and Vattenfall Heat UK, Sweden's nationally owned energy company, and specialists in low and zero-carbon networks. It's a long-term partnership – twenty years – during which the companies will work to deliver a low-carbon energy infrastructure for the city. There's no UK government finance for the project: capital funding to the tune of a billion pounds, with half of that in the first five years, has come from private-sector partners. It will take 150,000 tonnes of CO_2 out of our future emissions. We've given these firms the access they need to our heat networks and our buildings: we've given them the space to come in, invest and get a return from Bristol.

It is the first deal of its kind. It took five years of work and £7.5 million of our budget to pull together. We set up a global procurement process to find the companies we wanted to work with. In total, we had almost a hundred expressions of interest and serious discussions with over twenty firms. The deal itself was incredibly complex – we had to get the details right. The city was going to be tied to whatever we signed for the next twenty years.

The process wasn't entirely smooth – after the first round of procurement, we discovered an error, which meant we had to start the whole process again. And, while we were negotiating, Bristol's opposition parties were criticizing our approach – not just the Conservatives and the Lib Dems, but the Greens as well. The idea was pie in the sky, I was told. Too high risk. I was handing Bristol over to private companies, who would use the deal to extract vast profits. I didn't understand – if a climate emergency isn't the time to take risks, when is? Then, when we announced the deal, the criticism swung the other way. One of the questions at the press conference was: 'This deal seems amazing. Is it too good to be true?' Sometimes, it really does seem that you can't win.

What the City Leap deal shows, though, is what can be achieved at this level of government. It's not the sort of deal that could be done at a national level, but it's big enough to make a difference. It's another example of where cities can work more effectively and efficiently than governments. What we lack is the political power to make more decisions locally and the finance needed to make local decision-making meaningful. The City Leap deal is a leap forwards in terms of what can be achieved, but that process needs to be replicated and made easier. One grouping that could be useful here is 3Ci, the Cities Commission for Climate Change, which brings together Core Cities across the UK, together with various councils and authorities. One of its aims is to work out how to raise the finance for similar ventures.

A couple of years ago, I was invited to the Open Society Foundations. This organization was set up by George Soros and provides funds to groups working for justice, democratic governance and human rights. It was a strange time for me: we were back at Mum's house, the same house she, Dionne and I had moved to in 1978, while work was being done on my house, yet here I was, flying to New York to take part in the Foundation's work. I went to their board meeting and said, 'Here's what we should do. We should get people like George, Warren Buffett, Bill Gates and their friends, put them in a room with 250 mayors around the world, make the match and

get stuff done.' There was something very simplistic about that statement, of course, but something profoundly true as well – if only there
was a way to get the money in the room with the people you know
can make things happen.

The City Leap partnership will focus on areas such as Solar PV,
heat networks, heat pumps and energy efficiency across scale. Efficiency here is crucial. Because while new homes can be built to the
latest environmental standards, the challenge of how to tackle existing houses and other buildings remains. The UK has some of the least
energy-efficient housing stock in Europe: it is estimated that out of
the 29 million homes in the UK, just 8 million reach the highest
energy standards.

If we are serious about climate change and decarbonization, this
is one of the battlegrounds: how do you retrofit the homes that are
already there? Decarbonization isn't just about finding renewables.
The less sexy part of the process is creating homes that require
less energy and produce less waste. Insulation is never going to be
a headline-grabbing topic. But homes that require less energy to be
heated help the environment. When it comes to transport, shifting
buses to electricity and biofuel is great, but there are other things
we can do too. Building homes in active travel distances of work, for
example: if people can walk or cycle to the office, that's energy saved.

Retrofitting isn't cheap. I recently moved house and Kirsten and
I decided to fit an air-source heat pump, together with underfloor
heating. It means we won't need gas central heating, and the house
will be more efficient and use less energy. We've put solar panels on
the roof as well. It won't make us self-sufficient, but it should heavily
reduce our bills. I'm also planning to buy an electric car, which will be
charged from our own solar power. None of this is cheap: I'm lucky
that I can afford to do all of this. Even with the grants available, it
is still very expensive – far too expensive for the sort of mass take-
up we need to make a real dent in our decarbonization targets. But
it's not all about the economic return – if I'm pushing the city into
becoming more environmentally friendly, then I've got to be seen to
be contributing to saving the planet as well.

* * *

In November 2021, Glasgow hosted COP26, the United Nations Conference on Climate Change. It was widely seen as crucial in terms of bringing the world together to commit to working together to combat climate change.

The year before, as planning for the conference got underway, I took part in an all-party parliamentary group to discuss the aims of the conference. There were, as the name suggests, MPs of all stripes on the call. When it was my turn to speak, I warned my colleagues that one of the biggest dangers we faced was that we would come away from COP with a bunch of commitments that might sound impressive at first glance but had no finance attached, no measurable outcomes and no deadlines. Frustratingly, that's what we ended up with.

I also emphasized my belief in the importance of cities in finding an environmental solution: 'I think one of the best things the UK could do would be to make COP the COP of cities, beginning the process of shifting the emphasis from national governments to the decarbonization of cities.' I suggested developing a plan for this – showing what we could do with UK cities and offering it as a template for the rest of the world to follow. In the run-up to COP, however, no one from the government asked the Core Cities group to talk about this.

This lack of interest in cities played itself out at COP. I was invited to Glasgow and spoke at several events. The conference timetable meant the focus on cities was not until the final day: long after many of the world leaders had made their speeches and left. It was the wrong way round – cities should have had a much more prominent role and been discussed at the start.

The events I went to were all positive and well-received, though. Most people there were informed about the issues and receptive to our message – that most of the world's population live in cities, that cities were ready to decarbonize, but that they needed the finance to do so. But turning that receptiveness into action proved harder. There was a lot of talk at COP about money and it was announced that $130 trillion of private capital would be committed towards the goal of net zero. But as Mark Carney, the former governor of the Bank of England, said the challenge with the finance was about 'plugging it in'. The problem isn't the money itself – it's about getting it to the people who are going to spend it on real programmes. I subsequently heard that the general secretary of the UN told one leader that cities were going to have to lead on climate change because the national governments were not going to deliver.

In the aftermath of COP, one of the frustrations was that while the meeting had generated momentum, it lacked the vehicle to build on that momentum: the abstract announcements at its close weren't concrete enough. At the next COP meeting in Baku, Azerbaijan, there needs to be a change in attitude. I worry that the negotiations will continue to be dominated by national governments – and national governments that still don't understand the importance of city leadership in decarbonizing the world's cities. My concern, too, is that these conferences will lack any plan for how cities can work together to achieve this.

In terms of what has been agreed at COP, little has changed in how Bristol deals with the environment. There's been no further funding, no programmes to enact or new targets to hit. Instead, we'll continue to do what we can, innovate with projects such as City Leap, and offer up our model for others to follow.

One thing I wanted to do to help tackle climate change was to make sure we had the best minds working on solutions for the city. Bristol is fortunate to have two world-class universities and I wanted to use their intellectual firepower. Just as there is a national advisory committee on climate change, so we set up a Bristol Advisory Committee to help plan our strategy as a city.

The committee members pored over our proposals, eventually delivering a report in which they made their suggestions as to what we should do. It was a really meaningful process. They weren't there to take it apart, but neither did they have any particular loyalty to our plans. Instead, we gave them the space to properly stress test what we wanted to do.

The link between universities and cities is important. Yale was a $20 billion organization in one of the ten most violent cities in the United States, living in its own little Ivy League world. Then, one of its students was shot. The university realized that it couldn't continue to live in a bubble and began a process of real engagement with the local community. When the sub-prime mortgage crisis hit, Yale offered pro bono legal support to those who were struggling. And when maintenance jobs and other work came up, they made sure to offer contracts to local firms and residents.

In 2012, wanting to find out what people believed the role of the universities in city management should be, I had discussed this with leading figures at the University of the West of England and the University of Bristol. We had all agreed that Bristol was part of their university's brand. When students are deciding which university to go to, they want to feel like they're coming to a great place. They also want to feel that they're part of and safe in the city they've chosen to move to. It's therefore in the interests of the universities to invest in that city.

Once I became mayor, I adopted the same approach and set up an environmental board to make suggestions for the city's policies. I don't run it: I co-chaired it at the beginning to ensure people knew we took it seriously but soon left them to run their own agenda. The board meets every few months and, crucially, interacts with the other boards I've set up to tackle different issues facing the community. None of these happen in isolation. It's a great set-up, with the best minds in the city working on solutions, and people with different experiences and backgrounds pulling together to create a plan for the city.

It's the sort of constructive, creative approach that is politics at its best – a world away from sloganeering and grandstanding. Stepping back and letting the people who know what they are talking about have the space to do what they can do is the best kind of leadership.

Our ecological strategy came straight out of a discussion at one of these meetings. The focus of the discussions had all been around decarbonization, but one of the board members, Ian Barrett, chief executive of Avon Wildlife Trust, pointed out that we needed to go further, warning us that it was possible to solve CO_2 issues yet still lose elements of the natural world. The ongoing threat to biodiversity and the risks of mass species extinction would remain a huge concern, he went on, above and beyond the hard work we were putting in on the climate. And failing on ecology would harm the work on climate.

This was in November 2019. By February 2020, with Ian's help, we had convened a working group consisting of not just the council, but the local health services, the universities, the voluntary sector and more, all coming together to declare an ecological emergency. We were the first UK city to do so.

All these different groups manage land in the city, so their input was crucial. And so was our response. There are so many alarming statistics but one that always sticks in my mind is that the songbird population has declined in Bristol by 96 per cent. We set up four clear goals in our emergency strategy: to ensure that 30 per cent of the land in Bristol is managed for the benefit of wildlife; to reduce the use of pesticides in Bristol by at least 50 per cent; for all our waterways to have sufficient water quality to support healthy wildlife; and to reduce the consumption of products that undermine the health of our wildlife and ecosystems.

Managing land for the protection of wildlife takes us back to house-building. Of course, we need to find homes for Bristol's growing population. But where we put them has repercussions. Building out takes land away from nature: putting as many people as possible in the same bit of land allows us to protect those green spaces, and the green spaces within the city.

Our BoKlok development on Airport Road, for example, is an interesting scheme in this respect. The site has a stream running through the centre and for a long time, it's been used as a bit of a dumping ground. When we gave BoKlok the contract, I explained that the city wanted not only to try to measure ourselves against the Global Sustainable Development Goals but to deliver on them. BoKlok were of the same mind: part of the development was to rehabilitate the stream and allow nature to re-establish itself along its banks. It's a good example of how housing development, done in the right way, can support the natural world.

Another challenge is how we use pesticides, which are one of the key factors in the decline of the insect population, which underpins our entire ecosystem. And it's not just insects that suffer: the use of pesticides is also damaging to birds, bees and rivers. And it's not only pesticides. Glyphosate, a common ingredient in weedkiller, was declared a possible carcinogen by the World Health Organization in 2015.

Bristol, like many councils, decided to stop using dangerous pesticides and glyphosate weedkillers. To control weeds across the city, we've experimented with different alternatives, and we've had pesticide amnesties, where people can bring them in and have them disposed of safely. The truth is, from a council perspective, making the declaration has been easier than the delivery. We've found the alternatives to be ineffective, costly and the source of other problems and complaints. But we've also reclassified plants that we used to target – some of them are wildflowers that benefit the ecosystem.

How we look after our waterways is also crucial for a city like Bristol. We have to tackle pollution to get the water quality we need to support the city's wildlife. Chemicals that run off agricultural land further upstream cause problems, as do overflows from the water companies – our sewage system is not equipped for the growing population. Then there are microplastics microfibres, and other pollution from single-use plastics. Part of the answer here is education – making people aware of the consequences of their lifestyle choices. Another part of it is providing alternatives: with Bristol Water, we've installed water fountains across the city to encourage people to use reusable bottles. It's an ongoing challenge that can only be met by the whole city pulling together.

The same is true of our fourth goal, to think about the wider footprint of the city, which involves inspiring both businesses and consumers to think about their choices – to be more aware of the environmental impacts of the products they make and buy. Again, it's partly down to awareness and alternatives. If we can make it easier for businesses to adopt more sustainable sourcing policies, then that is to the benefit of us all.

Interconnectedness is key. It's how the city's different policy boards work together. At City Hall, the decisions I make as mayor have an impact on the environment, but company and individual choices matter too. And interconnectedness is important in a wider sense, too. The environment does not respect borders. Over the next thirty years, urbanization is going to see an additional 2.5 billion people living in cities, with 90 per cent of that increase in Asia and Africa.

We can do what we can to combat climate change in Bristol but our policies work in tandem with what happens in Freetown, say, or Kampala. A city's footprint is global – and if we don't recognize that, we will tread on those we need to help.

The twenty-first century has been the century of the city and cities, and city leaders have a vital role to play in tackling the world's problems, problems that are only going to become more challenging in the years ahead.

For more than two centuries, the nation state has been the building block of how the world has worked. But the world has moved on. Ed Johnson, the former mayor of Asbury Park, New Jersey, summed this up perfectly. He once told me that we have the best model of governance the 1960s could ask for; the problem is it's the 2020s. The way we live is different now. Mobility and connectivity are everything. People live beyond national boundaries. And the challenges we face are no longer confined to national borders. Whether it's climate change, migration, economic stability, poverty, political stability or extremism, these issues are transnational, and we need transnational solutions to solve them.

In terms of land mass, cities occupy less than 3 per cent: if you put them all together, you could fit every city in the world into India. And yet, cities are home to over half the global population: 55 per cent at the time of writing and projected to grow to just over 66 per cent by the middle of the twenty-first century. Cities are responsible for 75 per cent of CO_2 emissions and consumers of 80 per cent of the world's energy. Any response to climate change should have the environmental and ecological policies of the world's cities front and centre.

But the growth of cities creates huge possibilities, too. Their size and density, their adaptability and capacity for invention mean that we have the potential to do more with less. Cities are one of the most effective tools that we have at our disposal for generating efficiencies when it comes to our use of land, of energy, and of dealing with waste.

So if you want to do anything, achieve anything, the quickest way to do so is not through national governments, but through a network of international cities. There is a nimbleness and directness to how cities act that national governments can't always follow.

Cities, meanwhile, are starting to group and get their collective act together, both on a national level, with groupings like Core Cities, and on a transnational level. The C40 Cities Climate Leadership Group is a network of ninety-seven of the world's largest cities, coordinating action on climate change. The U7, or Urban 7, is a grouping of G7 city leaders that meet as part of the annual G7 summits. In the US, meanwhile, the State Department now has a specific lead for subnational politics and diplomacy. That's the way the world is going: not country to country, but city to city.

Not everyone understands this. When I watched the recent TV coverage of the local elections in Northern Ireland, the BBC reporter described local politics as being about 'bin collections and potholes'. When I was elected as mayor in 2016, I had a limited appreciation of the global role that cities can play. But since then I've grown to understand what cities can do, especially when they do it together.

For bin collections, read recycling; for potholes, read transport choices. These are just two of the many ways we need to tackle climate change. It might start locally, but the response, if cities act together, can have an effect across the globe.

In 2019, I met with Rob Scott Cook, the founding pastor of the Woodlands group of churches. He said that we needed to talk about hope in Bristol because sometimes people can feel a little hopeless. When I first ran for mayor, I had wanted to talk about hope. But I knew what would happen if I did. Everyone would have turned round and said, 'Oh, he's just trying to be Barack Obama.' A white politician would probably have got away with it, but as much as I wanted to speak about hope, I didn't feel I could.

Having talked to Rob, the notion of hope was suddenly back at the forefront of my mind. A short time after our conversation I spoke at an event for the Rockefeller Resilient Cities programme. The programme, funded by the Rockefeller Foundation, invited one hundred cities around the world to create a 'resilience strategy', and Bristol was one of five UK cities chosen to participate.

Not for the first time, I found myself without any pre-prepared script, but I remembered a Scriptural passage from the Book of Romans that has always been important to me: 'we rejoice in our sufferings, knowing that suffering produces perseverance, and perseverance produces character, and character produces hope.' So, there I was, doing what I said I wouldn't do, and talking about hope. There must have been something in the water, because later that day I was scheduled to do an interview at a cafe for homeless people, run by a local charity, In Hope. I did the interview and ended up talking about hopelessness. Some people do feel hopeless, I said, but I went back to Romans: if people can overcome their challenges, they'll find resilience, and from there they'll find hope. We can't always do that alone, but – especially with the support of organizations like In Hope – it is possible.

About six months after that interview, Rob came back to me with an idea.

'I'd like to present the city with a plaque,' he said. 'I want to declare that Bristol is a city of hope.'

I was both moved and taken aback. It was quite a statement. At first, I was also a little bit cautious: Rob's a leader of the biggest church group in the city and I didn't want anyone to feel excluded. But I talked to my friend and colleague Mohammed Elsharif, a prominent member of the local Muslim community, and it soon became clear that everyone was happy to be involved. We unveiled the plaque in front of members of all of our communities, and Bristol being a city of hope is a central part of our council strategy. In terms of a city being a community act, it's a great place to start.

EPILOGUE

In the lead-up to the 2020 mayoral election, the Liberal Democrat candidate stood on a 'back me to scrap me' platform. They didn't only want to defeat me, but to get rid of the mayoral system altogether. When Covid hit, the election was delayed to 2021. By then the Liberal Democrats had changed their candidate, but not their policy. And the Conservatives had joined them. Together, they raised the issue of local government and city leadership in their leaflets and at every hustings. They argued that the mayoral system had usurped the role of local councillors, undermining democracy by putting power into the hands of just one person.

Neither the Green candidate, Sandy Hore-Ruthven, nor I engaged with it in any meaningful way during the campaign. He was a strong candidate and, justifiably, thought the Greens could win. For me, the role of the mayor was a non-issue. There were much bigger things to discuss: Covid recovery and the inequalities it had shone a light on, the housing crisis, climate change and the loss of biodiversity. I also believed, and I think Sandy did too, that the mayoral system was the best way of getting things done, and was genuinely delivering for the city.

The reason that it had become an issue was because we were approaching the tenth anniversary of Bristol having a mayor. Three years after the 2012 referendum introduced the mayoral system, Barbara Janke, the former Liberal Democrat leader of Bristol City Council who was by then in the House of Lords, tabled an amendment to the Devolution Bill, making provision for a second referendum to decide on the shape of local government, including getting rid of the mayoral system. In the end, this was restricted to a ten-year moratorium with the earliest possible date being 2022.

In the election, I came first and the Greens second, securing 74 per cent of the 140,599 votes cast between us.* Or to put it another way, the 'scrap the mayor' campaigns secured only 26 per cent of the vote. But the question wasn't settled. If a majority of councillors in the chamber voted for a referendum, there would be one.

In 2016, when I became mayor, Labour won thirty-seven of the seventy council seats. In 2021, we lost thirteen seats while the Greens won thirteen, taking them to twenty-four, the same number as us. With the Liberal Democrats having eight seats and the Conservatives fourteen, the opposition parties held forty-six seats and a majority in the chamber. Once that became clear, the Greens, having lost the mayoral election, switched positions and joined the campaign for the role to be scrapped. At Full Council on 7 December 2021, the opposition parties put forward a motion for a referendum, which they won by forty-one votes to twenty-four.

As soon as the referendum was announced, I was asked which way I thought it would go. Like boxers, politicians are supposed to talk up their chances of winning. But I was completely frank and suggested that it was highly probable Bristol would vote against the mayoral system. I could see how things would unfold: a poor-quality debate focused on the row rather than one that discussed the strength of the argument – both for and against; a strong anti-politics message, a low turnout and disproportionately motivated anti-mayor and anti-Marvin voters. We'd seen these factors lead us into Brexit.

Even before my re-election in 2021, Kevin and I had talked about the role I should take in any referendum campaign. I had already made it clear that I would not be standing for a third term. I had thought for a long time that eight years would be enough of me and for me.

---

* HORE-RUTHVEN Sandy: Green Party – 45,663
REES Marvin Jonathan: Labour Party – 59,276
Eligible electorate: 341,682
Total of ballot papers verified: 140,599
Turnout: 41.15 per cent

I thought the city should reinvent itself around a new mayor, with a new style and new priorities, or at least new approaches to existing priorities. I also wanted time and space to reinvent myself.

So we agreed that if a referendum was called, I would put the case at the beginning, setting out my position, and then leave it up to the city to decide. I was worried that I would be a distraction. While some of the 'scrap the mayor' campaign was about getting rid of the system itself, some of it was about getting rid of me. I tried to make it clear that if people were going to vote to get rid of me, they had misunderstood the issue. The mayoral system wouldn't end until May 2024, and I had already announced my intention to stand down. So all the vote would do is stop anyone from becoming mayor after me. By standing back, I hoped there would be more space for a reasoned debate about what model of local government leadership would best deliver for Bristol.

As the arguments spiralled into hyperbole, it was a real challenge not to dive in. The anti-mayor campaigners claimed that one man – me – made all the decisions. While the mayor has executive power, given the role of the council, let alone the many other city organizations, it's simply not possible for one person to dominate. But they kept repeating the idea that having a mayor undermined democracy, even though the mayoral system gives voters the chance to choose that person, as opposed to one where the councillors chose the leaders on the voters' behalf. Another argument was that the mayor wasn't accountable. Here, I think they were confusing accountability with control. I'd say mayors are more accountable because they are so visible – far more so than the anonymity of a committee system.

For all the ins and outs, my key concern was that this was a debate among councillors, for councillors, about councillors. At no point did I hear any attempt to explore, understand or explain what kind of political leadership would best serve the needs of Bristol, with the challenges and opportunities before it.

I'm not saying that a city governance model where the leader is decided by councillors can't work. It has worked very well in cities like Manchester and Cardiff. But in Bristol, political energy had been sucked into the council because the leader's position depended on keeping their councillors happy: I'd experienced this kind of leveraging when I was first selected and some of the older Labour leaders had tried to exert power over me. A mayor, by contrast, is directly dependent on the people, which offers a degree of immunity from inner- and cross-party shenanigans.

When the result was confirmed on polling day, with 59 per cent support for scrapping the mayoral role on a 29 per cent turnout, the combined Conservative, Liberal Democrat and Green councillors stood shoulder to shoulder and gave a huge cheer.

The parties had led the city to vote for a committee system, a decision that will bring its own challenges. Key among them is to ensure the city's political focus continues to look up and out, rather than just looking inward. The city will also need to work out how to ensure the progressive urban voice remains strong in a combined authority made up of three local authorities, two of which are rural with a strong conservative political tradition. Most of all, they must take a lead from Barack Obama, who, when asked about entering leadership, said 'Just learn how to get stuff done'. The danger is that rather than taking action, the committee will be consumed by talk and disagreement.

On the day of the referendum result, the press asked me what I thought. I reminded them that I had said at the start I didn't think it would be good for Bristol. 'But now Bristol has made this decision,' I concluded. 'I hope I was wrong.' I still do.

For the foreseeable future at least, I will be the last directly elected mayor of Bristol. My team and I have had a good run. I think we've made a difference. You could liken the experience of being mayor to the Greek myth of Sisyphus, the founder and king of Ephyra whom Hades punished by forcing him to roll an immense boulder up a hill only for it to roll back down every time it neared the top, repeating this action for eternity. We've made progress but the challenges of leading a city are never solved.

Maybe it's a political skill I should have mastered but I couldn't separate myself – Marvin Rees – from the mayoral position. It felt personal. It allowed me to experience the profound joy and sense of achievement in securing the homes and jobs that have brought hope into people's lives. I would go as far as to say that those occasions have given me a real taste of the purpose I have pursued since I was a child.

Now it's on to the next chapter. Let's see what happens.

ACKNOWLEDGEMENTS

My thanks go to my family — my wife and children in particular. Too often I have thanked others and failed to properly and publicly acknowledge the part my family has played in motivating, supporting and believing in me. And they have paid a price for that. I have often been away. Sometimes when I have been home I have not been fully present. And I know Kirsten in particular has felt the effects of this. Thank you. My prayer for you all is that you continue to grow into the purpose found in your fullest selves. I must also thank Tom Bromley.